Yale Romanic Studies, Second Series 25

THE DIALECTICS OF ISOLATION

Self and Society in the French Novel
from the Realists to Proust

Richard Terdiman

New Haven and London
Yale University Press
1976

Library of Congress catalog card number: 75-18187
International standard book number: 0-300-01888-6

Designed by John O. C. McCrillis
and set in Baskerville type.
Printed in the United States of America by
The Alpine Press Inc., South Braintree, Mass.

Published in Great Britain, Europe, and Africa by
Yale University Press, Ltd., London.
Distributed in Latin America by Kaiman & Polon, Inc.,
New York City; in India by UBS Publishers' Distributors Pvt., Ltd.,
Delhi; in Japan by John Weatherhill, Inc., Tokyo; in Australasia by
Book & Film Services, Artarmon, N.S.W., Australia

To Daniel
and his whole family

Combien je souffrais de cette position où nous a réduits l'oubli de la nature qui, en instituant la division des corps, n'a pas songé à rendre possible l'interpénétration des âmes!

Proust, *La Prisonnière*

Contents

Preface

This study examines the tradition of the French novel during its most prestigious period. Necessarily, therefore, these pages do not claim to be a fully balanced study of Proust, nor indeed of any of the major figures treated. The strategy here is different, and it accounts for the somewhat unorthodox division of the discussion into two unequal parts, employing in the main two different kinds of analysis.

The first of these parts attempts to define—in an examination of the nineteenth-century Realist novel—a central concern which since the French Revolution it has been the task of fiction to explore. The forms of this exploration animate the tradition in which Proust must be placed, and of which he was acutely aware. But the concept of the tradition implies something more. Among the forces which determine the novel's progression from Stendhal to Proust, the most essential is not the relation of book to book or writer to writer, but the relation of each writer's effort to the object of his effort, of each successive book to the evolving social reality which it attempted to comprehend. The tradition's coherence is thus a reflection—a very profound and illuminating reflection—of the real movement of human history. The orderly progression of masterpieces in this period is the dynamic record of attempts to understand the individual's situation in the face of an evolving crisis which placed the individual in unprecedented peril. The techniques of these novels are innovative because the crisis was unprecedented; the novels are crucial because the crisis was crucial.

But there is a difference between the rate at which social crisis evolves and that of the conceptual formulations—what we ordinarily call their "visions of experience"—which are writers' responses to it. In examining the Realist paradigm in Part I, my emphasis is on delineating the character of this nascent crisis, which is the explicit subject of Realist novels and determines the techniques they employ. In this period individuals experienced a devastatingly rapid alteration of social relations and responded with attempts to understand what was, in fact, happening to people. The Realist novel was born, one might say, of a social emergency, and it brilliantly saw that the first necessity was to discover what in the world outside might explain the individual's disorientation. Seeking individual meaning in the material world is thus central to the tradition, though as time progressed continuing on this path became extremely difficult. The difficulty itself is immediately reflected in the forms of fiction.

By the time of Proust, the outward characteristics of the individual's crisis were thoroughly known; the sense of emergency, its accompanying atmosphere of abrupt movement and tragic discovery, had died out long before. Proust had time to fill in a portrait the Realists had only been able to sketch. Stendhal for example worried continually that he had neglected detail in his haste to get on with the story whose events carry his meaning, his judgment of experience. Proust's leisurely pace, his exhaustive detailing, his exquisite consciousness of his own artistic practice, are all symptoms of his position at the other end of this long sense of crisis.[1]

1. See Stendhal's marginal notes to *Lucien Leuwen*: "*For me. Rule:* Do physical portraits of all the boring, secondary characters. I left these out in *Julien* [*Le Rouge et le noir*] . . . ." "Impression of the first twenty-seven pages of the fifth volume of *Rouge et noir:* true, but dry . . . ," *Lucien Leuwen,* p. 968, n. 2. Proust almost seems to echo this latter judgment in a crucial moment of *La Recherche.* At the Vermeer exhibition, just before he dies, Bergotte is reflecting on the failure of his last novels and comparing them with the luxurious but significant detailing he observes in the "View of Delft" (the famous "petit pan de mur jaune"): " 'That's how I ought to have written,' he said. 'My last books are *too dry,* I should have built up the layers of color . . . ' " (III, 187). The implied characterization of, and justification for, Proust's own practice is clear.

Of course Proust's task was not simply to resume. *A la recherche du temps perdu* culminates a whole evolution of attempts to understand the predicament of post-Revolutionary man by advancing the analysis of the predicament to a new level of penetration. But Proust accomplished this breakthrough (as so often in intellectual history) by conceiving his object of study more narrowly than had been done before. The task as he defined it had been suggested insistently since the early Realists, but never realized to the same degree before *La Recherche*. Proust decisively "moved inside." The impression of hypertrophy we have in reading *La Recherche* is the immediate sign of how much inner territory was opened up when Proust outwardly narrowed the object of previous novelistic investigation. His work illuminates the history of this entire movement by brilliantly unfolding its most profound implications for individual consciousness.

In this sense, what fascinates in Proust is not *new*, but *more*. Techniques for "moving inside" had been developing for a very long time;[2] Proust took them through an astonishing quantum jump in the course of evolving his system. The result is that discoveries in the world of *La Recherche* are to be made in detailed exploration of the novel's form, specifically in investigating how it developed the forms that were its tradition. If the connections between his techniques and parallel aspects of earlier fiction sometimes seem obscure, this is only because in following out impulses that surfaced in the Realist paradigm Proust so thoroughly realized their previously disguised potentialities. Placing him in the tradition means explicating these relations of form, means demonstrating how what seem newest in Proust are precisely those aspects of his system

---

2. Erich Kahler offers a provocative analysis of this extended process in *The Inward Turn of Narrative*. His very Hegelian account of the means by which the focus of fictions slowly and progressively "moved inside" ends just around the point at which the account of the fictional tradition in the present study begins.

which subsume the implications of preceding systems and retrospectively reveal their latent content.

It follows that, in exploring the Realists, Part I employs a dialectical method and insists on the sociohistorical matrix in which the patterns of Realist plots developed. On the other hand, the techniques used to analyze Proust's novel in Part II are primarily formalistic. This difference arises in the immediate character of the material discussed: the Realists take the dialectical process as their explicit subject, while Proust insistently denies it. To be sure, the reason for his denial is to be discovered in the movement of the dialectic itself, and will be considered in its place. In any case, it is not in denying the dialectic that Proust is original; it is in his extraordinary effort to carry through the analysis of this position in the realm of novelistic form. Thus even though we may judge Proust's *perception* of social reality to be an inadequate view forced upon him by the unprecedented difficulty of the individual's situation around the turn of the century, his novel embodies a powerfully accurate *feeling* of society's crisis in his melancholy account of the soul's isolation.[3] Placing Proust in the tradition of the novel requires exploring the techniques through which his portrayal of this isolation superseded all of the tradition's previous attempts to express it.

EDITORIAL NOTES

Emphasis in quotations: Emphasis in material quoted has been added, unless otherwise stated. Proust almost never used italics for emphasis. But because of the length of his sentences it is often necessary to call attention through use of italics to the part of a quotation central to surrounding discussion. The same convention has been followed in the case of other quoted material.

Translations: Not everyone who is a reader of Stendhal or Proust reads French easily. For this reason English ver-

3. This general distinction between "perception" and "feeling" is Christopher Caudwell's in *Illusion and Reality*, p. 36.

sions have been provided for passages in French quoted in my text. To lighten the flow of the argument, an English version alone appears for relatively short quotations whose style and language are not the principal focus of surrounding discussion, and which present no special translation difficulties. Inevitably the English versions involve compromises, and therefore reference is always given to the original French text which can thus be easily checked. The translations are my own in all cases, though I have found consulting the following editions helpful:

Flaubert: *Madame Bovary*, trans. Paul de Man (Norton).
Montesquieu: *Persian Letters*, trans. J. Robert Loy (Meridian).
Proust: *Remembrance of Things Past*, vols. 1–6, trans. C. K. Scott-Moncrieff; vol. 7, trans. Andreas Mayor (Random House).
Stendhal: *The Charterhouse of Parma*, trans. Margaret R. B. Shaw (Penguin).
Stendhal: *Red and Black*, trans. Robert M. Adams (Norton).

Marcel: A convincing case has been made for ending the traditional practice of calling the hero of *La Recherche* "Marcel" (see the articles by Michihiko Suzuki and Harold Waters in the list of works cited). I have used this name as a convenience, distinguishing by it the protagonist engaged in the unfolding fictional time of the story from the retrospective narrator who tells of him.

ACKNOWLEDGMENTS

During the development of the idea of the French novel tradition which is represented here, I have accumulated debts which it is a pleasure to acknowledge. I would like particularly to mention, among my teachers of years ago, Henri Peyre, Jean Boorsch, Victor Brombert, and Martin Price. Among present and former colleagues, Robert Alter, Stephen Arkin, Pierre Barbéris, Jean-Claude Barré, Thompson Bradley, Robert Cantor, R. V. Cottam, Joseph Duggan,

Fredric Jameson, Robert Rozà, and Susan Smith. Among my students, all those with whom I read the nineteenth-century Realists and Proust, and particularly Laura Basker-ville Adjemian, Linda Colman, Roswitha Mueller, and Mary Larner. I hope each of them will recognize the places in the discussion below where their influence has been most strongly felt; but of course responsibility for the shortcomings which remain is my own.

I would like to thank Mme Florence Callu of the Manu-script Department in the Bibliothèque Nationale, who facilitated access to the Proust material there; the Beinecke Library of Yale University for the opportunity to consult material in their possession; Joan Spangler for her careful typing of my manuscript and for her assistance generally. I am grateful to Mme Suzy Mante-Proust for her kind permis-sion to publish extracts from the Proust manuscripts in the Bibliothèque Nationale. An earlier version of my discus-sion of Flaubert was published (in French) in the *Revue des Sciences Humaines.* The typing and copying of my manuscript have been supported by grants from the Uni-versity of California, Berkeley, and from Mills College.

Part I

Notes on the Great Century

Le roman doit raconter, c'est là le genre de plaisir qu'on lui demande.

Stendhal

1

The Coherence of the Tradition

It was almost exactly a hundred years from the brilliant flowering of the French novel in 1830 to the appearance of the last volume of *A la recherche du temps perdu.* So coherent is the shape of this great century of the novel in France that each succeeding masterpiece seems the next necessary stage in the fulfillment of the idea "Novel." It is almost as if we were observing the unfolding of a Hegelian category independent of the individual craftsmen who worked to perfect it. The evolving tradition appears to determine the character of each successive book; the structural and psychological problems which each new novelist comes to grips with seem to develop directly from those which occupied his predecessors. So compelling is the movement of the tradition that the genius and the autonomy of these creators—which from one perspective we value beyond anything else in modern literature—seem to evaporate. Suddenly the Novel seems autonomous; genius seems to belong to the genre. Its needs call forth the writers' responses, and with perfect orchestration they provide them: *Le Rouge et le noir, La Chartreuse de Parme, La Peau de chagrin, Eugénie Grandet, Illusions perdues, Madame Bovary, L'Education sentimentale, L'Assommoir, A Rebours, A la recherche du temps perdu.* In such books the attempt to grasp the real world through fiction traverses a magnificent period.

The logic of this brilliant evolution must be sought in the unprecedented pressures placed upon the individual by the rapid social changes which in France accompanied what Eric Hobsbawm has called the "age of revolution." Mate-

rialist criticism has made the argument compellingly. The
general view of the novel which Lukács has provided (most
coherently in *Studies in European Realism*) and the recent
work of Pierre Barbéris on Balzac and of Sartre on Flaubert[1] suggest that the progression of the genre reveals the
continuing effort on the part of writers to reconceptualize
the rapidly changing relationship between the individual
and his society. The forms of this conceptualization are
those of the French novel during the great century of its
attempt to stay abreast of the reformulation of the world.
This is what the novel in this period is about, and it is from
this perspective that Proust needs to be placed in the tradition.

The evolving relation of the protagonist of these novels
to the action which the novels portray is central to the effort to understand this process. The changing situations of
novelistic heroes over the period in question reflect the
evolution of social forms, and reveal the deepening difficulty, as the century progressed, of making sense of the
pressures focused upon the individual. For these novelists
the effort to understand the individual, his social possibilities, and his dreams took the form of a story whose plot
represents an exemplar of human fate in a definite historical situation. The plots of these novels seek to reveal truths
about the world of everyday life which the confusion of
everyday life disguises.

The case for such cognitive value in novels is not difficult
to make. One need go no further back in the tradition than
the "philosophical" novels of the eighteenth century to
find a form based in large part upon the idea that truths
about the world are to be perceived through the events—
one might say the "strategies"—of a story. Roger Caillois's
idea of the "sociological revolution"—the hypothesis that

---

1. Pierre Barbéris, *Balzac et le mal du siècle: Contribution à une physiologie
du monde moderne*; *Balzac: Une Mythologie réaliste*; *Mythes balzaciens*; *Le
Père Goriot de Balzac: Ecriture, structures, significations*; *Le Monde de Balzac*.
Jean-Paul Sartre, *L'Idiot de la famille: Gustave Flaubert de 1821 à 1857.*

important discoveries about eighteenth-century society flowed from the simple ruse of imagining plots in which foreigners visited France or, alternatively, Frenchmen went off to view and judge other lands—provides a good case of a concept which situates the meaning of these novels in the manner in which they permit their audience to conceptualize social facts which otherwise they might never have possessed so clearly.[2] The absolutist ideology of the *ancien régime* denied the dreams of change which emerged from the increasing sense that life as it was, was unsatisfactory. But this official ideology proved, over time, completely incompatible with the comparative habit of mind fostered by these "foreign traveler" fictions. They, in turn, sharpened consciousness of the antithesis, of the immense distance between the developing dreams of a society and its present reality. Indeed, this comparative tendency in the eighteenth century is far more generalized; it is at the heart of many novels of the period not embodying the "foreign traveler" device. As a pattern of thinking, it reaches its highest expression in the constant dialectical interplay that characterizes the writing of Diderot.

Once again, the internal development of the genre seems to have been guided by a logic which must largely be accounted for by contemporary social facts. The comparative tendency was surely not new; it is one of literature's important resources for generating meaning, and the "foreign traveler" device can be traced back through Montaigne's "Cannibals" to the satires of Lucian. But perhaps never before in European literature had the problems which writers were thinking through in their fictions so clearly seemed to demand the increasing dialectical sophistication which these forms elaborated and made socially available. As consciousness grew of the barriers against the development of individuals by official ideology and accepted social forms, contemporary fiction gave a means of organizing these diffused perceptions of dissonance and

2. Roger Caillois, preface to Montesquieu, *Oeuvres complètes*, I, v.

isolated feelings of dissatisfaction. In a society based upon
rigid stasis, fiction thought the unthinkable and imagined
what change would be like. Against the divinely sanctioned
givens of the here-and-now, the dialectical turn of mind
functioned to conceive a future which might be other than
the past. Before 1789, there could have been no greater
crime of *lèse-majesté*. Caillois is thus right when he applies
the term "revolution" to this intense search for persepctive
through fictional means, and by his term associates it with
the immense social reorganization which closed the eighteenth century.

But each historical period has its own characteristic dissonance, and the artistic "thinking-through" proper to
each problem must generate its own appropriate form. It is
probably easier for us to see the connection between the
fictional types created by the *philosophes* and the social
problems it was the task of their ideological creations to
reform, than to see this same relationship in the post-Revolutionary period. The dissonance which eighteenth-century
forms attempted to make sense of is brought into focus by
the stunning period of social change which followed, by a
serious historical attempt to work out in real life what was
implicit in the "philosophical" vision. The concrete effort
to realize these changes renders previous imaginings of
them in literature objective in a way which has no parallel
in the post-Revolutionary period.

On the other hand, the main reason it is so difficult for
us to understand just how the forms of nineteenth- and
twentieth-century literature relate to their social bases is
that, unlike the period before 1789, the problems which
writers tried to come to grips with after the Revolution
still remain unsolved today. That is why our identification
with the heroes of nineteenth-century literature is so profound while (with the exception perhaps of Diderot) such
identification is something we hardly feel to the same degree with their eighteenth-century forebears. Since there
has been no concrete resolution of the problems which

writers since the Revolution have tried so courageously to think through, it remains difficult for us to see just what problems these writers may have thought themselves to be imagining solutions to. No doubt it would be otherwise if any of the revolutionary attemps of the nineteenth century had actually succeeded in realizing the social ideals held out for them in their initial phases. But the failure of these movements, which parallels the failure of the hero in the nineteenth-century novel, is one of the facts we have so well learned to live with that perhaps it is hard for us to imagine that hopes could ever really have been otherwise.

If we examine the plots of the eighteenth-century novels we admire, and compare them with nineteenth-century plots, some significant differences emerge in the kinds of stories told. Perhaps in the death of Roxane, Montesquieu's *Lettres persanes* prefigures the tragic situation of the nineteenth-century hero losing the battle for autonomy and freedom within the larger society. Typically, however, eighteenth-century plots (particularly those within the "philosophical" tradition) do not end with deaths, but rather open outward in a more or less hopeful view of human possibilities, a mirror of the optimism of the pre-Revolutionary period.

The atmosphere after 1815 is crucially different. Nineteenth-century plots may begin with the prospect of happiness—that "new idea in Europe"—and may suggest in their initial situations that the hero's self-realization is not excluded. But in the first great period after 1830, plots typically end with the death or the suicide of the protagonist. A fictional plot is an exploration of the causality of experience, and these novelistic deaths are verdicts—profoundly pessimistic verdicts—concerning the possibilities of the individual's realization in a particularly trying socio-historical context. Even the corpse of Roxane in *Les Lettres persanes* represents a very different sort of moral than the corpses of Julien Sorel, of Lucien de Rubempré,

of Emma Bovary. Roxane dies by her own hand, an angry
martyr to the eighteenth century's developing idea of freedom:

> Comment [she writes to Usbek in the final letter]
> as-tu pensé que je fusse assez crédule pour m'imaginer
> que je ne fusse dans le Monde que pour adorer tes
> caprices? que, pendant que tu te permets tout, tu
> eusses le droit d'affliger tous mes désirs? Non! J'ai
> pu vivre dans la servitude, mais j'ai toujours été libre:
> j'ai réformé tes lois sur celles de la Nature, et mon
> esprit s'est toujours tenu dans l'indépendance. . . .
> Tu étais étonné de ne point trouver en moi les trans-
> ports de l'amour. Si tu m'avais bien connue, tu y aurais
> trouvé toute la violence de la haine. [Classiques Gar-
> nier ed., p. 334] .

> (How could you have thought that I was naïve
> enough to believe that I was born only to gratify your
> whims? that, while you allow yourself everything, you
> had the right to forbid all of my desires? No! I may
> have lived in a state of servitude, but I have always
> been free: I have rewritten your laws according to Na-
> ture's, and my spirit has always maintained itself in
> independence. . . .
> You were surprised that I did not exhibit love's
> transports for you. Had you understood correctly, you
> would have felt in me instead all the violence of my
> hatred.)

But in contrast there is something abject in the deaths of
the nineteenth-century heroes we admire. Even in the
spirited courage of Julien Sorel facing his jury and accusing
them (in terms that almost sound pre-Revolutionary) of
grave social injustice, we miss the suggestion of a tran-
scendence that might redeem the individual in the world
instead of reserving his redemption, in profoundly ironic
terms, for the afterlife, in the silent hearts of Mathilde or
Mme de Rênal.

One sees clearly in these books of the first great period of the Realist age that the deaths of these characters symbolize the closing down of crucial possibilities in the real world of human action. It is of course in this world that men first seek the possibility of happiness. They fall back upon other loci for such happiness only when it proves impossible to discover in concrete, immediate social activity. Much of the evolution of the French novel during the period after 1830 represents a series of fall-back positions when, through the successive explorations of the possibilities that are represented by the plots of each succeeding novel, these possibilities are discovered to have failed, and the individual seeking his fulfillment is obliged, *faute de mieux*, to seek elsewhere. The evolution of fictional forms in the period up to Proust thus resembles a Flaubertian plot: each dream of happiness is deflated in a way that directly parallels the successive defeats of Emma Bovary, Frédéric Moreau, or Bouvard and Pécuchet, until the closing down of possibilities leaves only the alternatives of suicide for the more courageous and impotent alienation for the less.

A la recherche du temps perdu comes into focus against the background of these nineteenth-century attempts to make sense of life's possibilities. The changing fictional forms of the nineteenth century pass into the form of Proust's novel somewhat like a protracted process of natural change seen in time-lapse photography. Stendhal, Balzac, Flaubert and the post-Naturalists thus need to be considered in the light of what their forms evolved into, so that in turn these later forms can reveal the use they made of the developing tradition, and the modifications forced by new perceptions and new circumstances. With each successive masterpiece during the novel's great period, the possibilities of the relationship between an exemplary hero and the larger society are worked out. The overall shape of this exploration is a closing down of possibilities, a drying up of chances for self-realization, a tightening of the noose around the individual consciousness until, at a stage which lies beyond Proust but toward which his book points, this consciousness has only itself to reflect upon.

Moreover, there were not an infinite number of possibilities to explore; the strategies for seeking individual self-fulfillment were far from unlimited. Each of these in turn proved itself unavailable, implying a negative verdict on the possibility for human happiness in a given social configuration, and necessitating further modifications in the formal organization of fictions to take account of the new situation and try somehow to generate a source of value to replace the preceding failed one.

Pierre Barbéris outlines the beginnings of this evolution after the Restoration.[3] He suggests locating a crucial change in the consciousness of writers around the time of the severe economic reverses of 1827. The precise details of this crisis, and the exact dating of the change, are not what is of concern here. Rather, it is Barbéris's account of the change in the ideology of this period to explain the sudden acceptance of Romanticism by young, liberal bourgeois. The first phase of post-Restoration Romanticism was limited almost exclusively to sons of the aristocracy, who through their poetry expressed their sense of loss in a world which denied them the one thing that their fathers had thought inalienable—the sense that nothing could change.

Historically, the Restoration, though it made an outward show of returning privilege to the aristocracy, was the beginning of an immense appropriation of social control by members of the bourgeoisie. So the sense of disorientation felt by the aristocratic Romantics is relatively easy to understand. They were in fact dispossessed. While the revolution that has driven him out is triumphing at home, Vigny in India discovers Shakespeare's touching lines which express his sense of powerless exile:

3. See his "Mal du siècle ou d'un romantisme de droite à un romantisme de gauche," and (less schematically) his *Balzac et le mal du siècle*.

Eating the bitter bread of banishment,
While you have fed upon my seignories,
Disparked my parks and fell'd my forest woods.[4]

Beginning with Mme de Staël and Chateaubriand, this is the spirit which defines the familiar elegiac themes of the aristocratic Romantics: exile, death and wasting away, solitude, regret, and so on.

But why should the sons of the progressives who made the revolution of 1789, the liberal bourgeois, have found to their taste a literary style—indeed, an entire ideology— directed not toward a hopeful future, but rather toward a past wreathed with impotent nostalgia? Why in the midst of one of the most expansive periods in history, and precisely at the time most propitious for the realization of the dreams of their own class? Initially, the bourgeoisie was resolutely anti-Romantic. In *Illusions perdues*, Lousteau accurately explains this to Lucien de Rubempré fresh from the provinces: "Les royalistes sont romantiques, les libéraux sont classiques" ("The royalists are for Romanticism, the liberals are for Classicism"). In January 1830, the *Constitutionnel*—the leading liberal paper—put it more polemically, calling the Romantics "Messieurs du Moyen-Age."[5] But the expectations that liberalism had aroused among the young were betrayed when, in a series of unexpected economic disasters, society discovered to its surprise that it could not utilize the pool of talent which it had tempted out of the provinces into the capital. This was the lesson (and dictated the form) of *Illusions perdues*: the dream of Paris, the bitter reality, the abject retreat.

Whatever happened in detail, it is clear that members of the bourgeoisie, in almost all cases progressives who had viewed the course of events since 1789 with optimism, turned against the confidence of their class. The historical

---

4. See Barbéris, "Mal du siècle," p. 165. The lines are William Shakespeare, *Richard the Second*, III. i. 21-23.
5. Barbéris, "Mal du siècle," p. 169.

moment at which they abandoned the liberal dream and, in whatever guise, took up the long lament which we call *mal du siècle* represented a fundamental change in the French consciousness. Its immediate result in literature was the rise of Realist fiction.

Some of the ways the early novels of the Realist period represented verdicts against the possibility of human self-realization in the post-Restoration period have already been suggested. But these books were more than verdicts, they were critiques. For the first time, bourgeois values came under serious attack by bourgeois—an attack more destructive than any mounted against middle-class society in France under the banner of working-class socialism. Beginning with Saint-Simon and his followers, with Lamennais, with Stendhal's sarcastic pamphlet entitled *D'un nouveau complot contre les industriels* (1825), from scattered sources and in diverse ways, the ideological preparation for an analysis of the failure of liberal society began. When the impulse to conceptualize the dilemma of the lapsed liberal consciousness came to fruition in the plots of early Realist fiction, it was natural that these books, written from a perspective within the bourgeoisie itself, would chronicle how the tension between individual aspirations and the inimical demands of the larger society developed and, finally, destroyed those aspirations. I have already spoken of the revolutionary sound of Julien Sorel's speech to his jury. The jury he addresses with such ill-contained bitterness is made up, however, not of hated aristocrats, but of bourgeois. To conclude this first masterpiece of the Realist era, Stendhal creates a situation which symbolically expresses the essential perception in the Realist critique: the enemy is no longer "out there," and can no longer be swept away in a beneficent social house-cleaning resembling the fervor of 1789. As the relationship of subject and object, of aspiration and obstruction thus became more internally conflicted, it was natural that plots should lose the optimistic schematism of the pre-Revolutionary period.

Frank Kermode writes that "fictions are for finding things out, and they change as the needs of sense-making change" (*Sense of an Ending*, p. 39). But in the Realist period, what could be found out through fiction increasingly suggested that the problems had no real solution, that the dissonance which could at last be heard in all its unpleasant clarity was built into the social instrument itself. No amount of tuning, it seemed, would remove it. The prestigious corpses of so many novelistic protagonists simply cannot have resulted from mistaken identity or "administrative error." These heroes die in the early Realist period because there is no way for them to live. Once fiction had found this out, some of the energy which it had possessed left it. Progressively the forward thrust of plot which carried us along in the early novels of Stendhal and Balzac began to melt away.

The "need to make sense" of which Kermode speaks led under these new conditions to a subtle but definite inward turn in fiction. There would be, in the nineteenth century, no more picaresque jollity; the enterprise had become deadly serious, even solemn. Of course, conditions outside the novel were also evolving, and the process of "finding things out" did not take place only in writers' minds. But it is worth noting here that the subdued, introspective character which only became obvious in novels later in the century, and which reached its formal apogee in Proust, was built into novelistic texture from the beginning of the Realist period. Indeed, Proust caught this crucial note exactly in a brilliant jotting on Stendhal: "En un sens les beaux livres ajoutent aux événements une tranche d'âme coïncidente. Dans *Le Rouge et le Noir*, chaque action est suivie d'une partie de la phrase indiquant ce qui se passe inconsciemment dans l'âme, c'est le roman du motif" (*CSB*, p. 655; "In a sense, great books add a congruent slice of the soul to their account of events. In *The Red and the Black* every action is followed by a section of the sentence indicating what is going on unconsciously in the soul: it is the novel of motives").

So the nineteenth-century novelists conceived in imagination—and sent forth their heroes to confront—a social
situation which time after time proved fatal to their aspirations for happiness. But the effort to understand why led
to a dead end within the psychology of the protagonist.
The more profoundly novelists analyzed the mechanism
which defeated the hero's desires, the more the inimical
force turned out to be indivisible from the questing hero
himself. The profound detail with which the hero's inter-
action with the world outside is depicted and the density
of analysis of his internal dilemma thus reflect the same
underlying cause, the inability of nineteenth-century
writers to locate outside the thinking and feeling subject
solutions to the life problems which pressed in on them.

The desires which drive the heroes forward and the mechanism by which these desires are defeated are not separable.
The desires cannot remain while the destructive mechanism is defused. The aspirations and their antitheses are
part of the same organic social nexus, whence the series of
crucially divided, internally "flawed" heroes in Realist
novels: Julien Sorel, who cannot sort out his profound desires, on the one hand for personal purity, on the other for
success and power through hypocritical dissembling;
Raphaël de Valentin, who within the fantastic myth of
La Peau de chagrin discovers that his desires bear within
them their own antithesis, that the means by which he attempts to attain self-realization lead him, through a totally coherent, irreversible process, to self-destruction;
Lucien de Rubempré, whose artistic talents are no match
for the destructive muscle of bourgeois-controlled Restoration society, but whose ambition is generated by precisely
the social forces that prevent its realization; Frédéric
Moreau, whose weakness parallels and prolongs the weaknesses of his predecessors, and in whom we discover that
inaction in no way slows the process of destruction, since
it turns out to be no more possible to defeat inimical social
forces by attempting to elude their influence than by attempting to triumph over them in head-on battle.

In eighteenth-century "philosophical" fiction the conflict in the social dialectic which was mirrored in novelistic
plots seemed to have a solution. Between aristocratic privilege and some ideal of human equality, a clear choice could
be made—in imagination by writers, in fact by revolutionaries. The situation of the Third Estate would immediately change with the elimination of aristocrats and privilege: in this middle-class conceptualization, the thesis and
the antithesis appeared clearly differentiable one from the
other.

The nineteenth-century dialectic proved—and still proves
—much more intractable, for there seemed, and seems, no
way to separate its terms from each other. Throughout the
novel in the nineteenth century we find a search for some
contemporary equivalent of the "aristocrats" whose expul-
sion would resolve the problems of the individual. But the
evil to be expelled has not been successfully divided from
the characters who undergo its effects. Whatever the synthesis of these opposing forces might be, it has not yet appeared in novels as an imaginative suggestion. It still
appears, as it did after 1830, that solving the problem
ultimately implies destroying the self that suffers from it.
The divided consciousness and self-alienation we impotently
recognize as characteristic of modern existence arises in
this post-Revolutionary dilemma.

As a result, it begins to become clear just what in the
nineteenth-century novel progressively drove action out of
fiction and modified the idea of traditional plots until they
disintegrate into the agonizing stasis of *L'Education sentimentale* or the bitter ritual repetitiveness of *Bouvard et
Pécuchet*. But this was a discovery which took a substantial
part of the novel's great century to come to artistic consciousness. Let us examine how things stood in Stendhal.

2

Stendhal: Unhappiness in Action

In the long love affair they have had with him, what seems to charm critics most profoundly is Stendhal's exquisite vulnerability. His dilemma is acute, but it rarely makes him solemn. He faces a sense of loss and confusion no less intense than that which produced such enervation and sentimental excesses in the Romantic poets, but Stendhal remains faithful to a complex view of experience in which his anguish, though extreme, is always tempered by attempts to grasp and gain control of it. This bivalence characterizes everything in the Stendhalian world, and provides a powerful source of energy in his plots. Stendhal always insists on having things both ways—how comforting, we feel, that his weaknesses should prove so like our own.

Victor Brombert's examination of the "analyst" and "amorist" strains in Stendhal, Jean-Pierre Richard's "connaissance" vs. "tendresse," and other similar pairs have brilliantly demonstrated how deeply ingrained in the Stendhalian view of the world such bivalence is. Jean Starobinski and Robert M. Adams have shown the variety of Stendhal's masks, and have revealed the logic behind the impulse to have things both be and not be, to be in two places at once, to be both young and old, wise and naïve, that underlies Stendhal's tendency to disguise himself and his heroes.[1]

But the tragic quality of this bivalence and of these dis-

1. Victor Brombert, "Stendhal, Analyst or Amorist?"; Jean-Pierre Richard, "Connaissance et tendresse chez Stendhal." Jean Starobinski, "Stendhal pseudonyme"; Robert M. Adams, *Stendhal: Notes on a Novelist.*

guises needs to be emphasized here. The desire to have things both ways is immensely seductive in Stendhal, but it is a doomed desire, not very different from most of the dreams of his own heroes or of others in the Realist period. This man who, born in 1783, is the only great nineteenth-century novelist with any worldly experience of the period before the Restoration, finds himself spanning his two centuries in no posture of strength, but rather in disequilibrium, often embarrassingly close to an ignominious tumble.

Stendhal is moreover the first of the Realist writers in whom we find a paradoxical tendency, despite his often proclaimed political progressivism, to embrace with powerful reactionary nostalgia the pre-Revolutionary "dark ages" before Liberty, Equality and Fraternity. The defeat of the hopes, not only of Stendhal but of numerous nineteenth-century writers, leads to this attitude. Increasingly through the century that follows the Restoration, the need to conceive in imagination a world in which the problems of contemporary society might be rationalized leads writers either to dream confusedly of a "lendemain qui chante"—a frequent tendency in Stendhal—or, more characteristically, to fantasize a return to the past. A well-known quotation from Talleyrand expresses the emotion behind this nostalgic impulse: "Qui n'a pas vécu dans les années voisines de 1780 n'a pas connu le plaisir de vivre" ("Those who did not live around 1780 have not experienced the joy of living").[2]

For Stendhal, the sweetness of pre-Revolutionary life is a dream of his own childhood. The memory of this time, rather than fading with the passage of years, grew stronger

2. This is not the form in which the thought is usually quoted (generally, the tradition has Talleyrand speaking more grandly about the period "before the Revolution"; it is this form that Bernardo Bertolucci adopted in the title of his fine film). This common form, however, seems apocryphal; the source appears to be François Guizot's *Mémoires pour servir à l'histoire de mon temps*, I, 6, quoting a remark Talleyrand made to Guizot.

as, against the desolation of the present, Stendhal embroidered the past with a glow very much like that with which the aristocratic Romantics surrounded the period before the emigration. For these dispossessed individuals, this is the past whose disappearance forms the fundamental element in their regret. Their experience prefigures Proust's lament over the lost paradise of childhood and has the same meaning: the purpose of this nostalgia remains constantly to criticize by comparison the unhappiness that awaits the adult in modern society. There is such a strong impulse in these writers to turn back in time!

Throughout his career Stendhal's political position was moderate constitutionalism. But he describes in his *Journal* an important discovery of political nostalgia which took place during his trip to Italy in the fall of 1811 (he was then twenty-eight). Until that point in his life, he writes, he had rejoiced at the French Revolution and the changes it brought. However, he continues:

> Depuis quelque temps seulement, j'avais quelque idée vague qu'elle [the Revolution] avait exilé l'*allegria* de l'Europe pour un siècle peut-être. . . . J'avais pris tous les regrets de nos vieillards pour le radotage d'un *laudator temporis acti*. . . . Je vois, par ce que j'apprends de Venise et de Milan, qu'il pourrait y avoir du vrai. . . . [*Journal*, 2 Sept. 1811, p. 1073]

> (Only recently have I entertained the vague idea that the Revolution may have exiled *allegria* [joy] from Europe for perhaps a century. . . . I had taken our elders' nostalgia to be the babbling of a *laudator temporis acti* [glorifier of the past]. . . . But I see, by what I've learned in Venice and Milan, that they may have been right after all.)

But in Stendhal, bivalence is constant. The best comment on this touching discovery of nostalgia comes in a note he added to the passage on 22 October 1817—that is, several years after the Restoration began.

> J'avais encore un peu de cette illusion en 1814 à la chute de Napoléon. La terrible expérience que nous faisons m'a illuminé. L'Europe ne peut pas plus être ce qu'elle était en 1760 qu'un homme de 30 ans être le folâtre jeune homme de 15.

> (That illusion still tempted me a little in 1814 at the time of Napoleon's fall. But the awful period we are passing through now has enlightened me. Europe can no more be what it was in 1760 than a man of 30 [Stendhal is 34] can remain the lighthearted adolescent of 15.)

Indeed, the ironically-named "Restoration" irrefutably demonstrated how futile was the nostalgia which Stendhal never stopped experiencing—"Oh! how much better it would have been to have been born two and a half centuries ago, in 1600!" (*Lucien Leuwen*, second preface, 1836)— and which, because it is never allowed entirely to bolt away with his feelings, provides a major part of his charm. In this way, the fantasy of a past where life could be lived fully, without the *bassesse* which for Stendhal defined the dreary nineteenth century, is nonetheless accompanied constantly, and constantly balanced, by the idea that such a past is irretrievable, and that the present, however disagreeable, is the only arena for realizing human happiness. It is inevitably the present that the novelist must judge.

The most charming, most deceptive of Stendhal's ideas is "la chasse au bonheur" ("the pursuit of happiness"). The vigor, the refreshment we feel in reading the early parts of his novels sometimes expands in our minds until this enthusiasm seems to characterize the entire Stendhalian world. But bivalence is always present, and happiness never lies at the end of the hero's quest. In fact, the dialectic of experience in Stendhal is no different from that in Balzac, Flaubert or Proust: desire is always followed by defeat—indeed, seems mechanically to call it forth. Although energy bursts out in each renewed effort to realize the hero's dream, although frequently in these books situations are described in which a character finds himself "mad with joy" or "transported with happiness," such privileged moments are always painfully scuttled.

This happens because of the constant, irreducible distance in Stendhal between the world of mind—with its passions, its sensitivities, its fantasies—and the world of action, rational, effective, solid, but for Stendhal's heroes always beyond their grasp. What Stendhal terms "that delicate plant we call happiness" (*La Chartreuse*, p. 167) constantly withers when his hero comes upon it in the world. Stendhal is lucid about this, as shown in two judgments from *Le Rouge et le noir*. The first occurs as Julien Sorel is just beginning his quest: "In a word, what made Julien a superior being was precisely what prevented him from enjoying a pleasure that lay directly in his path" (p. 82); the second when he is nearing its tragic end: "His whole life had been nothing but a long preparation for misfortune [*malheur*]" (p. 453). The assertion is constant: happiness will elude these beings.

When happiness proves unattainable in the world of concrete social activity, the fall-back position is to transform in imagination the solitude to which the individual is condemned into a privileged locus for his self-realization. Proust, whose experience of the plight was more profound than that of any novelist who preceded him—because his isolation was more total—was logically the first of Stendhal's admirers to identify how this strategy of solitude takes form as a Stendhalian theme: "Chaque fois que Julien Sorel ou Fabrice quittent les vains soucis [Proust's revealing term for what I have called the world of concrete social activity] pour vivre d'une vie désintéressée et voluptueuse, ils se trouvent toujours dans un lieu élevé (que ce soit dans la prison de Fabrice ou celle de Julien)" (*CSB,* p. 611; "Whenever Julien Sorel or Fabrice leaves illusory concerns behind him and is able to experience unselfish and sensuously free existence, he is always somewhere high up (for example in Fabrice's prison, or in Julien's)"; the idea reappears in *La Prisonnière* during the lesson of art criticism which Marcel gives Albertine; *La Recherche,* III, 377). Stendhal himself tells us that Julien alone on the mountain was "happier than he had ever been in his life" (*Le Rouge,* p. 69). He thus does his best to put an optimistic face on the tragic discovery which is the central moral judgment in his novels, that the organization of society makes it impossible for the sensitive person to be happy in the real world. Stendhal understood the mechanism quite clearly. One need only read his bitter description of the "ordinary course of things in the nineteenth century" (*Le Rouge,* p. 141)—it led inevitably to the destruction of the "homme de coeur"—to understand the burden of disappointment in the apostrophes to his own age which run through Stendhal's works (for example, in the made-up epigraph to Chapter 29 of the second part of *Le Rouge*: "Oh unhappy nineteenth century!" [p. 398]).

Julien Sorel, a peasant trying to force his way into respectable society, is the subject of Stendhal's most detailed attempt to conceptualize this "ordinary course of things in the nineteenth century" in terms of the concrete social dialectic. The result is sufficiently definite for Stendhal to feel he need not repeat the same fatal experiment again (of the unfinished *Lamiel* more will be said later).

At the other end of the scale, Fabrice del Dongo is his most protected hero, in terms of social position and, more important, in terms of his action in the novel. Yet it is remarkable how desultory is Fabrice's "chasse au bonheur"; it leads him, rather sheep-like, to a progressive shrinking of the orbit in which he moves: from prison before Waterloo to exile in Romagnon, to prison in the Tour Farnèse, to retreat in the monastery at Velleja, and finally to the charterhouse where his life simply fades out. The extraordinary freshness of *La Chartreuse de Parme* hardly compensates for this powerful movement toward social quarantine, though the two phenomena are surely linked. Indeed, the charm of the book is achieved at the cost of resolutely isolating Fabrice from the real.

Most obvious is the constant protection of Fabrice by his aunt, Mosca, and others. But there is something in the very texture of their characterization that makes Fabrice (and Clélia Conti too) seem like fairy-tale figures within the more general Realist convention present in the novel. Fabrice and Clélia have a kind of Peter Pan complex. They *won't* grow up, and Stendhal is their constant accomplice in indulging their adolescence. When the pressure of the real on this arrangement proves too great, Stendhal kills them off before adulthood can make them grave.

In the meantime, the book curiously controverts what now seems the classic pattern of novels of the Realist period. Stendhal's task is not to "educate" Fabrice—he had learned the cost of this with Julien—but to allow him to remain uneducated; not to fit him for life in the modern world, but to render him increasingly unsuited for it. He thus seems a fairy-tale character, a figure from olden-days; and yet, in spite of the protection which surrounds him, the social dialectic manages to exert its malignant force. From Fabrice's point of view, the action of the novel is a "chasse au bonheur," but it is difficult to understand why happiness, in any lasting sense, always eludes him. Insulated from apparent pressure, he remains a deeply troubled person. His primary symptom betrays a psycho-social malady hardly less grave than something one might find in Jean Genet: Fabrice's capacity for love is profoundly distorted.

The imprisonment which alone releases in him the ability

to love is seen by Stendhal as a heightened case of the charm of isolation. But how radically pessimistic is this solution to the problem of the individual! With a bit of perspective, it is immediately apparent how far into absurdity Fabrice has been driven. What a mad world must lie outside the prisons which Fabrice actively seeks (see *La Chartreuse*, pp. 357, 368, 378) to make such insanity seem reasonable! When Fabrice covers with passionate kisses the bread Clélia has sent him in his cell, Stendhal excuses his odd behavior with a classic plea for tolerance: "he was in love" (p. 355). But the larger movement of the novel, which forces the hero from prison to prison and permits him no peace during his increasingly rare times on parole, reveals this enchanting excuse as simply another example of Stendhal's continual feinting to distract himself and us, with a consummately charming mumbo-jumbo of false hope, from his distressing knowledge of the fate of individuals as he discovers it through fiction.

Whatever its intermittent charm, love in this novel always fails. The same pattern, however disguised, always intervenes, as in this moment with Clélia and the immediate comment of the narrator: "Fabrice embraced her, beside himself with surprise and happiness. . . . The happiness which began that evening lasted but a few days" (*La Chartreuse*, p. 491). No matter how bewitching, this is a world of personal disaster. Flaubert's profound pessimism is not far off.

The irony of the end of *La Chartreuse* is total. Mosca has become immensely wealthy, but has lost the reason for which he wanted riches. Gina "united all appearances of happiness" (as Stendhal cruelly puts it), and she, too, soon loses her reason to live, as Fabrice, sapped by the deaths of Clélia and their son Sandrino, passes away. The hecatomb rivals the classics, but its meaning is more immediate, for Stendhal insists that the catastrophe of his world is historically determined, that the villain is the "triste dix-neuv-

ième siècle" whose shadow lies over all his worlds like a
curse. In a sad perversion of the initial hope, the "pursuit
of happiness" becomes a "chasse au malheur."

What happens in love—most devastatingly in *La Chartreuse*, but to some degree in all of these novels—is symbolic
of what happens in Stendhal to all human relationships.
Something always cuts off Stendhal's protagonists from
their experience of others. In the case of Julien Sorel, the
self-distortion he elects in order to win success in the world
—his ambition, hypocrisy, and so on—leads to a painful
state of alienation, in which the self that relates to others is
not the real self, while the real self finds relation impossible. The individual internalizes the pressure he is under,
until even self-honesty is excluded. For five hundred pages,
Stendhal tries to remain lucid about Julien, coddling him
with his protective irony and obliging him to deeply moving efforts of self-analysis after each successive triumph.
Characteristically in the famous "n'est-ce que ça?" ("is
that all it is?") Julien takes the measure of the disappointment each triumph turns out to be.

But it requires a profound paroxysm to reveal the depth
of the self-deception his situation has forced him to. Julien
has learned through practical experience of the social dialectic—having been beaten by his father, despised by his
brothers, held in contempt by M. de Rênal and the bourgeois of Verrières—to see social situations as constant ad-
versary proceedings. As he says soon after he enters the
seminary in Besançon, "here I am at last in the world I
must live in till I play out my role, surrounded by real
enemies" (*Le Rouge*, p. 171). This perception becomes his
mode of consciousness of others.

But how tragic it is that this internalized assumption of
the world's hostility should cause him to experience even
the women he loves as adversaries: "His glances the next
morning, when he saw Madame de Rênal again, were odd:
he was studying her like an enemy with whom a battle was

inevitable" (*Le Rouge*, p. 50). "Enemy" echoes through the novel until Julien attempts to kill Mme de Rênal after she seems to have become the agent of a grave set-back to his ambition. Seen internally, his conduct is logical. The reversal which follows, however, lays bare the excruciating tension within Julien which is the product of this distorted dialectic. In the sudden welling-up of love for the woman he tried to murder, he finally understands how he should have lived.

But we must be careful not to see this discovery as a classical redemption. Concretely, it points nowhere. In a few days time the discovery—"Give me five more years, to live with Madame de Rênal" (*Le Rouge*, p. 482)—will cost Julien his head. There is no solution in this life for the kind of self-distortion which Julien finally understands: "Parlant seul avec moi-même, à deux pas de la mort, je suis encore hypocrite. . . O dix-neuvième siècle!" (*Le Rouge*, p. 481; "No one around, talking to myself, two steps from the scaffold, and still I'm a hypocrite. . . Oh, nineteenth century!").

The situation of Fabrice is different. Stendhal's recognition through Julien that concrete contact with the world inevitably distorts the "âme sensible" leads him to isolate Fabrice so totally from the real, and to cut him off so completely from any direct experience of the social dialectic, that he is never sure whether his experiences are authentic or not. On the surface, his situation might seem less problematic than that of Stendhal's other heroes: "En sa qualité de noble, [Fabrice] se croyait fait pour être plus heureux qu'un autre" (*La Chartreuse*, p. 100; "As a nobleman, Fabrice believed he was made to be happier than ordinary people"). But his life, defined by the protection accorded him and by the unmodified naïveté of his passions, so removes him from the conflicts of society that his existence becomes totally internalized. Material comfort is something Fabrice is not aware of, social concupiscence something he cannot understand. He is without external attachments; Mosca and Gina enable him to live without having to make a single material decision. Even on his trip to Waterloo he finds himself so protected from the consequences of his actions—not least, as the bullets fly, by Stendhal himself—that he remains unsure whether these themselves were real.

For us as for Stendhal, Waterloo represents a political struggle which changed millions of lives, a battle in which thousands died. But the magic which surrounds Fabrice and asserts his fairy-tale quality is at odds with the atmosphere of a military massacre. Fabrice continues, for himself and for us, to be queerly abstracted. Shortly after meeting Clélia Conti for the first time, he questions his capacity to love with the same innocence with which he had questioned the reality of Waterloo (see *La Chartreuse*, p. 131). And locked in a cage at the top of the Tour Farnèse, surrounded by hideous guards who intermittently attempt to poison him, fed on little more than bread and water, he asks himself with undiminished naïveté: "Mais ceci est-il une prison?" (*La Chartreuse*, p. 329; "But is this really a prison?").

When romance goes this far, what happens to reality? In his prison Fabrice remains, in the midst of the most malevolent elements of the real, oddly insulated from the real. Thus Stendhal in his greatest novel comes to define the authenticity of his hero in terms of his radical incapacity for authentic contact with the world. The degree of self-distortion here is fully as great as in Julien, and in view of later developments in the novel during the great century, it is strikingly prophetic.

The case of *Lucien Leuwen* is more complex because Lucien finds himself at neither of the extremes we see in Julien and Fabrice. Neither peasant nor aristocrat, he lacks the means available to Stendhal's other heroes for defining himself at one or the other limit on the social scale. In his experience, as in the entire novel that depicts it, there is something uncertain and indecisive which mirrors his social situation. For Lucien, because he is profoundly unclear about where he is, the constant question becomes, what should I strive to be? His father delights in taunting him on this point. In a family conference concerning his problematical son's future, M. Leuwen puts it this mocking way: "l'objet de l'ordre du jour: 'Sera-t-il dieu, table ou cuvette?'" (*Lucien Leuwen*, I, 1072; "The question on today's agenda: 'Should he become this, that, or the other thing?'"). But Lucien has already answered the question: "In truth, I don't know what I am" (I, 986).

Lucien Leuwen reveals something which neither *Le Rouge* nor *La Chartreuse* could deal with adequately. Those books show that the extreme positions are not tenable, but *Lucien Leuwen* is well on the way to showing that *no* position is. In his intermediate situation, Lucien has available to him the material wealth of Fabrice, and still has social reason to feel the ambition of Julien. The experiment with him as subject is thus more complex and more critical than the other two; but its results are no more encouraging. In a position to make what seem like real choices, with the material capacity to make them, Lucien flounders. Neither solitude nor society, neither wealth nor austerity, attracts him strongly enough to win real commitment. From one end of the book to the other, no real choices are made, and Lucien's exasperated "I don't know what I want" (I, 823) becomes the novel's motto.[3] The roles which Lucien bluntly declines are numerous; others, inattentively tried on, prove vaguely disappointing (his "is that all it is?" [I, 1346] after seducing Mme Grandet precisely echoes Julien's). He jokes desultorily about various possible poli-

---

3. Near the end, even Lucien's cynically positive father contracts the disease: " 'Well, yes,' he finally said, 'I've had an attack of ambition, and what's comic is that I don't know what to desire' " (I, 1328).

tical allegiances (I, 851), but nothing really serves. Only true love tempts him. And on the question of true love the novel founders.

Mme de Chasteller, the pure beauty who captures Lucien's heart, more completely resembles the "belle dame sans merci" than any of Stendhal's other heroines. Yet we know from Stendhal's outlines for the novel that—alone of all his major works—*Lucien Leuwen* was to have had a happy ending.[4] But Stendhal never wrote it.

The author who fails to finish a book presents us with a problem of analysis as tantalizing as does any completed novel. It is difficult enough to imagine an ending which would complete the overall harmony of the form in a work (like *Lamiel*) interrupted by its author's death. But in the case of a book simply abandoned, inevitably we ask ourselves whether its noncompletion betrays a discovery on the writer's part that concord between the end of the story and its developing texture was impossible to establish.[5] That may well be the case of *Lucien Leuwen*.

The fundamental difference between this book and the two major novels Stendhal completed is that Stendhal wanted his bourgeois hero to end up happy where his peasant and his aristocratic heroes failed. In this novel, the social dialectic was to have come out differently. Not that Lucien was to be any less naïve than other Stendhalian heroes, or the world in general any more attractive a place. But in *Lucien Leuwen* love was to have found a way, and the magic which is only an aura surrounding Fabrice was to have become an element of the plot. Though Stendhal willfully complicates the course of love for poor Lucien and Bathilde de Chasteller, his intention remained firmly to marry them off at the novel's conclusion. But in the end, perhaps he was unable to bring off what Henry James (in the preface to *Roderick Hudson*) called the "distribution

4. See Henri Martineau's preface, I, 740.
5. "Concord" is Frank Kermode's term in *The Sense of an Ending*, p. 4.

at the last of prizes, pensions, husbands, wives, babies, millions, appended paragraphs, and cheerful remarks." A clue to why the happy ending may have proved out of reach is found in Stendhal's apostrophe to himself: "Tu n'es qu'un *naturaliste*, tu ne *choisis* pas tes modèles, *mais* prends pour *love* toujours Methilde et Dominique" ("You're nothing but a *naturalist*, you don't *choose* your models, *but* always use for *love* Méthilde and Dominique")—that is, Mathilde Dembowski and Stendhal.[6] Desperately, Stendhal loved the woman he called Méthilde from 1818 to 1821. She did not love him. And though in *Lucien Leuwen* the grounds are laid for a marriage between Mme de Chasteller and Lucien, the shape of such a dénouement must have seemed wrong to a man for whom the most intense experience of love in his life rather paralleled the habitual course of experience elsewhere in his novels: failure and collapse.

Around the time he began writing *Lucien Leuwen*, Stendhal noted the following on the fly leaf of his copy of *Le Rouge*: "M. de Tracy me disait: on ne peut plus atteindre au vrai . . . que dans le roman. Je vois tous les jours davantage que partout ailleurs c'est une prétention" ("M. de Tracy used to tell me: the only way to get hold of what's true is in novels. Every day it becomes clearer to me that anywhere else it's just a pretension").[7] The thought most likely reflects upon the epigraph from Danton which he had chosen for that novel—"La vérité, l'âpre vérité" ("The truth, the bitter truth"). But truth as Stendhal knew it was infinitely more bitter than the planned conclusion of *Lucien Leuwen*. For Stendhal, it seems that the logic of experience, since *Armance* and here as elsewhere, required nonconsummation.

6. Stendhal's italics. Quoted by Martineau in his preface to *Lucien Leuwen*, I, 745.

7. Quoted from Martineau's older Classiques Garnier edition of *Le Rouge* (p. 539), since a part of the passage appears to have been inadvertently omitted from the Castex text (p. 493).

What are the consequences of this logic for the portrayal of action in Stendhal's novels? For Stendhal's heroes, "la chasse au bonheur" becomes increasingly desultory. Once we leave behind the *arriviste* energy of Julien Sorel, who has concrete obstacles to battle, and join Lucien in Nancy or Fabrice in the Tour Farnèse, we float in a diffuse and languorous dream of exaltation which, as far as its energy-content is concerned, is not so very different from the Romantic "vague des sentiments." "Le roman doit raconter, c'est là le genre de plaisir qu'on lui demande" ("The novel has to tell a story; that is the sort of pleasure we expect from it"), Stendhal noted in the margin of *Lucien Leuwen* (I, 1581). In this spirit, narrating his heroes' ethereal love affairs—which at the same time he believed were the highest expression of their authenticity—must have been like trying to make contact with someone who is woolgathering: "M. Leuwen talked for quite a while without being able to involve his son in conversation. He didn't like Lucien's dreamy air" (I, 1110).

The behavior of Stendhal's heroes, progressively alienated from concrete experience, is becoming internalized. Increasingly in these books, the hero does not act and, though an object of intense interest, ceases to be a source of narrative energy. In the perspective of developments later in the century, his passivity—one might almost say, his enervation—is immensely suggestive. The character of the protagonist (from the Greek for competitor) is changing under the pressure of an increasingly unmanageable social world outside. Life is apparently becoming a competition which the novelistic hero must lose.

Yet history was moving, and Stendhal was trying hard to believe in it. *La Chartreuse de Parme* opens with a brilliant evocation of the drama of Napoleon's conquest of Milan. Suddenly, Stendhal tells us, governments and hearts are changed. Similarly, Mme Leuwen insists that things are changing: "Praise God, dear Lucien, you're thirty-eight

years younger than the King. Think about the changes
that have occurred in France in thirty-eight years. Why
shouldn't the future be like the past?" (I, 1082-83). But in
this conversation, situated more than thirty years after
Napoleon's victory in Italy, the tone (cast as a negative
interrogation) is crucially more tentative. For Stendhal,
contemporary salvation was much harder to believe in.

Yet his world remains full of energy, though it is not
always incarnated in his heroes. Complicated political plots
and personal intrigues animate his novels with all the vigor
of adventure tales. "Le vague," Stendhal wrote, "tue la
politique" (*Mélanges intimes*, I, 368; "Vagueness kills politics"). He might have said the same of novels, and his own
remain alive because the intermittent vagueness of his heroes is counterbalanced by the energy of other characters.

The force that moves history and the force that moves
stories are the same force under different disguises. In both
cases, *desire* propels the dialectic forward, in one world
toward change or revolution, in the other toward dénouement. There is no problem of energy in *Le Rouge et le
noir* because Julien's desires have clear social roots and
materially thrust him forward on his fatal course. But increasingly the desires which motivate action in the other
novels are found in subsidiary characters, while (as we
saw in *Lucien Leuwen*) the principal "actors" all seem to
have contracted some profound paralysis of the will.

The result in *Lucien Leuwen* and *La Chartreuse* is a curious fragmentation of energy. Lucien and Fabrice, with
their exquisite sensitivity and in their effective isolation,
are freed to live out the spiritual plight of the "homme de
coeur" in the nineteenth century. In the meantime, the
field of action is occupied—indeed, preempted—by figures
like the extraordinary Dr. Du Poirier. Consider this passage,
describing Lucien's first meeting with Du Poirier, who
comes to examine the wound Lucien has received in his
duel:

M. Du Poirier était un être de la dernière vulgarité,

M. Du Poirier was a person of the lowest vulgarity

[*This first touch augurs badly.*]

et qui semblait fier de ses façons basses et familières; c'est ainsi que le cochon se vautre dans la fange avec une volupté insolente pour le spectateur.

who nonetheless seemed proud of his base manners and of the liberties he took, like the pig that wallows in the mud with a voluptuous pleasure that insults the viewer.

[*At this point, the reader is ready to abandon the horrible physician.*]

Mais Lucien n'eut presque pas le temps d'apercevoir ce ridicule extrême;

But Lucien hardly had time to note this extreme ridiculousness;

[*Things begin to turn around.*]

il était trop évident que ce n'était point par vanité, et pour se faire son égal ou son supérieur que Du Poirier était familier avec lui.

it was perfectly obvious that it was not out of vanity, or because he pretended to be Lucien's equal or his superior, that Du Poirier took liberties with him.

[*A kind of rehabilitation seems to begin here.*]

Lucien crut voir un homme de mérite, entraîné par le besoin d'exprimer vivement les pensées dont la foule et l'énergie l'oppriment. . . .

Lucien thought he detected a man of talent, carried away by the need to express thoughts which frustrated him with their number and energy. . . .

[*Du Poirier begins to appear a kind of "Rameau's Nephew."*]

"Mais non, se dit Lucien . . .

"No, after all," Lucien said to himself . . .

[*Yet another change of direction.*]

cet homme est un hypocrite; il a trop d'esprit pour être entraîné, il ne fait rien qu'après y avoir bien songé."

"this fellow is a hypocrite; he's too smart to let himself be carried away, he doesn't do anything without having planned it all out carefully."

[I, 846–47]

The movement within this description is striking. A man who appears contemptible turns out complex, and forces admiration in spite of his vulgarity. For whatever he may be, Du Poirier is a figure of real energy (see for example his powerful speech to the Chamber of Deputies much later on—I, 1291 ff.), and is thus saved from ridicule. He is a rascal, but not riffraff. All the real "actors" in Stendhal exhibit to some degree the roguishness of this "coquin singulier" (I, 1084).

Stendhal's relationship to these characters is as ambiguous as anything in his novels. Let us recall his admiration for the "actors" of history—beginning with Napoleon—and the fascination with which he deciphered old chronicles of crimes of passion, read the memoirs of the Cardinal de Retz, the *Gazette des Tribunaux*. Energy haunted him. But energy in his world could never be pure in the way he imagined it in the past that he spent so much effort creating as an antidote to his present. The effective characters who fascinated him at the same time absolutely deny the isolation which he invented as a privileged state for his cherished heroes. Fabrice, Lucien, even Julien were the "âmes sensibles" ("sensitive souls") whose glory was to be out of tune with their century. The actors in harmony with it, who manage somehow to come to terms, though they fascinate Stendhal, are to that degree discredited. But then action itself is discredited in these books, since it represents a threat to the protective idealism which is Stendhal's most intimate psychological defense.

To put it another way, there is in this conflict an imbalance that gravely threatens the enterprise of the Realist novel. Between the necessity of revealing the hero's soul in action and the impossibility of his action, Stendhal stands attempting to battle a tension which, within an astonishingly short time, will shake the forms of fiction to their foundations.

The fragmentary *Lamiel*, which Stendhal was working on when he died, attempted to come to terms with this tension. Fictional forms are not free—Stendhal's inability to see *Lucien Leuwen* through to its happy ending is sufficient indication of that. In logic there may have seemed two ways to resolve the formal impasse which *La Chartreuse* concealed beneath its brilliant enthusiasm. In fact, however, "action" would prove increasingly irrelevant as the tradition of the novel progressed. The genre was moving decidedly in one direction only, toward Flaubert's epochal experiments with immobility. *Lamiel* fights a rear-guard action in attempting to follow out the implications of the other course. Its effort is to rejoin in one character the energy which had fragmented in previous books. Julien, Lucien, and Fabrice had, progressively, become divided individuals. As their alienation from the rotten society that surrounded them became a self-alienation which paralyzed them from within, their conflict with the world had increasingly been veiled by their protective isolation, and the social dialectic carried on through a series of intermediates (Chélan, Pirard; M. Leuwen, Coffe; Mosca, Ferrante Palla, La Sanseverina) whose vigor compensated for the heroes' increasing passivity. But Lamiel's alienation was to be completely open, her revolt was to be brutally frank. Her violent opposition to French society around 1830 was to abolish the mystification of the earlier books.

Much of the shape of *Lamiel* flows from this underlying logic: Lamiel is more clearly a peasant than Julien Sorel (whose delicacy always seemed charmingly somewhat above his station), more clearly an orphan than he, and a woman besides! Stendhal thus accumulated for his heroine elements of profound social frustration, and gave her a mentor, the extraordinary hunchback Sansfin, who immediately detects her anger and provides it a focus and direction through his cynical instruction.

> —Le monde, lui disait Sansfin, n'est point divisé, comme le croit le nigaud, en riches et en pauvres, en hommes vertueux et en scélérats, mais tout simplement en dupes

et en fripons; voilà la clef qui explique le XIXe siècle depuis la chute de Napoléon. [II, 945–46]

("The world," Sansfin told her, "is not divided (the way fools believe) between rich and poor, or virtuous and villainous, but between con men and their dupes; that is the key which explains the nineteenth century since Napoleon's fall.")

This contemptuous judgment (which echoes also in Balzac) is the moral equivalent of the formal division Stendhal had discovered in his earlier novels, between the reverie of the sensitive hero on the one hand and the manipulative pragmatism of the characters who advance the action on the other. To return for a moment to Du Poirier, who is the most important antecedent of Sansfin, it is important to recall that the contempt Lucien feels for Dr. Du Poirier is evenly matched by that which the physician feels for him. Du Poirier knows that Lucien's wealth is the result of birth, not of talent, and that given the right circumstances, he, Du Poirier, can become as wealthy. It is not money Du Poirier prizes, but the force of character necessary to acquire it. In this, he completely agrees with Lucien's father, who profoundly despairs at his son's virginal idealism. Whence the call to "friponnerie" which M. Leuwen makes to the uncomprehending Lucien: "'Serez-vous assez coquin pour cet emploi?' Lucien tressaillit" (I, 1072; "'Are you rogue enough to handle that job?' Lucien shuddered"). But Lamiel understands rascality.

In her relationship with the outlaw Valbayre, which Stendhal only sketched, she joins the tradition of the criminal at war with society that reveals so much about the tensions in nineteenth-century France. Like Balzac's fascination with Vidocq, and his titanic creation of Vautrin, Stendhal's "scoundrels" imply much more than a taste for the exotic. These surreal figures exist in the Realist novel

to show the dialectic naked. Stendhal's plan for the first
meeting between Lamiel and Valbayre is profoundly suggestive:

> Valbayre rouvre la porte un instant après que l'amant
> de Lamiel vient de sortir; elle se cache pour lui faire
> une plaisanterie et voir ce qu'il vient faire; elle voit
> Valbayre qui jette un coup d'oeil et se met sans délai
> à ouvrir un secrétaire. Lamiel se présente à lui, il saute
> sur elle un couteau ouvert à la main, il la prend par les
> cheveux pour lui percer la poitrine; dans l'effort fait,
> le mouchoir de Lamiel se dérange, il lui voit le sein.
> —Ma foi, c'est dommage, s'écrie-t-il. Il lui baise le
> sein, puis lâche les cheveux.
> —Dénonce moi, et fais-moi prendre, si tu veux, lui
> dit-il.
> Il la séduit ainsi. Voilà du caractère! Elle ne se dit
> pas cela, elle le voit et en subit les conséquences.
> —Qui êtes-vous?
> —Je fais la guerre à la société qui me fait la guerre.
> Je lis Corneille et Molière. J'ai trop d'éducation pour
> travailler de mes mains et gagner trois francs pour
> dix heures de travail.
> Quoique traqué par toutes les polices, et avec acharne-
> ment personnel, à cause des plaisanteries qu'il leur
> adresse, Valbayre la mène fièrement au spectacle; cette
> audace la rend folle d'amour. [*Lamiel*, II, 1031]

(Valbayre opens the door a moment after Lamiel's
lover has left; she hides to play a joke on him and find
out why he has come back; instead, she sees Valbayre
who glances around quickly and immediately begins to
break into the desk. Lamiel interrupts him, he jumps at
her with a knife, grabs her by the hair and is about to
stab her; in the struggle, her fichu is pulled aside, and
he sees her breast.

"My God, it would be a shame," he cries. He kisses
her breast, then lets go of her hair.

"Turn me in, have me arrested if you want," he says.
He seduces her this way. What spirit! She doesn't tell
herself that; she experiences it and submits to it.
"Who are you?"
"I'm at war with the society that makes war on me. I
read Corneille and Molière. I've had too much education to do manual labor at three francs for a ten hour
day."
Although pursued relentlessly by the police because
of the contemptuous tricks he plays on them, Valbayre
proudly takes her to the theater; his audaciousness
makes her fall madly in love.)

Some of the details concerning this precursor of Arsène
Lupin betray how far Stendhal had to reach into imagination to create Valbayre; the outlaw's literary tastes are almost comically *beyliste*. But the desire to take what one
wants by force, the extraordinary energy and the fascination of rapacity, the identification of sexual and social tension, make even *Le Rouge et le noir* seem timid. Stendhal
discovers in criminality a mode of "naturel" (II, 1005), an
impulsiveness and a radical refusal of the larger society
which outdistance anything he had already composed.

But action, which thus reenters Stendhal's fiction here
at the heroic center, does so at the price of a grave displace-
ment of the hero's possibilities. In the unmitigated revolt
of Lamiel, Stendhal has been driven completely out of
contact with the world of real social activity. The projected
end of *Lamiel*, perfectly logical within the fiction, nonetheless shows how completely the form represents an impasse. Valbayre is driven to commit several murders, and is
finally condemned to death. Lamiel's response is to pre-
cipitate a sort of social Götterdämmerung which she cannot survive. Here is how Stendhal sketches the end of
the novel: "She sets fire to the Palais de Justice to avenge
Valbayre; in the debris of the fire are found half-calcined
bones—they are Lamiel's" (II, 1033). The charred remains

of this *auto da fé* are symbolically those of Stendhal's
doomed attempt to join the ideals of action and authenticity in the "triste dix-neuvième siècle." Stendhal died,
interrupting Lamiel, in 1842. The traditional hero and the
form in which he once was able to move by then were
nearly burned out.

3

Balzac: The Logic of Failure

Balzac's career stands as evidence of the pressure the changing forms of social life exerted on the form of the novel. To the end of his career, Balzac attempted to resist the fragmentation of energy and interest that dogged Stendhal as he tried to keep his heroes free. The details of Balzac's form flow from very different beliefs about the world. But Stendhal and Balzac agreed about the artistic problem to be faced. How to relate the hero to action was the question for both of them.

Critics have explicated their dissimilarities for nearly a century and a half. But their more basic agreement is what makes this effort interesting. Their divergent solutions clarify the shape of the literary situation after 1830. The suddenly aroused, complex tension between the self and the world which generated their formal innovations evolved inexorably during the novel's great century. At its close, Proust cannot be well understood without the background of Stendhal's and Balzac's responses to the problem he had to face in a more acute form than they.

But around 1830, what self, and what world? Balzac's world, of course, is broader, filled out in half a hundred novels compared to Stendhal's fewer than half a dozen. Given the profusion of Balzac's plots, how can we identify one shape as essentially "balzacien"? What orients us is the use tradition has made of Balzac. And the tradition has clearly laid out a central series of books from Stendhal to Proust whose forms and concerns respond to each other.

In these novels, the self is a young protagonist endowed

with talent and sensitivity—in Stendhal's phrase, an "être d'exception." The world outside resists his efforts to force its recognition of his quality. Simultaneously he discovers deep conflict in himself as he attempts to maintain his own purity. Eventually, things end badly for him, but even at the last the century seems unmoved by his tragedy. His passion and the world's impassivity define the conflict that is played out in these books. Other periods explored other dissonances; it was the task of the novel during its great century to work out what happens when the heroic impulse of the young is indiscriminately smothered.

We have seen how Stendhal's charm depends upon delaying to the last possible moment his hero's defeat. By the protection he weaves around his protagonists until this final instant, he flatters our need to imagine that things are better than they are. Under the influence of his sleight-of-hand, however, the brilliant irony of the narrator and the volatility of the protagonists' behavior generate a view of experience that, though we cherish it, has strong elements of caricature. Underneath his charming enthusiasm and his unconvincing cynicism, Stendhal is confused by the turn life has taken and not overeager to explore the details of its new direction. Instead, he simplifies—both the happiness of the lost age and the vileness of the present.

Consider the central element in his theory of love, crystallization. As with the supersaturated raincloud, suddenly, inexplicably, the vapor condenses and the downpour begins. Things in Stendhal characteristically go through such violent, unanalyzed changes of state. Lucien's love affair with Mme de Chasteller contains innumerable reversals of this kind. For long periods, "our hero" is thoroughly inane. But his boorishness can be instantaneously transformed: "Upon hearing Madame de Chasteller's remark to him, Lucien suddenly became a different person" (I, 923). Reality is complex for Stendhal, no doubt. The range of the pendulum-swing in his portrayal of experience is great and provides the incomparable vigor of his books. But though he gives us the heights and the depths, his techniques are not as well adapted to show the intermediate movement— the subtle modulations of consciousness which will occupy Proust, or the inexorable mechanism which gives experience its tragic shape in Balzac's portrayals.

The elements of reality for Stendhal are thus divided into opposing groups or clusters of phenomena at the extremes of his admiration or his disapproval. For Balzac, on the other hand, reality is a continuous system of constant, necessary relations. Contrary to Stendhal's practice of in-sulating elements from each other to protect those he val-ues, Balzac's impulse is to trace the connections which explain—even if they simultaneously destroy—what he admires.

There are protected enclaves in Balzac, areas of goodness and of insight whose existence within the overall corrup-tion he describes he never explains. The "Cénacle," the group of dedicated blood-brothers with whom Lucien de Rubempré briefly associates after arriving in Paris, is of this kind. But d'Arthez, Michel Chrestien, and the others are far from being the protagonists of *Illusions perdues*. Their function as reflectors of values betrayed by Lucien has clear utility (though it may seem heavy-handed to us). But their active role in events is so small that their existence does not really compromise the profoundly pessimistic lesson of the book. The Cénacle, one feels, is not of this world. If in inventing it Balzac allowed himself a bit of wish fulfillment, he does not share Stendhal's constant tendency to locate such protected anomalies at the very center of his fictions. Unlike Stendhal's, Balzac's prisons are *prisons*.

A more interesting case of protection is *Eugénie Grandet*. Eugénie is cited as an example of noncorruptibility in a corrupted world.[1] Balzac's intention, however, seems to have been more subtly critical. The novelist warns us in the middle of the book, in one of his frequent professorial

1. For example by Harry Levin, *The Gates of Horn*, p. 192.

passages, that no human conduct is without its material causes:

> Assez souvent, certaines actions de la vie humaine paraissent littérairement parlant, invraisemblables, quoique vraies. Mais ne serait-ce pas qu'on omet presque toujours de répandre sur nos déterminations spontanées une sorte de lumière psychologique, en n'expliquant pas les raisons mystérieusement conçues qui les ont nécessitées? Peut-être la profonde passion d'Eugénie devrait-elle être analysée dans ses fibrilles les plus délicates; car elle devint, diraient quelques railleurs, une maladie, et influença toute son existence. Beaucoup de gens aiment mieux nier les dénoûments que de mesurer la force des liens, des noeuds, des attaches qui soudent secrètement un fait à un autre dans l'ordre moral. [p. 122]

> (Frequently, certain actions of human life seem, literarily speaking, unlikely, although they are true. Is this not because we fail to clarify spontaneous decisions by providing a kind of psychological illumination, fail to explain the mysterious generation of the reasons which made these actions necessary? Perhaps Eugénie's profound passion needs to be analyzed in its most delicate fibers, for it became, as some mocking spirits might say, a disease, and influenced her entire existence. Many people would prefer to deny a denouement rather than measure the strength of the bonds, the knots, the chains that weld one fact to another in the moral order of things.)

The implication here, insistent even in this relatively early novel, is that no human conduct can be isolated from the material effects of outside forces. The structure of *Eugénie Grandet* is somewhat immature; the opposition of forces (Grandet's cynical rapacity vs. his daughter's pure openness to love) is almost Stendhalian in its schematism. But

differences are immediately visible, first in the structure
and later in subtle elements of psychology. The chapter
entitled "Promesses d'Avare, Serments d'Amour" ("Mi-
ser's Promises, Lovers' Promises"; pp. 127-83) powerfully
throws together the two impulses whose relative power
Balzac is testing in this fiction. Eugénie's discovery that
she loves her cousin Charles is nearly submerged in dense
pages recounting Grandet's derisive double speculation, the
sale of his gold and the fraudulent offer to liquidate
Charles's debts. This chapter, at the exact center of the
novel, is a precise accounting of the good and evil forces
which Balzac sets in operation: "Ainsi le père et la fille
avaient compté chacun leur fortune: lui, pour aller vendre
son or; Eugénie, pour jeter le sien dans un océan d'affection" (p. 159; "Thus father and daughter had both counted
their fortunes: he, in preparation for converting his gold
into cash; Eugénie, in preparation for throwing her gold
into a sea of affection").

Eugénie is a martyr to the power of the outside to destroy the inside, however strong the defenses the individual
erects against such penetration. The heroine of this novel,
who remains a virgin to the end and is even protectively
sequestered for a period in the middle of the novel, is
nonetheless despoiled. Against the malignant materialism
represented by her father, her idealism can conserve only
the outward appearance of integrity. The inside subtly
sours, and the process is irreversible. One of the more impressive effects in the novel is the corrosive passage of time
which marks the conversion of Eugénie's purity to barren-
ness:

> En toute situation, les femmes ont plus de causes de
> douleur que n'en a l'homme, et souffrent plus que
> lui. L'homme a sa force et l'exercice de sa puissance:
> il agit, il va, il s'occupe, il pense, il embrasse l'avenir
> et y trouve des consolations. Ainsi faisait Charles.
> Mais la femme demeure, elle reste face à face avec le

chagrin dont rien ne la distrait. . . . Ainsi faisait Eugénie. Elle s'initiait à sa destinée. [p. 184]

(In all situations, women have more causes for pain
than do men, and suffer more than they do. Men have
their strength and the exercise of their power: they
act, they move about, they keep busy, they think, they
plan the future and find consolation in this. So Charles
behaved. But women remain, they confront their suffering, from which nothing distracts them. Thus did
Eugénie. She was being initiated into her destiny.)

The seven year story of Eugénie's patience is not one of
redemption by fidelity; Balzac rather calls it a cruel "bourgeois tragedy" (p. 187). The victim of the conflict is
Eugénie's never-to-be-realized happiness: "At thirty,
Eugénie had yet to experience any of life's felicities"
(p. 227).

Her resistance, her spiritual force, has been immense—
perhaps greater than Balzac would have shown it later in
his career—but the toll has nonetheless been taken: "Eugénie had begun to suffer" (p. 227). The threat she has
faced in her father reappears where she (and perhaps,
sharing her naïveté, we) least expected it, in herself.
Charles's idealism has been vanquished with despairing
ease. Enriched, ironically, by slave trade, ennobled by a
cynically loveless marriage, he returns to France: "Terrible and total disaster" (p. 242). Money has appropriated
all the privileged places in Eugénie's life, and in the details
with which Balzac ends the book, we learn how powerfully
the colossal fortune which has passed to Eugénie has con-
taminated the possibilities of her idealism.

Money never comes free, Balzac had learned through the
gothic myth of La Peau de chagrin three years earlier. But
like Charles Grandet, Raphaël de Valentin was already corrupted by desire. The lesson of Eugénie is graver, resembling the moral of Fabrice's defeat in La Chartreuse de
Parme: Fabrice and Eugénie are both radically pure, and

without desire. But insulation is impossible; the inside cannot resist the outside. Stendhal's romanticism arranges for
Fabrice's death, but in a sense the realism of what happens
in Eugénie's "bourgeois tragedy," though less grand, is
more grindingly pathetic. Slowly, experience closes her up.
And though Balzac had warned us in his sententious assertion concerning denouements that experience develops
along lines of material force, the disaster that befalls her is
the one we had probably not even imagined as a threat:
heiress to her father's seventeen million francs, she begins
to resemble him:

> Là Eugénie rendit froidement la lettre sans l'achever.
> —Je vous remercie, dit-elle à Mme des Grassins;
> *nous verrons cela ...* [p. 247; Balzac's italics]

> (At that point, Eugénie coldly returned the letter
> without finishing it.
> "Thank you very much," she said to Mme des
> Grassins, *"we'll consider that ..."*)

Two pages later she contracts her *mariage blanc* with M.
de Bonfons, who dies leaving more money to fall into her
lap: "God thus threw piles of gold to his prisoner" (p.
255). And Eugénie, who Balzac tells us was born to be a
wife and a mother, lives on childless and alone in her
father's cheerless house. Is it in filial faithfulness to his
memory that she allows the fire to be lit only on days
when he would have permitted it? The book's end remains
ambiguous, for Balzac does not tell us clearly whether her
father's materialism has corrupted her innermost heart.
But by the time of *Illusions perdues* (written between
1837 and 1843), this vestige of sentimentalism will have
disappeared. Lucien de Rubempré lives out his fate in the
shadow of Paris, where the forces of the outside are
brought to focus on individuals more powerfully even than
those which old Grandet concentrated on his daughter sitting by their melancholy fire in Saumur.

The title of *Illusions perdues* would lead one to expect a
mood of almost Stendhalian nostalgia. But the absence of
authorial sentimentalism is striking. The protagonists in
this magnificent novel take a very long time to come to the
state of disabused realism in which Balzac stands at the
very beginning of the book. He allows his characters their
mistakes—indeed, their mistakes provide the substance of
the story. But unlike Stendhal he does not indulge them.

To judge by the techniques and structure of the novel
itself, Balzac's object was to explicate the necessity both
of the illusions his characters hold and of their destruction
by events. The perspective from beginning to end is developmental, the overall attitude largely dispassionate. To be
sure, Balzac has very strong feelings; his propensity for
ventilating them has made him seem less subtle a writer
than Stendhal (whose feelings were no less strong, but who
protected himself by veiling them in his irony). But Stendhal's beliefs are in constant tension with the destinies of
his heroes. He would like them to succeed, but his sense of
their possibilities forces them to fail. Such tension is virtually absent in Balzac's case, since he "believes" that
things must go as they do in fact go. His sententious ser-
mons on the way of the world are fully consistent with the
pattern of the fictional material in his books.

Because of the consistency between his beliefs about
the world and what he finds himself able to show in his
fiction, Balzac can make action fully carry the significance
of his novels. Action may need to be explained and commented upon—but nothing is real without it. Unlike the
case of Fabrice, what "happens" to Eugénie Grandet, the
meaning of her experience for us, is not her long sequestra-
tion from the world, but the growing sense that her quarantine has not been—could not have been—successful. The
immobility, the dreaminess, the isolation of Stendhal's
heroes are thoroughly foreign to Balzac's intentions.

For him as for no other novelist of the nineteenth century except Tolstoy, what happens to people happens to

them in the world, in society, and there is no privilege granted to the kind of introspection which makes us call Stendhal and Proust "psychologists." For Balzac as for Tolstoy, what goes on inside the mind is not a "higher reality," but only an imperfect and mostly inaccessible version of what is being played out in the arena of the world. Lucien de Rubempré and Constantine Levin introspect intensely, of course, but their creators do not believe that their ambiguities and confusions can be worked out in thought. *Conduct* is the question, and action the means by which the question is answered. What interests Balzac and Tolstoy is not principally the existence of our passions (though they accept these profoundly) but their results in real behavior, their consequences for the hero and for the others in his world.

There is thus no discordance in Balzac's tendency to force the significance and the emotions his narration must carry into every corner of the story. For him, this is nothing more than expressive heightening. The idea of the "physiognomy," so popular in his time, is a characteristic element in his almost medieval belief that everything in the world corresponded to the general direction in which events led. Balzac believed in a great chain of meaning, if not of being. In his world phrenology can be an effective science because he found it reasonable to expect people to look like their destinies. Albert Béguin in "Balzac visionnaire" identifies the energy with which in Balzac every level of the story adds consonant elements:

> Les passions y éclatent dans les gestes ou les jeux de physionomie, les grimaces, les rides; la pureté et la vie spirituelle y produisent, sur les fronts et les visages, des flammes, des étincelles, des lumières rayonnantes; la démence fait craquer les os, les peurs et les colères rugissent plus fort que ne crient autour de nous les hommes. Quand le drame atteint à sa phase mortelle, sa sauvagerie est extrême et le sang versé empourpre

tout le décor. Ni l'Espagne, ni les élizabéthains, ni le mélodrame populaire ne vont à de tels excès, ou surtout ne réussissent à leur conférer cet air de vérité dépourvue d'exagération.[2]

(Passions burst out in gestures or the play of physiognomies, in grimaces, in the lines of a face; purity and spirituality produce flashes and shining glows on foreheads and faces; madness cracks bones; fear and anger howl louder than real men can scream. When the drama reaches its fatal phase, its savagery is extreme and spilled blood colors all the scenery. Neither Spain nor Elizabethan England nor popular melodrama go to such excesses, nor do they succeed in creating Balzac's atmosphere of unexaggerated truth.)

So action in Balzac is evolutionary, but powerfully progressive; the events and descriptions with which the novelist begins connect with what will eventually happen, and with the meaning of what happens, with iron links. From the first moment, everything moves massively and materially toward the conclusions which establish the "concord" of the book and the moral lesson which Balzac is drawing through the represented experience.

Such is the case in *Illusions perdues*. But the case is a privileged one, for in this novel the conduct at issue, the passions in question, are those at the vexed center of the problems raised by new conditions after the Restoration. *Illusions perdues* is the heart of the great tradition of the nineteenth-century novel in France. The title itself is a brilliant condensation of the issues. All the themes, all the tropes are present: province vs. Paris; the cynical glitter of high-life in the capital counterposed to the grinding poverty of the young people just arrived and on the make; the heady feeling of upward mobility and the intense joy of

2. *Balzac lu et relu*, p. 43.

conquest; prostitutes with hearts of gold and traitorous friends who would sell one for a small sum; eternal love affairs and love affairs based on the most disingenuous manipulation; a duel with all the social trappings; the mysterious, quasi-supernatural figure of a consummate criminal living out his opposition to the established order; the pair of young heroes and their as-yet unsullied friendship; a cruel, rejecting father; a dedicated, self-sacrificing mother; the intermittent threat of suicide; and above all, Lucien Chardon de Rubempré, not simply a crass bourgeois, nor yet a recognized, superior nobleman—the weak but brilliant hero who evolves at the center of this complex action, and provides the standard against which his confreres in other novels (Julien Sorel, Lucien Leuwen, Fabrice del Dongo, Joseph Delorme, Eugène de Rastignac, Frédéric Moreau and the others up through the Marcel of Proust's *Recherche*) must be judged.

Balzac's first effort to deal with the theme which comes to maturity in *Illusions perdues*, and the first book he signed "de Balzac," was *La Peau de chagrin*. Barbéris's exploration of the significance of this strange novel written on the heels of the July revolution identifies the thematic and technical innovations in the story of Raphaël de Valentin (see *Balzac et le mal du siècle*, II, 1417–1616). At the center of the book is an intensely felt and powerfully imagined critique of the possibilities open to young people of talent and ambition in the post-Restoration world.

The graphic shrinking of Raphaël's talisman may be an unsubtle symbol, but it communicates. Moreover Balzac does not make it the cause of what happens to Raphaël. Like the Rubempré cycle, *La Peau de chagrin* makes use of supernatural elements, but as everywhere in Balzac, these function as expressive heightening. The laws of French history, of Parisian economics and sociology, still rule action, here as elsewhere. Raphaël's recapitulation of his miseries and his downward slide into despair in the second part of the novel and Balzac's dark description of him in the gambling-house as the book opens provide the material background for what befalls the hero of this book.

In spite of the gothic trappings, Raphaël is thus first in the lineage of Balzac's *enfants du siècle*. Although an older, cynical Rastignac appears in *La Peau de chagrin*, Barbéris shows persuasively that the immediate descendent of Raphaël is the very different Rastignac of *Le Père Goriot*, which Balzac began work on about three years later.[3] Finally, the filiation leads to Lucien de Rubempré, the Balzacian image of the *enfant du siècle* in fully developed form.

Why is Lucien weak? And does this not limit the degree to which we can take his plight as typical of young people after Napoleon's fall? Or is Lucien's fragility somehow a constitutive element in the portrait of the post-Restoration hero? Musset suggests an answer in the first chapter of his *Confession*, which appeared in February of the year Balzac began work on *Illusions perdues* and parallels the portrait in Balzac's novel in a number of important respects:

> Ayant été atteint, jeune encore, d'une maladie morale abominable, je raconte ce qui m'est arrivé pendant trois ans. Si j'étais seul malade, je n'en dirais rien; mais, *comme il y en a beaucoup d'autres que moi qui souffrent du même mal*, j'écris pour ceux-là. [*La Confession d'un enfant du siècle*, p. 1]

> Having contracted, while still young, an abominable and fatal illness, I shall tell what happened to me over a three year period. If I were the only sufferer, I would not speak of this, but *since there are many others besides me who are victims of the same illness*, I write for them.)

What Musset calls the "ardent, pale, nervous generation"

---

3. *Balzac et le mal du siècle*, II, 1448. The descendent of the cynical, manipulative Rastignac of *La Peau de chagrin*, on the other hand, is Vautrin.

(p. 1) defines the heroes of the Realist novel in its early period. That element in Lucien which Balzac so clearly judges a fault—what Musset calls a "je ne sais quoi de vague et de flottant" (p. 7; "an indefinable vagueness and indecision")—was a crucially characteristic one.

When we recall Rastignac's strength at the end of *Le Père Goriot* as he challenges the heart of power in Paris from the heights of Père Lachaise, it is hard not to wonder why Lucien, Balzac's next *enfant du siècle* (Balzac specifically calls him that, p. 541) spends his scene in the same cemetery in a state of neurasthenic despair (see p. 537). From the side of Goriot's grave, Rastignac swaggeringly challenges the capital. Lucien, at the side of Coralie's, acknowledges that Paris has beaten him. He flees the capital on foot, in defeat, back to Angoulême.

The explanation for the change which occurred in the three or four years between Rastignac and Rubempré is perhaps to be sought in what happened to Rastignac himself after the bravado ending of *Le Père Goriot*: Rastignac succeeded. He became a rogue in the grand style, accumulating wealth and power. Doctor Sansfin, we remember, divided the century between "dupes" and "fripons" (*Lamiel*, I, 945-46). The Vicomtesse de Beauséant had used precisely the same terms in her Vautrin-like lecture to Rastignac on the ways of worldly success (*Le Père Goriot*, p. 94). The Vicomtesse suggests that Rastignac can find a third term as he moves up the social ladder. But experience proves this hope for success with purity is vain. Stendhal and Balzac assert the same thing: you must choose between being a rogue or a fool. But Balzac adds more clearly than Stendhal a chilling corollary: *neither choice will make you happy.*

On one side of the balance, then, Balzac placed the rogues—Rastignac and numerous lesser incarnations. Vautrin, the supreme "actor" in the novels, who tests through his social experiments the relative strength of the conflicting impulses toward purity and toward power, tries first to gain control of Rastignac. But Eugène, intent on succeeding whatever the cost, refuses to be dominated by Vautrin and achieves his success—such as it is—alone. The logic of roguishness requires Rastignac's refusal of Vautrin. So Balzac must look to the other side of the balance, to the heroes tormented by the impotence of their purity: to Lucien. The transition is contained in a curious moment at the end of *Illusions perdues*. Lucien and the mysterious Abbé who has stepped in his way as he was off to kill himself pass by Rastignac's estate. Lucien is bitter: "Voici, dit-il, d'où est parti le jeune Rastignac qui ne me vaut certes pas, et qui a eu plus de bonheur que moi. . . . Moi, je me suis laissé aller à la poésie; lui, plus habile, a donné dans le positif" (p. 709; "So this is where young Rastignac started from. Surely I'm better than he, yet he has had more *bonheur* ["success"/"happiness"] than I have. . . . I let myself drift into poetry; he was smarter and stuck to realities").

But in playing tantalizingly on Lucien's word "bonheur," Balzac does not entirely agree with him. Rastignac has been more successful, but he has not been happier. However, Lucien's distinction between two groups, the poets and the pragmatists, is accurate. This is precisely the division that gave rise to the fragmentation of energy in Stendhal, as his heroes proved unable to combine purity and effectiveness. Balzac makes this discovery more explicit. As Barbéris puts it:

> Rastignac sait que sa réussite n'est que façade et comédie. Il joue, pour les autres (mais en le sachant), à celui qui a réussi. Mais il n'est pas heureux. Il lui a fallu, pour parvenir, mettre entre parenthèses les exigences de sa jeunesse. Michel Chrestien n'a pas triché. Seulement, it est mort. *Nul ne réussit innocemment.* Nul n'est pur, *et* continue à vivre. Le monde des hommes est régi par des lois qui condamnent les purs à l'exil, et font des heureux des complices. [Barbéris's italics; *Balzac et le mal du siècle*, I, 130]

(Rastignac knows that his success is a farcical façade. For others, cynically, he plays the role of someone who has succeeded. But he is not happy. To "arrive" he has had to put aside the aspirations of his youth. Michel Chrestien [the republican member of the Cénacle, killed tragically in the Cloître Saint-Merry repression] never compromised his ideals. But he is dead. *No one can succeed in innocence.* No one can be pure *and* still continue to live. The world of men is governed by laws that condemn idealists to exile and make accomplices out of those who "succeed.")

The choice between rogue and dupe is thus to be read as a choice between profound disappointment, unrealized aspirations, and the sour taste of betrayed idealism on the one hand, and on the other a final impotent assertion of purity in suicide (the cases of Lucien, Julien Sorel, Lamiel) or total withdrawal (to which Fabrice is driven). Weakness succeeds roguishness—Lucien replaces Rastignac—because the tragedy is *purer* in Lucien. The meaning of their experience, however, is the same.

In *Splendeurs et misères des courtisanes*, Vautrin provides an extraordinary epitaph for Lucien which condenses all these perceptions into the most heightened image of the *enfant du siècle* that one finds in Balzac's work:

Ah! jamais une bonne mère n'a tendrement aimé son fils unique comme j'aimai cet ange. Si vous saviez! le bien naissait dans ce coeur comme les fleurs se lèvent dans les prairies. Il était faible, voilà son seul défaut, faible comme la corde de la lyre, si forte quand elle se tend... C'est les plus belles natures, leur faiblesse est tout uniment la tendresse, l'admiration, la faculté de s'épanouir au soleil de l'art, de l'amour, du beau que Dieu a fait pour l'homme sous mille formes!... Enfin, Lucien était une femme manquée. [p. 613]

(Ah! No mother ever loved her only son more tenderly

than I loved that angel. If you only knew! Goodness grew in his heart like flowers grow in a meadow. He was weak, that was his only fault, weak like a lyre string, which can be so strong if you tighten it... The finest characters, their weakness goes together with tenderness, admiration, the capacity to flower in the light of art, or love, or the beautiful which God has made for man in a thousand forms!... Well, Lucien was really a failed woman.)

The extraordinary beauty of Julien Sorel at Mme de Rê-nal's gate for the first time, the soft hands and delicate grace of the poetic Rubempré; in fact, all the constant feminine imagery which surrounds the heroes of Realist novels is a way of asserting their lack of fitness for the world of action, and thus their creators' rejection of middle-class confidence, pragmatism, infuriating self-satisfaction. When young men of sensitivity have only the choice between the bourgeois vulgarity of M. Prudhomme and a neurasthenic "vague des sentiments," of course they will want to resemble Rubempré rather than Rastignac. It will be the same in Proust.

The technical problem for the novelists was still one of motivating the action. Having elaborated the appropriate fictions, ending with the appropriate disasters, to embody their sense of life's possibilities after 1815, they found time after time that the story's energy fragmented, leaving the hero on its outskirts, a more or less paralyzed, per-plexed victim of the implacable forces that destroyed him, unable to generate any sort of adequate individual re-sponse.

In both Stendhal and Balzac, the tendency for heroes like Lucien de Rubempré to replace heroes like Rastignac was inevitable as the novelists saw more clearly the real dilemmas which their stories were exploring. The imageries, the contents of their plots, the shape of the heroes' fates, all evolved in consonance with the advancing discovery of how deep the crisis of the individual was. In the early thirties, Julien Sorel and Rastignac explored roguishness; but by the end of the decade the outlines of the problem were sadly clearer. In this perspective, how like Fabrice's retreat into the charterhouse is Lucien's retreat from Paris.

The elegiac tone which the aristocratic Romantics had begun exploiting thirty or forty years earlier here catches up with the bourgeois Realists. And by the time of Flaubert, the results of the tentative experiment which Balzac and Stendhal were conducting were in. For Flaubert and those after him, the only stance remaining was lamentation, the only possible action was inaction. In turn, the roots of the stasis, the frequent tedium which, whatever our admiration, characterizes the three thousand pages of Proust's *Recherche*, are to be found in the collapse of Fabrice's love affair with Clélia Conti, and in Paris's double rebuff of Lucien de Rubempré. Once lost enough painful times in the action of these fictions, the illusions so dear to Stendhal and so fascinating to Balzac simply ceased regenerating. Flaubert and Proust wrote after the fall.

Yet the strategies of the writers who followed the early masters of the Realist period did not alter their novelistic "project" in essential detail. They still kept trying to bring the world to book. From Stendhal to Proust, from the nervous Julien to the neurasthenic Marcel, they set a young hero in a network of social complication, to discover what life would force him to become.

But after the fall, the novelists' initial hopes for their hero became more modest. No one after Flaubert expected to discover whether the hero could be happy in the world; such happiness by now was known to be impossible. Rather, an important fall-back position was being prepared. More can be discovered about this evolution by examining how the later writers understood their predecessors than by any other method.

Proust was astonished that Balzac preferred truth to

beauty. This is the central judgment in his long consideration of Balzac and the Realist novel, and the whole changing relation of the writer to his created world can be
elicited from it. According to Proust, Balzac failed to
"spiritualize" experience; reality in his novels is "too little
transformed."[4] The result for Proust was that our pleasure
in reading Balzac is hardly different from the pleasures we
can find in life—and this was radically insufficient. Indeed,
Proust goes even further than this in his demands upon the
novel. His extraordinary insistence is implied when, still
speaking of Balzac, he writes in *Contre Sainte-Beuve*:
"Bien souvent ses personnages seront réels, *ne seront pas
plus que réels*" (Proust's italics; *CSB,* p. 268; "Very frequently his characters are real, *but nothing more than
real*").

To the degraded, pessimistic sense of reality which
emerges from the Realists' fictive explorations, this is a
logical reaction. In impotent but faithful contact with a
deeply humanist tradition, the novelists during the great
period continued to believe that there ought to be—had to
be—something finer in experience than the insistent pattern
of failure which defined the Realist hero's contact with the
world. Or to put it another way, they continued to search
for the proper techniques to uncover and express that which
remained positive and fine, after it became clear that the
techniques developed by Stendhal and Balzac to explore
the hero's encounter with the world turned up only defeat
and collapse.

Proust saw that the illusions lost in Stendhal and Balzac
were critically linked to these writers' insistence on chronological specificity. Realist disasters necessarily occur in
real time. The typical Balzacian beginning which Proust
pastiched ("In one of the final months of the year 1907
. . ."; *CSB,* p. 7) unavoidably contains within it, as time's
fatal dynamism, the graveyard scenes which punctuate

4. "Journées de lecture" (written in 1905 as preface to Proust's translation
of "Sésame et les lys"); *Contre Sainte-Beuve,* p. 171n. (hereafter cited as *CSB*).

disasters at the other end of Balzac's stories. An emptiness remains after the heroes' corpses are laid in their graves. To respond to it, attitudes related to the projective quality of time in the early Realists had to be replaced by a new emotional configuration. Fulfillment of the individual could no longer be tied to the complexities of his relation to the outside, but would somehow have to become independent of these ruinous relations.

For Proust, the attitudes toward the portrayal of experience that he criticizes in Balzac are summed up in one word: vulgarity (see *CSB*, p. 263). In turn, Balzac's view of the world as an arena for the working out of passions and desires—in ambition, in romantic love, and so on—is for Proust the root cause of this vulgarity: "He considered the object of life to be the satisfaction of the basest ambitions" (*CSB*, p. 263). Proust is explicit on this point: "Aussi continuerons-nous à ressentir et presque à satisfaire, en lisant Balzac, les passions dont la haute littérature doit nous guérir" (*CSB*, p. 268; "Thus we continue, in reading Balzac, to experience, and almost to have stimulated in us, the passions which great literature should rather cure us of").

But the degree to which Proust perceives the resemblance between Balzac's books and concrete social life as a fault is astonishing when viewed with perspective: "Moreover, Balzac explains things with the help of images . . . which make us understand them the same way someone might explain something in a conversation" (*CSB*, p. 269). What can possibly be wrong with making oneself understood, and why is it an error to explain rather than suggest? Why the desperate need for harmony, as long as the reality depicted is understood, and represented so that it can be understood?

The gulf that divides Proust from his predecessor and accounts for this critique is that Balzac believes in history and Proust does not; Balzac believes in action, and that a character's concrete action *is* his meaning. Proust's attitude on the issue was still forming at the time of *Contre Sainte-*

Beuve, and was not fully mature even when he composed *Du côté de chez Swann*, parts of which (notably "Un Amour de Swann") retain obvious links with the structure and techniques of Realist fiction. But progressively while writing the seven books of *A la recherche du temps perdu*, his long sense of discordance with Balzac found its proper technical response, in the style of the middle and late volumes of *La Recherche*. By the time of his seminal essay on Flaubert in 1919, the consequences of the divergence between him and the early Realists were apparent on both theoretical and practical levels; the structure and the techniques had been devised which could replace the Realists' dependence upon narrated action to create fictional meaning. The Flaubert essay is a monument to the new synthesis. In clarifying Proust's use of Flaubert and Flaubert's own relation to the tradition, these brilliant pages define the central element of the change.

It had become apparent through the shape of Realist plots that history had failed the novel. The exciting, action-filled "roman d'aventures" which so enchanted young Marcel during his reading in Combray (*La Recherche*, I, 83) was superseded as he grew older by more poetic, introspective novels, in spirit resembling Proust's own—just as the Balzacian novel gave way to new fictional forms after 1848. The task of writers after Balzac became to divorce the portrayal of the individual from what Proust contemptuously called the "parasitisme des anecdotes et des scories de l'histoire" ("A propos du 'style' de Flaubert," *CSB*, p. 595; "the parasitism of anecdote and the dross of history").

Flaubert was the first to have sensed the need and found the forms. The 1919 essay admits that Proust's admiration for Flaubert's novels was far from total, but their relevance was intense. After Flaubert, one no longer expected to find truth baldly presented in the "styleless" manner of Balzac (see *CSB*, p. 269). Truth now increasingly seemed to need clothing in a kind of beauty which, preoccupied as

he was by the effort to seize the connections and capture
the intensity of events in the world outside, Balzac would
simply not have understood. In the Realists, meaning is
fundamentally discursive, revealed in a series of charged,
progressive human acts. In Flaubert and Proust, meaning
tends to become metaphorical, and it is increasingly created by the articulation of images: "What until Flaubert
was action becomes impression" (*CSB*, p. 588). The most
characteristic aspect of Proust's fictional system, the anti-
dramatic, antichronological quality of extreme stasis, de-
rives from Flaubert's attempt to metaphorize Realist
causality—or as Proust beautifully put it, to "turn time
into music"(*CSB*, p. 595).

4

Flaubert and After: Failure Formalized

Flaubert's world is a brutal one:

> Elle souhaitait un fils; il serait fort et brun, elle
> l'appellerait Georges; et cette idée d'avoir pour enfant
> un mâle était comme la revanche en espoir de toutes
> ses impuissances passées. . . .
> Elle accoucha un dimanche, vers six heures, au soleil
> levant.
> —C'est une fille! dit Charles.
> Elle tourna la tête et s'évanouit. [*Madame Bovary*,
> p. 91]

> (She hoped for a son; he would be strong and dark;
> she would name him Georges; and this idea of having a
> male child was like an anticipated revenge for all her
> past powerlessness. . . .
> She gave birth on a Sunday, at about six, as the sun
> was coming up.
> "It's a girl!" said Charles.
> She turned her head away and fainted.)

The Realists had explored the logic of the hero's defeat.
For Flaubert this logic is increasingly irrelevant. Not that
his diagnosis alters theirs; his protagonists are neither more
nor less doomed than the Realists'. But, as Malraux once
wrote, Flaubert's heroes are Balzacian characters "conceived in failure,"[1] and this is an essential difference.

1. André Malraux, "Laclos," p. 421.

Consider the passage from *Madame Bovary* just quoted. What distinguishes it from defeats in the Realists' worlds is a subtle change of illumination. Stendhal amused himself with creating ignominious setbacks for his heroes—for example Fabrice's unhorsing at Waterloo:

> Le maréchal des logis s'approcha de Fabrice. A ce moment notre héros entendit dire derrière lui et tout près de son oreille: C'est le seul qui puisse encore galoper. Il se sentit saisir les pieds; on les élevait en même temps qu'on lui soutenait le corps par-dessous les bras; on le fit passer par-dessus la croupe de son cheval, puis on le laissa glisser jusqu'à terre, où il tomba assis. . . .
>
> Désespéré, bien moins de la perte de son cheval que de la trahison, il se laissa tomber au bord du fossé, fatigué et mourant de faim. Si son beau cheval lui eût été enlevé par l'ennemi, il n'y eût pas songé; mais se voir trahir et voler par ce maréchal des logis qu'il aimait tant et par ces hussards qu'il regardait comme des frères! c'est ce qui lui brisait le coeur. [*La Chartreuse*, pp. 54–55]

(The sergeant came over toward Fabrice. At that moment our hero heard someone behind him say, close to his ear, "This is the only one that can still run." He felt himself seized by the feet; they were lifted out of the stirrups at the same time as someone grabbed his body under the arms; he was lifted over his horse's rump and fell to the ground, where he landed sitting down. . . .

In despair, not so much at the loss of his horse as at the treachery, he collapsed by the side of the ditch, exhausted and dying of hunger. If his fine horse had been stolen by the enemy, he would not have thought twice about it; but to be betrayed and robbed by the sergeant he liked so much and by the hussars whom he had thought of as brothers! That is what was breaking his heart.)

It is not that Fabrice's hopes for his experience in battle were less profound than Emma's at the birth of her child. Both characters have, and require, their dreams: Fabrice of a pure heroism à la Tasso; Emma of a new beginning with her son. And both dreams are unceremoniously shattered. But Stendhal keeps his sympathy for Fabrice, and soon gets him back in the saddle. The situation for Flaubert's protagonists is much graver. Flaubert's impassivity leaves Emma at precisely the depth that corresponds to her disappointment.

Happiness is an illusion for all the great novelists of the nineteenth century. But Stendhal's romantic sense of its pursuit infuses the action of his books with the illusion, which he himself seems to share until the very end. Balzac's pessimism is more concerted, but he is careful to show how the illusions that guide their lives were generated in his characters, out of what clearly defined social hopes and personal needs. The process which destroys illusions unfolds with compelling verisimilitude in his novels. But Flaubert endows his characters with the most extravagant dreams, then simply slaps them down. No one has ever cut the ground from under his heroes with greater cruelty. The social process by which illusions are lost in the early Realists becomes in Flaubert a formal mechanism by which they are coolly crushed. The Balzacian sentence has as its referent action in the world of concrete social reality. As early as *Madame Bovary* Flaubert's sentences begin to become events of pure language. The disasters they recount are increasingly rhetorical rather than experiential. Whence the well-known arch shape of the Flaubertian narrative block: a hopefully ascending beginning; a middle section of intense desire; and a conclusion which deflates the dream, cuts the hopes to pieces. For Flaubert there is no redemption in experience, and he will provide none out of sentiment.

His pessimism appeared quite early:

> C'est étrange comme je suis né avec peu de foi au bonheur. J'ai eu, tout jeune, un pressentiment complet de la vie. C'était comme une odeur de cuisine nauséabonde qui s'échappe par un soupirail. On n'a pas besoin d'en avoir mangé pour savoir qu'elle est à faire vomir.[2]

> (It's strange how I was born lacking faith in happiness. When I was very young I had a complete presentiment of life. It was like a nauseous kitchen odor which filters out through a vent. You don't have to have eaten their cooking to know that it would make you vomit.)

In *L'Idiot de la famille*, Sartre provides a detailed interpretation of the psycho-social mechanism which generated Flaubert's "nausée de vivre" (I, 392). His feeling expressed to Du Camp in the letter of 1846 has its roots, according to Sartre's exploration, considerably earlier, but it develops organically, dominating Flaubert's emotional life and dictating the form of his novels. At the center of the emotion is a conflict between the empiricist ideology which was Dr. Flaubert's legacy to his son, and Gustave's own existential experience of misery.[3] The bourgeois sees experience as sequential, progressive, analyzable: this is the view that gives action its characteristic shape in the novels of Balzac and Stendhal. To men like his own father, Flaubert's view seemed absurdly mystical; to Flaubert, his father's ideas were naïvely optimistic. Indirectly quoting the passage from Gustave's 1846 letter to Du Camp, Sartre explains:

> Telle est la première contradiction qui, sur le terrain de la connaissance, oppose Gustave à son père sans qu'aucun d'eux s'en aperçoive: Gustave *sait tout*, une unique expérience lui a donné un pressentiment com-

---

2. Letter to Maxime Du Camp, 7 April 1846; *Correspondance*, I, 201.
3. Sartre, *L'Idiot de la famille*, I, 483-90.

plet de la vie; Achille-Cléophas en bon empiriste tient, au contraire, l'expérience pour la somme—jamais achevée—de toutes les expériences particulières qui se produisent non pas seulement au cours d'une vie humaine mais depuis la naissance de l'humanité. [Sartre's italics; *L'Idiot de la famille*, I, 483–84]

(This is the first contradiction which, in the realm of knowledge, divides Gustave from his father without either of them being aware of it: Gustave *knows every-thing*, a unique experience has given him a complete presentiment of life; on the other hand, Achille-Cléophas [Flaubert's father], as a good empiricist, believes that experience is the never-ending sum of all particular experiences which have occurred, not only during the life of an individual human being, but since the birth of humanity.)

But Flaubert knew he knew better than his father. At the center of his fiction is an ideology of omniscience. Balzac and Stendhal discover the fates of their heroes; Flaubert *knows* the destinies of his because he knows the total shape of life: "L'analyse *est déjà faite* et . . . il sait déjà ce qu'elle lui apportera" (*L'Idiot de la famille*, I, 489; "The analysis *is already completed* and . . . he already knows what it will demonstrate"). Time is becoming metaphorized; experience is no longer fundamentally sequential for Flaubert. Miscarriage and collapse *define* the shape of life, which is lived not as a series of significant actions, but as an image of disaster in which the developmental, chronological element is no more than accidental.

In Sartrian terms, the meaning of experience is "totalized" in each Flaubertian instant, and the sum of these instants which make up a human life adds only imagistic depth to the unvarying diagnosis. The outward form of the novel corresponds to the empiricist ideology of the first post-Revolutionary generation, to the ideology of Dr. Flaubert. But as Sartre puts it, by Gustave's time the experiment was finished (see Barbéris, *Balzac ou le mal du siècle,* I, 147, quoting a remark of Sartre's). Flaubert's statement to the Goncourts, that in *Madame Bovary* he had been trying to capture "a tone, the mouldy color of the wood louse's existence" (Goncourts' *Journal,* 17 March 1861) implies both the ideology which dominates his fiction and the techniques which he developed in response. His writing problem became to construct a series of moments which, suffered one by one, would make the outward condition of his protagonists coincide with the fate he had chosen for them long before. The total quality of the Flaubertian instant is thus in conflict with the developmental impulse which propels the action of Realist novels forward. The conflict finally forced Flaubert beyond the Realist para- digm altogether, to the point where effective action virtually disappeared from his books.

Proust's admiration for Flaubert is based precisely on Flaubert's movement away from Realism. This is no doubt why in his 1919 essay he hardly mentions *Madame Bovary,* because the influence of Realist texture, though already in conflict with other tendencies, is still quite apparent in this novel.

Defeat is fundamental to the conception of *Madame Bovary.* The whole novel exists to guarantee it. The events of the story represent one side of a dialectic in which the hopes of the characters form the other. For the protag- onists, events are their experience of the world's resistance to the fulfillment of a desire: "Emma would . . . have pre- ferred a midnight ceremony by torchlight, but Père Rou- ault could not comprehend such an idea. So there was the usual country wedding" (p. 27). This rhythm of desire and frustration characterizes the entire novel.

Yet although it is total, defeat in *Madame Bovary* is never tragic, since there is a clear effort to eliminate even the smallest traces of the nobility which in other literary systems often transforms human downfall. In this novel, prophetically for Flaubert's later books, the sense of events remains resolutely cramped.

Flaubert's decision to begin the story with Charles instead of Emma was inspired. Charles can absorb a dose of mockery which would have destroyed Emma precisely because he is not the book's hero. By covering him with irony from the start, Flaubert undermined the novel's foundation before its heroine even appears. The hapless Charles becomes the scale we use to measure Emma's aspirations once we meet her. Her hopes, directed at an incurable fumbler, are thus lamed from the start.

The concerted attack on them then continues in a subtler way. When the newlyweds arrive in Tostes, the tone remains exceptionally relaxed for several pages. Emma and Charles are busy setting up house, and Flaubert is particularly absorbed in describing Charles's happiness. Then, in the last laconic paragraph of the chapter, we read: "Avant qu'elle se mariât, elle avait cru avoir de l'amour; mais le bonheur qui aurait dû résulter de cet amour n'étant pas venu, il fallait qu'elle se fût trompée, songeait-elle" (p. 36; "Before her marriage she had thought she was in love; but since the happiness that should have followed failed to come, she must have been mistaken, she thought"). Nothing in the emotional context up to this point prepares us for this reaction, since Flaubert has carefully kept Charles at center-focus since the beginning of the book. With the exception of a few vague details, we have never been in Emma's mind before. So the shock of this sudden penetration into her feelings is doubly great: the point-of-view is unaccustomed, and the emotion revealed is totally unexpected.

From now on Emma's point of view is the novel's. The change in perspective occurs at precisely the moment when Charles thinks he has finally found happiness and his wife discovers that she has lost all hope of it. Flaubert's implacable method characteristically annihilates each trace of optimism or happiness as soon as it can surface. Even after we learn in the following chapter how the puerility of

Charles's affection caused Emma's reaction, her moment of despair remains isolated from its causes. The end of Emma's love for Charles seems as mysteriously inevitable as it was unforeseen. In a world constantly looking forward to failure, this is the paradigm of what the future always holds.

More and more, the telling is built upon this sort of abstract juxtaposition of elements. Increasingly, Flaubert short-circuits the emotional logic which explains events so that they appear purely gratuitous. Defeat becomes an a priori quality in the story; irony, the first principle in its unfolding. The episode at La Vaubyessard depends upon such a series of structural juxtapositions. Emma's vision of luxury at the ball sets the dialectic going; her return to Tostes systematically confronts this vision with the meager reality of life with Charles. From her carriage coming back, Emma sees some riders passing, laughing and smoking cigars. The moment runs directly up against the following cruel description of her husband after they return: "Charles began to smoke. He smoked with lips protruded, spitting constantly. . . . 'You'll make yourself ill!' she said scornfully. He put the cigar down and ran to get a glass of cold water at the pump" (p. 57).

The dialectic of desire and defeat thus increasingly controls the organization of the tale. The systematic cruelty of the world that frustrates Emma's flights of enthusiasm is transformed into a verbal mechanism. Each optimistic sentence collides with another which negates it, and the entire novel comes to seem like an expansion of the Comices Agricoles:

—Cent fois même, j'ai voulu partir, et je vous ai suivie, je suis resté.
"Fumiers." [p. 153]

("A hundred times I have tried to leave, and yet I followed you, I stayed."
"Manure.")

This continual presence of stillborn transports is what creates the characteristically abrupt rhythm of events in *Madame Bovary*. The system requires great resilience in the heroine, a considerable capacity to renew aspirations in spite of past defeats. This is why everything in the novel occurs in series (Charles, Léon, Rodolphe, Léon again; Les Bertaux, Tostes, Yonville) without the characters seeming to learn anything from their repeated setbacks. Their sustained naïveté represents the essence of Bovarysme.

The techniques in *Madame Bovary* which slowly displace the novel's meaning from the psychological to the formalistic represent a tendency that Flaubert will develop more and more fully in succeeding books. *Madame Bovary* represents only the first step in this evolution; Flaubert is still quite far from the slapstick schematizations of *Bouvard et Pécuchet*. Emma's repeated defeats seem to echo one another as if the same mold had produced all of them; but there is still a limit placed on their continuation. After Léon, with the sort of psychological insight that recalls the Realists so often in this transitional book, Emma has no energy left to start the pattern again. At the end, her defeats have taken on enough weight to tip the balance against any new beginning. When her past catches up with her at last, it finds her emotionally exhausted.

The novel has always been peopled with antiheroes. The dissonances it explored always set a figure we are meant to admire against a reality outside, a set of accepted values, which the antihero's values are meant to supplant. "Anti-" in the phrase has a positive ring, reveals the operation of a social dialectic which seeks to resolve the contradictions of experience the novel portrays. Until the nineteenth century the system of values embodied by the antihero had implied a world in which conduct would become heroic again. An antihero dialectically implied his contrary, as the satirical or corrective purpose of the fiction explored what a better reality might be.

After the Restoration, however, this ceased progressively to be true. Balzac and Stendhal are, in profoundly different ways, reactionaries who seek their values in the pre-Revolutionary and republican periods. But Flaubert's values? To what point in history do they look? What are their ethical implications? The disaster they imply is that they look nowhere and imply nothing but disaster.

As is usual with a profound change in the ideology underlying a fictional system, the formal implications of the change are immense. Where precisely in time they occur is hard to specify simply, since Flaubert was innovating on many technical fronts at once. Perhaps the question is best answered by saying that the important inflection in novelistic form occurs between *Madame Bovary* and *L'Education sentimentale*. In its overall shape the plot of *Madame Bovary* still conserves a belief in experience as chronologically determined. History is still—even though painfully —the force that generates and reveals truth in the world. Everything in the novel projects forward with a rigor worthy of Balzac to Emma's definitive act, suicide. And between the point at which the story begins and this point of termination a series of actions punctuate the plot, each of them revealing another truth, another element of Emma's destiny.

By the time of *L'Education*, the sea-change in the narrative system had occurred. As Proust put it with unintended double meaning, "with *L'Education sentimentale* the revolution has taken place" (*CSB*, p. 588). Indeed, the revolution of 1848 (to which Proust was not referring), the event around which the novel is organized, is precisely the historical event which finally made it impossible for writers to believe in history. In 1846 Baudelaire had dedicated his *Salon* to the Bourgeois: "Un jour radieux viendra où les savants seront propriétaires, et les propriétaires savants. Alors votre puissance sera complète, et nul ne protestera contre elle" (Preface; "A glorious day will come when cultivated people will be rich, and the rich will be cultivated. Then your power will be complete, and none will protest against it"). Perhaps all prerevolutionary writers sound naïve today, but it is astonishing to encounter this credulous Baudelaire.

The ideological effects of the revolution that attempted to join the ideals implied in this optimistic dedication (and its sincerity is real) have often been chronicled—Marx was among the first. But the depression caused in artists and intellectuals by the failure of the revolution has not been captured better than by Flaubert: the mood of *L'Education sentimentale* is the dark comedy atmosphere of these failed aspirations. The present is never much of a source of hope; now the future held none either. History stopped for middle-class idealists who lived beyond 1848. We will not find Baudelaire eulogizing the Bourgeois in *Les Fleurs du mal*.

In the novel, the change in ideology progressed in parallel fashion. Of course the reconceptualization of experience always requires a painful and prolonged psychological adjustment. *Madame Bovary* was begun in the wake of the new Republic, just before the coup d'état of December 1851. The consequences of this whirlwind of changes were far from clear at the time Emma's story was conceived. By September 1864, when Flaubert began composing *L'Education*, the results were in, and Flaubert had thoroughly digested them. Describing his new book, he wrote in a well-known letter to Mlle Leroyer de Chantepie (6 October 1864): "C'est un livre d'amour, de passion; mais de passion telle qu'elle peut exister maintenant, c'est-à-dire *inactive*" (*Correspondance*, V, 158; "It is a love story, a story about passion; but about the kind of passion that can exist nowadays, that is to say, *inactive* passion").

The word "inactive" identifies what is profoundly new in this novel. *Madame Bovary* may have read slowly, but in *L'Education* nothing seems to happen at all. (The novel shares this characteristic—and the critical disapproval that it at first entailed—with Proust's monument to narrative immobility fifty years later.) The most "inactive" scenes in Stendhal—for example, the chapters of Fabrice's long months in the tower—do not exhibit the stasis, the exhaustion, of Flaubert's story of Frédéric Moreau. Proust caught the point precisely in his 1919 essay: *"L'Education sentimentale* est un long rapport de toute une vie, sans que les personnages prennent pour ainsi dire une part active à l'action" (*CSB*, p. 590; *"L'Education sentimentale* is a long account of an entire life, but one in which the characters take virtually no active part in the action"). The problem of motivating the action has been at the center of the changes in novelistic form examined up to this point. Proust's essay goes to the heart of the question: what, if not action, is recounted in the "eternal imperfects" which for him defined the originality of Flaubert's narrative style in this novel (*CSB*, pp. 590–91)?

A distinction between two techniques—which can be called active and synthetic narration—begins to be useful here. The active mode of telling depicts the sorts of decisive events that change lives and animate forward-moving plots —precisely the sort of narration that characterizes the Realist novel. The synthetic mode, on the other hand, seeks to create images of representative atmospheres. It tends to dissolve chronology, and concentrates on portraying the mental landscapes so important in much of modern fiction. As a result, it saps the energy of the individual events that active narration accentuates. Active narration is based grammatically on the preterite, the tense which fixes, in objective time, definite acts expressed as already accomplished. The synthetic, on the other hand, principally exploits a special "veiling" quality available in the French imperfect, what Proust calls "le plan incliné et tout en demi-teinte des imparfaits" (*CSB*, p. 591; "the shadowy inclined plane [or "downward slide"] of verbs in the imperfect"). It is the narrative mode of choice for writers who no longer believe that their characters' hopes can be realized in the world of concrete social activity. The synthetic is the primary mode of narration in *A la recherche du temps perdu*, and Proust found it in *L'Education* because the view of experience to which both the movement of history and his own technical experiments drove Flaubert is virtually the same as Proust's. Together their view of human possibilities links them in opposition to the Realists. They lived after the fall, and synthetic narration is narration after the fall. In this sense, the action of *L'Education sentimentale* contrasts even with that of *Madame Bovary*, and the plot of *L'Education* provides the first test of the new concept of human possibilities after the debacle of mid-century.

People have argued that if Emma Bovary had been rich, if she had been a man, if she had never married, her life would not have been such a failure. *L'Education sentimentale* disproves the argument conclusively. Frédéric Moreau is an Emma who is free, rich and male; but his defeat is nonetheless total. His slow decline, up to the book's "rat-tail ending" (as Flaubert described it in an early outline[4]), represents a failure which is all the greater because Frédéric's freedom offered so many greater possibilities.

L'Education does alter the balance of the narrative factors—psychological and realistic on one side, purely formalistic on the other—which are in such conflict in *Madame Bovary*. Since Frédéric is freer than Emma, his failure in the novel has to depend less upon the "fatality" that poor Charles Bovary blamed for his wife's adultery and suicide than upon a certain number of unfortunate coincidences and a good dose of simple bad luck. The sense of "fatality" in *Madame Bovary* flowed from the psychological rigor with which a set of material and emotional limitations circumscribed the heroine's destiny. The links with Realist causality are clear. But destiny in *L'Education* seems the result of chance. Consequently, this novel seems substantially more contrived than *Madame Bovary*.

4. See Marie-Jeanne Durry, *Flaubert et ses projets inédits*, p. 137.

The change can be measured by examining two of the technical elements of *L'Education*. The first is Flaubert's creation of a psychological symbol, "l'autre" ("the other"). Felt through the consciousness of the characters in the book, the strength of this device is organic. It seems to spring coherently from the emotional organization of the novel, and resembles the developmental logic that underlies Realist fiction. But the second of these elements, what might be called the technique of the constant obstacle, is perfectly fortuitous; it happens because Flaubert requires that it happen. It intervenes in the tale and violates the story's internal coherence. Yet of the procedures controlling the sense and direction of events in the novel it is by far the most influential.

For the "history of an entire generation" that Flaubert hoped his book would be,[5] the cast of *L'Education* is really quite small. Between the few actors a confusion of relationships grows up, pivoting around Frédéric, which finally the hero is no longer able to manipulate. The entire complex collapses under its own weight. The symbol of "l'autre" is associated with these moments when the structure of Frédéric's relationships begins to sway and shake. It appears like an evanescent extra character, nearly real and yet still clearly fictive, symbolizing for each of the relationships in which Frédéric tries to succeed the implacable outside force that prevents his happiness.

When Deslauriers accepts an invitation to come to Paris where Frédéric has been living unhappy and alone, Flaubertian fatality makes him arrive precisely on the evening when Frédéric has at last obtained a dinner invitation to the Arnoux's. Frédéric goes out anyway. He returns late that night, elated by his first prolonged contact with Mme Arnoux. Deslauriers is already asleep. Frédéric slowly recalls the presence of the other person, and Flaubert's sentences follow the psychological movement closely:

5. Flaubert used the phrase in the letter (6 October 1864) to Mlle Leroyer de Chantepie quoted above, p. 70; *Corr.*, V, 158.

"When he had closed the door, he heard someone snoring in the darkened room off the bed chamber. It was *the other*. He had forgotten about him" (II, 82).

Frédéric's life soon becomes hopelessly entangled. He had dreamed of the peace of one eternal love, but pursuing four women at once makes any calm impossible. He learns to lie, and his infidelities soon envelop him: "He repeated to one of them the pledge he had just made to another, sent them identical bouquets, wrote to them simultaneously" (II, 418-19). But what makes sustaining the situation impossible is that each of the characters in the melodrama his life has become knows that his rivals exist, knows who they are, knows what they want. The result is that Frédéric discovers it is psychologically impossible for him to be alone with any of them. The imagined presence of "the others" destroys every intimate moment: "'I love you as I always have!' 'Oh, no, that's a lie!' 'What?' She looked at him coldly. 'You're forgetting *the other* [woman]. The one you take to the races. The woman whose portrait you have—your mistress!'" (II, 388).

But the presence of this sort of obstacle to the happiness of the characters in *L'Education* still seems much less organically justified by the givens of the book than was the case in *Madame Bovary*. Structurally, the entire procedure is flawed. An incident at the Arnoux's, following an argument between Arnoux and his wife over his relationship with Rosanette, suggests the difference. Arnoux storms out, leaving Frédéric alone with Mme Arnoux: "Never had she seemed so attractive, so profoundly beautiful. . . . She closed her eyes, calm, inert. He came closer to her, and leaning over her, he gazed intently at her face. The sound of boots echoed in the hallway, it was the other" (II, 199). This is one of the tenderest moments in the long story of their love. But what necessitates the sudden intervention of the symbol, the unfortunate reappearance of Arnoux, the destruction of the intimacy? Only the logic of Flaubert's manipulation of the material.

Of course the characters in the novel are internally flawed

by their cowardice and their indecision. But their defi-
ciencies do not suffice to explain their defeat. Flaubert
had planned it that way in one of his earliest outlines for
the book: "Quant à l'empêchement de baiser quand tout
est mûr p[ou]r cela il n'y a pas que sa vertu qui l'empêche
mais une circonstance fortuite"[6] ("As for them not 'making it' when everything seems ripe, it's not just her virtue
that prevents them, but a *chance circumstance*"). Such
circumstances abound. In these five hundred pages, systematically, *every* moment of intimacy is interrupted by a
sound of boots in the hallway or something equally accidental. The repetition of such incidents creates the "constant obstacle" that defines the novel's rhythm. Whatever
"fatality" the book can be said to have flows directly from
this mechanical procedure.

It dominates the book's central love story. The first moment of contact, when Frédéric saves Mme Arnoux's shawl
from blowing over the side of the steamer, is interrupted
by Arnoux's raucous voice. At the pottery factory where
Frédéric goes to see her, the series of gratuitous interruptions is painful: "They passed close by a broken-down
shed where garden tools had once been stored. 'We don't
use it any more,' said Madame Arnoux. He replied in a
trembling voice, 'It could shelter our happiness together!'
The din of the forge blower made his words unintelligible"
(II, 227). Similarly, Flaubert takes great pains to describe
the little parchment tube vomited up by Mme Arnoux's
child Eugène—the object which on the day the revolution
began her at home instead of coming to meet Frédéric as they had planned. Such was the derisory object, the
"circonstance fortuite," which prevented the consumma-
tion of their love.

But things get worse. Toward the end, Frédéric and Rosanette's little boy dies hideously. Frédéric fails to arrive
on time with the twelve thousand francs necessary to save
Arnoux from bankruptcy. Having finally resolved to marry

Louise Roque, he discovers her leaving the church where she has just been wed to Deslauriers. Finally, Frédéric sees Sénécal shoot poor Dussardier—the ultimate symbolic blow, since Dussardier has been the only uncompromised character in the novel. The defeat of every hope, the obliteration of every positive value, is so total that the verdict of the bitter final chapter in which Frédéric and Deslauriers review their life—"ils l'avaient manquée tous les deux" ("they had both missed it")—does seem to take the measure of everything that has preceded.

The account of experience in *L'Education* is thus different from any of the fictions considered above, not so much in the final diagnosis as in the way the characters' failure seems to reflect backward and contaminate every element of their lives. The tone and the techniques are new, and more than anything else they suggest caricature. The task of writers since Stendhal had been to motivate the fates of their protagonists, to search out within their characters' souls and in the world surrounding them the profound origins of their disasters. But disaster in *L'Education* would seem pure caprice, were it not for the fact that Flaubert still sees his characters with seriousness. He has no love for them since he has no hope for the world. But we are not meant to laugh at their undoing, even though the techniques that insure it are so mechanical as to risk seeming comic. The manipulation is so overt and so tendentious that at some points it is a wonder we accept the story at all. With *L'Education*, the failure of the novelistic hero becomes a mere formality.

The constant obstacle in *L'Education sentimentale* thus represents the only significant intervention of the sort of active narration that changes lives (the only intervention, in other words, of history) in the novel. The world outside the characters' minds has become thoroughly hostile, and is thoroughly despised; the revolution at the ideological center of the novel (a revolution which before 1848 represented a hopeful possibility) is seen in retrospect as an exasperating hindrance or, worse, as simply irrelevant:

> Puis il [Frédéric] éprouva le besoin de voir Rosa-
> nette. . . .
> Elle se tenait près du feu, décousant la doublure
> d'une robe. Un pareil ouvrage le surprit.
> —Tiens! qu'est-ce que tu fais?
> —Tu le vois, dit-elle sèchement. Je racommode mes
> hardes! C'est ta République.
> —Pourquoi ma République?
> —C'est la mienne, peut-être? [II, 340]

> (At this point Frédéric felt he wanted to see Rosa-
> nette. . . .
> She was sitting by the fire, unstitching the lining of
> a dress. He was surprised to see her doing that sort of
> work.
> "Well, what are you doing?"
> "It's pretty obvious," she said curtly. "I'm mending
> my clothes. It's because of your Republic."
> "*My* Republic?"
> "Well, it sure isn't *mine*!")

As for the usual run of experience in *L'Education*, it
strongly resembles Proust's synthetic mode, and was well
described by him in his 1919 essay: "ce grand *Trottoir
roulant* que sont les pages de Flaubert, au défilement
continu, monotone, morne, indéfini" (*CSB*, p. 587; "that
long moving sidewalk of Flaubert's pages, gliding along,
monotonous, gloomy, indefinite").

It is worth noting in *L'Education sentimentale* how much
Flaubert's stance in relation to experience recalls that of
the Romantic poets thirty or more years earlier. Frédéric Moreau waiting for his boat to leave Paris at the beginning of the novel bears much more resemblance to Lamar-
tine on the shore of the lake than he does to Rastignac
ready to begin his campaign as *Le Père Goriot* opens, or to
Fabrice at Waterloo.

A comparison of Stendhal's use of Waterloo with Flaubert's treatment of the 1848 revolution—events each author
clearly felt as historical turning points—reveals how closely

Frédéric approaches the elegiac passivity of the Romantic persona. Stendhal's sense of the movement of history was real, immediate, visceral. His often-repeated "I fell along with Napoleon" describes the meaning of Waterloo for his own life and his own chances. But curiously, at the time of the battle, Waterloo is not seen in *La Chartreuse* as a disaster; it is seen as a confusion. Stendhal's sense of things seems to be that though the change is cataclysmic, and the military debacle complete, the modification of human possibilities it entails is left principally to Mosca to clarify much later on. Through Fabrice's participation, Stendhal makes us see Waterloo as live experience, with the immediate indeterminacy of real events.

In *L'Education* Frédéric's attitude as the revolution unfolds has a quality of disinterest, even vague disgust. Frédéric's role (unlike that of Flaubert, who in 1848 had been a member of the Garde Nationale) is distanced, hazily neutral. Where Fabrice was a naïvely hopeful participant, Frédéric is a world-weary spectator, too absorbed in his private uncertainties to involve himself in public problems. It is as if Frédéric *already knew* the disappointment the failure of the revolution would bring. His spontaneity is prematurely gone. Frédéric is an abstracted Fabrice who has learned too well the drawbacks of enthusiasm.

In a cynical parody of Romanticism, Flaubert feints at removing Frédéric from the reality of 1848 altogether. On a caprice, the hero leaves the capital at the most crucial point in the political struggle, the revolt of the June Days. With Rosanette as shepherdess, he is off to seek bucolic peace in the Forest of Fontainebleau. Word arrives of bloody battles in Paris: "The news did not surprise Rosanette or her lover," their creator dryly tells us (II, 355). At this point, as one of the crucial events in modern history plays itself out in the distant capital, Flaubert slips his protagonists into the most sustained passage of synthetic narration in the novel, their "honeymoon" (II, 358), a dense three-page idyll whose bitter moral significance repeatedly pierces Flaubert's impassive surface:

> Ils se trouvaient si bien dans leur vieux landau, bas comme un sofa et couverte d'une toile à raies déteintes! Les fossés pleins de brousailles filaient sous leurs yeux, avec un mouvement doux et continu. . . .
>
> Ils se croyaient loin des autres, bien seuls. Mais tout à coup passait un garde-chasse avec son fusil, ou une bande de femmes en haillons, traînant sur leur dos de longues bourrées. [II, 355]

> (They were so comfortable in their old carriage, low as a sofa and covered in faded striped cloth. The brush-filled ditches glided by smoothly and continuously. . . .
>
> They thought themselves far away from other people, completely alone. But suddenly a gamekeeper would pass with his gun, or a band of women in rags dragging bundles of firewood on their backs.)

The timeless imperfects function here (as they will in Proust) to insulate the material synthesized in the image from contamination by the movement of time outside the privileged moment. But at this point in *L'Education*, the outside is General Cavaignac's massacre of the poor in Paris, the brutal counterrevolution, the violent death of an imagined "fraternité" between the classes, the final burial of the liberal dream.

By 1864, of course, Flaubert knew all this, and had no illusions left. His effects were finely calculated in consequence. The painful scene (which follows almost directly) in which Père Roque casually executes one of the starving prisoners taken in the Paris repression makes the moral meaning of Frédéric's pastoral quite clear. Long before, Flaubert had told Louise Colet that irony seemed to him to dominate life.[7] By now he has reached an attitude toward the larger society of total outsideness. Like the aristocratic Romantics who mourned the passing of their world, his relation to concrete reality is one of elegiac contemplation, without even the earlier consolation of knowing just what had been lost.

7. Letter of 8–9 March 1852; *Corr.*, II, 407.

For Flaubert, the world outside is hardly recoverable for the thinking subject. Yet it is the only world he has. *L'Education* points forward to attitudes we associate with Mallarmé and Proust, the total primacy of literature over life, of mental over real events. But Flaubert's irony guarantees that the dying dialectical relationship between inside and outside still subsists (indeed, without such relation, his irony would not have been possible). In the 1848 scenes in *L'Education* through the escapism of the Fontainebleau episode, he makes irony a cruelly telling element in the narration. By juxtaposing the Fontainebleau rhapsody with the ravage in the capital, by counterposing the dream against the historical reality which makes the dream absurd, Flaubert completes the investigation the Realists began. The dilemma they started to explore is by now fully sketched out: there is no happiness in the world outside the individual; the soul flees inside attempting to find peace in isolation; the outside breaks through; the inside proves hollow.

The hollowness of the inside and the irruption of the outside are what *Bouvard et Pécuchet* is about. Elements of a caricatural view of experience have already been identified in the discussion of *L'Education sentimentale*. But *Bouvard* passes beyond these potentialities to complete Flaubert's revolt against psychological realism. It must have been drudgery for him in his earlier books to create characters who would seem worthy of sympathy, when he knew from the beginning they existed only to be annihilated at the end. He hated these beings who were doomed in advance; his letters to Louise Colet about Emma Bovary prove the point clearly. How much more satisfying, then, simply to watch his creatures run helter-skelter to destruction. He had only to drop the high seriousness he had maintained for so long concerning their destinies. So in *Bouvard* he transformed disaster into comedy, the better to express the "waves of hatred" he felt about the stupidity of his age.[8]

The characters in this new form had to be magic beings borrowed from children's stories: unbreakable, capable of sustaining the whole series of failures that caused Emma's and Frédéric's slow declines. He needed cartoon characters, or a silent movie duo, and this is what Bouvard and Pécuchet turn out to be. They are the perpetual victims we know as Laurel and Hardy, reacting just enough to the misfortunes inflicted on them to remind us that their experience is meant to have some connection with our own. "It's a fact," Flaubert wrote, "my two heroes are not interesting; but that's just what I needed."[9] The moral significance of the fiction did not change, of course. The action was devised, as in *L'Education*, to produce the greatest possible frequency of misfortunes; the heroes are simply more maladroit than before. Now, however, Flaubert was able to give free rein to his disgust without wrenching the realistic texture that had dominated his earlier books. As he wrote to Mme Roger des Genettes: "It seems to me no one has yet tried comedy of ideas ["le comique d'idées"] " (2 April 1877; *Corr.*, VIII, 26). And he discovered that this comedy was the most propitious terrain for expressing his abomination.

In the process, *Bouvard* ceases to be a novel in the traditional sense. The progressive movement of life which the novel had existed to depict is absent here. In 1839, at the book's opening, Bouvard and Pécuchet are forty-seven years old. And though the action lasts over thirty years, the two heroes are not perceptibly older at the end than they were at the start. The same conscious negligence of verisimilitude characterizes every level of the work.

<hr/>

8. Letter to Bouilhet, 30 September 1855; *Corr.*, IV, 96.

9. In conversation with Auguste Sabatier, quoted in Geneviève Bollème, *Le second volume de "Bouvard et Pécuchet,"* p. 11, n. 2.

Bouvard points forward toward the Absurd; Beckett himself might have written the tragicomic opening scene. It is easy to imagine the deserted stage: the sudden appearance of the two actors, the tall thin one balancing the short plump one; the queer symmetry of their mechanical gestures; the ridiculous conversation. Everything contributes to placing the scene and the characters in a world dominated by stylization and schematism. And so the story proceeds, as Bouvard and Pécuchet play out the bitter comedy that arises when life is made to function like a mechanism. Existence becomes a machine to produce disasters, a catalogue of calamities, an incomparable debacle. Sustaining it all is the comic nonchalance which Flaubert feigns in order to disguise the bitterest irony of his career.

That the purpose was more than slapstick humor is clear in this letter to Turgenev:

> Malgré l'immense respect que j'ai pour votre sens critique, je ne suis point de votre avis sur la manière dont il faut prendre ce sujet-là. S'il est traité brièvement, d'une façon concise et légère, ce sera une fantaisie plus ou moins spirituelle, mais sans portée et sans vraisemblance, tandis qu'en détaillant et en développant, j'aurai l'air de croire à mon histoire, et on peut en faire une chose sérieuse et même *effrayante*.[10]

> (Despite my great respect for your critical judgment, I don't agree with you about the way that subject [*Bouvard*] should be handled. If I treat it briefly, lightly, and concisely, it will produce a more or less humorous fantasy, but one having neither weight nor truth; whereas if I fill it with detail and develop it, I'll give the impression of believing in my own story, and it can become a serious—even terrifying—thing.)

The anthology of idiocy, the "sottisier," is the archetypal

10. 25 July 1874; *Corr.*, VII, 178. See also the letter to Mme Brainne, 30 December 1878; *Corr.*, VIII, 175.

Flaubertian work, extending from his adolescent comic fantasies about the quintessential Bourgeois he called the Garçon to the *Dictionnaire des idées reçues*. In *Bouvard* the "sottisier" reappears, victorious, for it alone can carry the weight of his monumental despair.

Bouvard et Pécuchet is a logical, indeed a necessary step beyond the proto-Naturalism of *L'Education sentimentale*. But its progeny, as indicated, lie mainly outside the tradition of the novel; it had, for example, no influence whatever on *A la recherche du temps perdu*. The texture of narration in *Bouvard*, which simply accumulates series of experiences (formalized disasters) told in the preterite, is worlds away from the techniques, deriving rather from some of the impressionistic scenes in *L'Education sentimentale*, that Proust will develop in *La Recherche*.

Nor will we find in the Naturalists elements of the tradition out of which Proustian narration emerges. The Naturalists were at some pains to furnish theoretical explications of what was new in their vision of the world. But none of their ideological innovations apparently required any formal ones, and Zola's narration adds virtually nothing to the techniques which Flaubert (and even Balzac) had already made available to novelists.

Rather, if there is a stage which intervenes between *L'Education* and *La Recherche*, it is probably to be found in another post-Naturalist work almost contemporary with *Bouvard* (and, like it, composed by a lapsed Naturalist): Huysmans's *A Rebours*. *A Rebours* has anecdotic connections with Proust which have become critical commonplaces: Des Esseintes and Charlus share a model in Robert de Montesquiou; Proust and Huysmans share an admiration for Mallarmé and bring his work into the texture of their novels (*A Rebours*, ch. 14; *La Recherche*, III, 455–56). But in this examination of Proust's tradition the importance of Huysmans's novel is not found in such details. Between the inactivity of Frédéric Moreau and the tech-

niques Flaubert devised to make a story out of it on the
one hand, and on the other the more radical passivity of
Proust's hero and more extensive departures from traditional narration which Proust developed to portray the experience of his characters, Huysmans's Des Esseintes stands
as a notable intermediate experiment.

In the preface he wrote in 1903 (the book had first appeared in 1884), Huysmans clarified his own attempt of
twenty years before. Naturalism, he wrote, had made no
real progress in the study of the soul since Flaubert; its
practitioners were going round in circles attempting to find
new material; his own Naturalist novels by 1884 seemed to
him irrelevant. He felt himself smothering in the novel and
longed to break the form open:

> C'était cela qui me frappait surtout à cette époque,
> supprimer l'intrigue traditionnelle, voire même la pas-
> sion, . . . concentrer le pinceau de lumière sur un seul
> personnage. [Preface, p. 21] [11]
>
> (What intrigued me at that time was to do away with
> the traditional plot, even with passion, . . . to focus
> the spotlight tightly on a single character.)

Des Esseintes objectifies tendencies toward inaction and
toward the total interiorization of experience that were

11. Huysmans's desire recalls Flaubert's, expressed in his well-known letter
of 16 January 1852 (*Corr.*, II, 345): "Ce qui me semble beau, ce que je vou-
drais faire, c'est un livre sur rien, un livre sans attache extérieure . . . , un livre
qui n'aurait presque pas de sujet" ("The thing that strikes me as beautiful, the
thing I'd like to do, is a book about nothing, a book with no external connections . . . , a book which would almost have no subject"). There is no
question of direct influence here, of course. Instead we see a parallel evolution
in two writers both insightful about the declining possibilities for fiction in the
Realist paradigm. Huysmans's movement from *Les Soeurs Vatard* to *A Rebours*
validates the logic of Flaubert's from *Madame Bovary* to the final *Tentation
de Saint-Antoine* and to *Bouvard*. Flaubert's letter of 4 December 1872 to
George Sand, associating *Bouvard* and *La Tentation* quite closely, sheds further light on this evolution.

not fully realized in Flaubert. The break with the outside, with the world of concrete social reality, and the isolation of the hero are here virtually completed. Flaubert was still bitterly fighting the outside; but for Huysmans in this novel (or at least in some of its most important scenes) the outside simply becomes irrelevant.

The most celebrated case is Des Esseintes's trip to London in chapter 11. England fascinates him and he dreams of a voyage (p. 167); sets out to purchase guidebooks (p. 169); loses himself in reverie over them (p. 170); enters an English-style café where his reverie continues (p. 173); drives to a restaurant near the railroad station and eats an English dinner there in preparation for taking the train (p. 174). But then he recalls how disappointing a previous voyage to Holland for which he had had great hopes had proven (p. 176). Finally he realizes that he has already experienced in his mind everything he wished to see and feel on the trip; and, without even having entered the station, he returns home as exhausted from his varied sensations as from a real journey.

The trope—that experience in imagination is so valuable that real experience becomes irrelevant—is schematic almost to the point of comedy. But Des Esseintes is not a comic being. He is the 1884 version of Julien Sorel or Lucien de Rubempré, a hero as authentically necessary as they, sent out to encounter the world by a novelist for whom, like Balzac or Stendhal, the hero's adventures in the world represent a serious attempt to explore and understand what the world holds for all of us. But virtually nothing of note happens to Des Esseintes in *A Rebours*; the events which do appear are so hollow as to be nearly nonexistent (he still gets into his carriage, but ends up going nowhere; he walks from one room to another, but does nothing when he gets there). Scenes of reverie dominate, and a large proportion of the tale is given over to minute descriptions of his tastes, his habits, his memories, his perceptions, his ruminations. As a result, verbs in the imperfect

and most of the other elements of synthetic narration a-
bound here; the book is built up of heightened images of
blocks of time seen in characteristic detail but isolated
from real chronology. Action seems to have no place in
this narrative system. These "inward" portions of *A Rebours*
share far more with Proust's narrative texture than they do
with Realist narration.

   Bouvard et Pécuchet and *A Rebours*, though they explore separate branchings in the post-Naturalist tradition,
nonetheless have profound similarity in an area important
for a consideration of Proust. Both of these books represent
in their own ways closer approaches to autonomous form
than do fictional works which preceded them. *Bouvard*
radically refuses psychology, and life inside the individual
virtually disappears in its headlong chronicle of multiform
disasters. *A Rebours*, on the other hand, denies the outside
and all connection with Realist texture, and expansively
explores mental landscapes of baroque splendor.
   These are books whose meanings are nothing but their
means; their techniques have been forced to extremes of
stylization that make their own schematic internal organi-
zations complete prisoners of the ideas which they respectively express. In them, from different directions, the
dialectic between the individual and his surroundings, between the inside and the outside, is finally abolished. They
are among the first radically formalist works in modern
fiction. In this sense their posterity is immense. An entire
literature about the creation of literature will follow from
the failure of life outside, of which these books stand as
early and prestigious indications.
   Proust received this tradition as a dominant atmosphere
and a prevailing set of techniques. He did not immediately
submit to it. *Les Plaisirs et les jours* and *Jean Santeuil* reveal explorations in other directions, which are still perceptible in the early parts of *La Recherche*. Nonetheless
the implications of the tradition which extended forward

from Stendhal and Balzac still remained to be traced out further on both ideological and technical levels.

The touchstone of the point the evolution had reached before Proust might well be Mallarmé's celebrated assertion: "Le monde est fait pour aboutir à un beau livre" ("The world is made to end up as a beautiful book").[12] In the perspective of developments in the novel since 1830, we need to consider what sort of book, possessing what sort of beauty, Proust devised to express his experience of the world's possibilities.

12. "Sur l'évolution littéraire" (enquête de Jules Huret; 1891); *Oeuvres complètes*, p. 872.

Part II

Proust: Reconceiving the Tradition

—Ah, Céleste, soupirait-il parfois, tout cela tombe un
peu en poussière. C'est comme une collection de beaux
éventails d'un autre siècle sur un mur. On les admire,
mais il n'y a plus de main pour les faire vivre. S'ils sont
sous verre, c'est que la fête est finie.
Céleste Albaret, *Monsieur Proust*

Our contemporaries afflict us because they have ceased
to believe. The most sincere of them will only tell us
what it is that happens to himself. . . . They cannot tell
stories because they do not believe the stories are true.
Virginia Woolf, "How It Strikes a Contemporary"

Introduction to Part II

The history of the nineteenth-century novel thus follows the waning course of the social dialectic. The outward events refracted through fictions seemed increasingly distant and hostile; the inner emotions which the Realists had progressively become skillful at portraying seemed increasingly disconnected with characters' actions in the world. Flaubert, surely, is the turning point. The enervation which pervades his world is what remains of the tense effort to harmonize the conflict between individual aspiration and social exigence that had animated *Le Rouge et le noir* or *Le Père Goriot*. Flaubert's fatigue is a peculiar second-generation phenomenon. It is the distress of the early Realist hero defeated in some grave social reverse, but now a despair floating free, no longer able to recollect the catastrophe that produced it, nor to believe there is any hope for recovery. In turn, Flaubert's enervation is the immediate ancestor of Proust's *angoisse*, the diffuse, desolate sense that the self is everywhere threatened and nowhere effective against the threat.

The forms of narration immediately reflect this evolution. In Proust the style of telling is the most sophisticated index of the change which has occurred in consciousness, as the concrete social process which had surfaced briefly as the explicit subject of fiction in the immediate post-Revolutionary period is again obscured. As the century advances the locus of meaning passes from the real content of the dialectic to the distant results of its process—results which are no longer even perceived as the product of movement outside the self. Instead, they are felt as pervasive "conditions" of existence, as desperately pessimistic universals responsible for the repeated defeats of experience, for human unhappiness generally. This perception decisively shapes narration in *A la recherche du temps perdu*.

Criticism necessarily follows its object. To the extent that writers are conscious of their practice, critics attend to those aspects that creators emphasize. Balzac's system insists that the social and historical context in which his books are embedded be dealt with at the center of discussion, and such discussion has been extensively provided in the studies of Guyon, Wurmser, Donnard, and Barbéris, among others.[1]

Proust's relation to criticism is very different. His vigorous attack on Sainte-Beuve, so thoroughly intertwined with the genesis of *La Recherche* around 1908–1909, suggests how. Proust begins by disputing Sainte-Beuve's critical method: "une botanique morale" ("a moral botany"; see *CSB*, p. 220, n. 2).[2] For Proust, Sainte-

1. An important distinction should be made between the critical study of a work's internal sociology, or even of the connection between the social world portrayed and its sociopolitical context, and attempts to relate the vision of human experience taken within the work (that is, its ideology) to the values, perceptions, and consciousness of a determinate social group. There is no lack of studies of Proust in the former category, from Ernst-Robert Curtius's summary but interesting article, "Les Bases sociales de l'oeuvre de Proust," to the recent books of Seth Wolitz (*The Proustian Community*) and P.-V. Zima (*Le Désir du mythe: Une lecture sociologique de Marcel Proust*).

Placing Proust in the tradition of the French novel since the Revolution leads one to examine his book from the second perspective. The problem is to interpret the insistence within *La Recherche* that the novel's vision of experience is autonomous, the product of no historical conditioning (in other words, universal), and that the book has been constructed and can be understood as a totality requiring no reference to forms or structures outside itself. In this perspective, studies in the former category, however valuable in themselves, have proven only marginally relevant.

2. A curious and important parallel exists between the methodology of Sainte-Beuve which Proust's idealism rejects and the methodologies of Sartre in his Flaubert study and of Barbéris in his work on Balzac. Sainte-Beuve may not have been a brilliant practical exponent of his own critical philosophy; his lack of success makes the philosophy itself overly easy to dismiss. In fact there is much affinity between Sainte-Beuve's naïve materialism and the more sophisticated materialism of Sartre or Barbéris.

Beuve's attempt to base explanation of a writer's work on the material circumstances in which it was produced is thoroughly beside the point. Genius for him has no connection with the material conditions in which it arises. The organization of a work of art, its language and images are, precisely, *sui generis* in Proust's view. Thus in his own novel, he gave his meticulous attention to working out the book's intricate architecture and its complex pattern of internal signs. His critical theory and his artistic practice are in this sense consistent: Proust defines art and its criticism as autonomous realms of mental activity, whose satisfactions, though they are immense, have little to do with the material reality which it is their task to transform and supersede. His world, like Mallarmé's, *is* a book. In exploring his novel, we tend to follow his lead. Criticism of *La Recherche* (like so much criticism of modern literature) is primarily formalistic because of the consciously formalistic organization of the novel itself.[3]

Of course this organization was no free choice on Proust's part. As the lessons of concrete experience which fictions reflected revealed ever graver meanings as the nineteenth century wore on, it is understandable that writers and readers increasingly focused on formal innovation rather than on moral exploration. The evolving tradition thus unfolded the defensive position Proust took as a natural consequence of the movement of history.

However, *A la recherche du temps perdu* takes this defensive impulse to a new level of formal coherence. What remains to be seen in terms of the form that this ideological inflection generated are the details and the inner design of Proust's new system. In a fragment from the period of *Contre Sainte-Beuve*, Proust insisted that Flaubert's syn-

---

3. Moreover, Proust was at the origin of much of the kind of criticism which often seems the most productive to apply to his own novel. Georges Poulet somewhere calls Proust the first phenomenological critic; and surely Proust's essays on Flaubert and Baudelaire make him the most original exponent of critical stylistics in the early part of this century.

tactical revolution had altered representation of the world as fundamentally as did Kant's formulation of transcendental idealism.[4] The very term of comparison is suggestive, since the idealist tradition of Kant and Hegel has deep resonances in Flaubert and Proust. But most important here is Proust's insistence upon the fundamental, unavoidable relationship between technique and vision, between the formal and the ideological levels of creation.

We may judge that Proust has the causation backwards, that it is rather the change in vision of the world, in underlying ideology, which motivates formal innovation in art—so that it is Flaubert's totalized pessimistic world view which determined the syntactical revolution Proust traced in his predecessor's novels. But whatever the case, the technical consequences of the change in Proust's own vision in *La Recherche* are far-reaching, as the immense body of Proust criticism persuasively demonstrates. What really results, however, is a reconception of the novelistic tradition that ties Proust to his predecessors. Like most modernist writers, Proust exalts originality as the brightest sign of the artistic imagination's autonomy. And it is certain that brilliant novelty characterizes *La Recherche*. Yet deeper down the tradition remains coherent *by way of* Proust's most thoroughgoing innovations. In fact, the surprise is not that things should seem so different in *La Recherche*, but that such a profound coherence of concern should turn out to animate all of the books in the tradition from the Realists to *A la recherche du temps perdu*.

Proust's book is the most prestigious example in France of a novelistic system that exists beyond the point at which the social dialectic ceased to be a perceptible force in the movement of reality. Like most substantially new fictional paradigms, *La Recherche* at first seemed to cause almost

---

4. "A Ajouter à Flaubert," *CSB*, p. 299. This 1910 fragment prefigures the major 1919 essay on Flaubert in numerous details, particularly in Proust's stylistic analysis of Flaubert's verbal system and his discovery of the perverse autonomy of objects in Flaubert's novels.

universal confusion. But taking the longer view, it has not required much time for us to see how clearly the novel fits into its tradition. Proust, being Proust, overdramatized the difficulty the world had in understanding his creation. In fact, *Jeunes filles* won the Goncourt Prize in 1919, and Proust received the Légion d'honneur in 1920. The memorial volumes that appeared at the time of Proust's death in 1922 and a number of the critical studies published within the next few years demonstrate that even early on, sensitive readers came to the novel with a shock, not of incomprehension, but of recognition. In *La Recherche* they found the system that had been implicit in the evolving tradition, brilliantly worked out in intricate and coherent detail.[5]

But grave tensions subsist in *La Recherche* despite the unifying power of Proust's reformulation of the novelistic paradigm. An examination of the novel's narrative structure begins to make these tensions perceptible. Not surprisingly, they develop from the dissonances that, unresolved, had animated Realism. In their heightened form in *La Recherche* they clarify the bearing of the tradition that led to and was subsumed in Proust's novel. In the period following the French Revolution the Realists had begun exploring the pressures isolating individuals. Carrying the fictional diagnosis further, *A la recherche du temps perdu* brings into clear focus this dialectics of isolation, which has been at the heart of novels since the rise of Realism.

5. As one revealing example, consider Virginia Woolf's reaction less than three years after Proust died, comparing *La Recherche* to *Mrs. Dalloway* on which she was then working: "I wonder if this time I have achieved something? Well, nothing anyhow compared with Proust, in whom I am embedded now. . . . He will, I suppose, both influence me and make me out of temper with every sentence of my own" (8 April 1925; *A Writer's Diary*, p. 71).

5

The Depreciation of the Event

Near the end of *Sodome et Gomorrhe,* Marcel leaves the Grand-Hôtel in Balbec to take the little train to La Raspelière, where Mme Verdurin is giving one of her summer parties:

> Ce qui me plaisait dans ces dîners à la Raspelière, c'est . . . qu'ils "représentaient *un vrai voyage,*" un voyage dont le charme me paraissait d'autant plus vif qu'il n'était pas son but à lui-même, qu'on n'y cherchait nullement le plaisir, celui-ci étant affecté à *la réunion vers laquelle on se rendait.* [*A la recherche du temps perdu*, II, 1036]

> (The thing that pleased me about these dinners at La Raspelière was that . . . they "meant a real *journey,*" a journey whose charm seemed all the greater to me because it was not an object in itself, and no one expected to find any particular pleasure in it, the pleasure being reserved for *the party we were bound for.*)

By this stage of the novel the reader, having experienced two thousand pages of Proust's manner, is acquainted with the kinds of scenes that habitually interest him. The *soirée mondaine* is part of a well-ingrained pattern of expectation, and Mme Verdurin and her guests are known quantities. All these elements seem to carry us, with the passengers in the little train, towards the next unfolding, at La Raspelière, of the ongoing tableau of society.

The train trip (the *stations du "Transatlantique"*) lasts

about sixty pages before the guests finally arrive at Douville, where they are met by the carriages Mme Verdurin
has sent to pick them up (II, 1095). The next sentence is
an extraordinary twenty-eight line period: one short ride
from the station through the darkness until the term of all
this created expectation is reached, "the brilliantly illumi-
nated *salon* and dining room." But then, with a vertiginous
movement, the tableau which seemed about to begin such
a large expansion is snatched away and replaced by a dis-
concertingly summary snapshot: "tandis que les services
nombreux et les vins fins allaient se succéder autour des
hommes en frac et des femmes à demi décolletées" ("while
the endless dishes and vintage wines followed one another
amid men in evening clothes and women in low-cut
gowns"). Suddenly the guests are out the door again and
find themselves back in the little train riding home. In the
course of this single sentence the soirée has simply evapo-
rated.

The effect is treated with an almost total lack of emphasis
and seems to carry no weight at all. Yet it is clear nonetheless that Proust has used the pattern of the train trip,
counting off the stations one by one, to rouse the reader's
anticipation of the conclusion of the voyage—the arrival at
Douville—and the expansive party scene to follow. His
escamotage of the evening at La Raspelière transforms
Douville, which should have been the last stop, into nothing more than a point at which the travelers change trains.

The meaning of such an elaborate mystification becomes
clear soon after the little train begins its shaky progress
home. The pattern of the trip fits into a higher and more
emotionally charged structure, the narrator's relationship
with Albertine, and the real moment toward which the
entire scene has been made to move without a glance in
that direction is the revelation, just a few stops later, of
Albertine's relations with Mlle Vinteuil and her lesbian
friend. Albertine's words, "spoken as we entered the
Parville station" (II, 1114), crush the narrator, and reveal

that Douville was only a decoy. The actual terminus of the train's rocking advance along the coast, a rhythm which has continued for more than eighty pages now, is Parville. By occupying the reader elsewhere Proust has left him as unprepared as Marcel for the sudden shock of a critical event.

Proust's freedom to manipulate events in *A la recherche du temps perdu* depends upon the insignificance of the event in his conception of narrative. The individuality of his conception is based on a series of patterns of deformation—for example the misdirection of attention in the scene just considered—which often characterizes his treatment of the tale. Not that there is any lack of real events in *La Recherche*: two dozen important deaths, including one or two possible suicides; half a dozen consequential marriages and corresponding noteworthy changes of identity; numerous liaisons and some shocking scandals; several meteoric rises and precipitous declines in the worlds of society and art; and assorted plots, intrigues, conflicts, rivalries, and crucial discoveries—all of these together might have provided the material of a stirring series of adventure novels.[1]

That such animated happenings should finally provoke so little suspense before they arrive, produce so little agitation in their passing, and cause so little significant alteration in the manner of telling once they are known results from the systematic way Proust has chosen to devalue the dynamic element they contain. His techniques for doing so are considerably more effective than any seen in Flaubert. Their object, to be sure, is the same. Whereas in the Realist paradigm events were treated as the centers of intensity

1. Jean-Yves Tadié discusses these phenomena in *Proust et le roman*, ch. 12, pp. 341–65. Tadié believes that Proust's alterations of earlier novelistic practice represent artistic progress and can be explained on normative grounds. This view differs from the one taken here, which sees Proust's innovations as a creative response to a narrowing set of artistic possibilities, determined ultimately from outside the novel.

around which the story naturally organized itself, accentu-
ating their passion, their drama, their inherent vigor, Proust
arranges these marriages, deaths, intrigues and revelations
to diminish the energy they would otherwise radiate. Their
animation is diffused, sapped, hidden or otherwise denied
wherever it threatens to irrupt into the center focus of the
narration. The entire concept of the event, its seemingly
irreducible singularity, its elemental hardness, and thereby
its very authenticity are altered by these procedures.

It was not always so. The treatment of episodes such as
Couzon's speech in the Chamber of Deputies in *Jean Santeuil* provides a norm against which the refusal of such procedures in corresponding passages of the later novel can
be measured. Couzon's courageous protest against the
Chamber's refusal to aid the victims of the Armenian massacre is a vigorous composition which makes the most of
the melodrama of politics. The scene's beginning is cast in
the present tense to achieve maximum reality of presentation: "He is at the rostrum and he waits, rocking back and
forth like a boat ready to depart though not yet untied,
but swinging in the current in anticipation. Once or twice
he says, 'Messieurs!' His voice is strong, almost astonishing;
an extraordinary degree of emotion makes it quiver and
shift" (*Jean Santeuil*, pp. 602-3). Then the telling shifts to
the preterite in order to emphasize the full singularity of
the event: "With the suddenness of a shot after the trigger
is pulled, the wild applause of the extreme Left answered
him" (p. 604). The orator is there at the rostrum, the force
of his emotion is felt by Jean in the gallery and through
him by the reader. At stake are the lives of "two hundred
thousand people." The suspense is exquisite, and Couzon's
sudden defeat by the majority's cloture vote is a shock
manipulated for maximum dramatic force. The entire
scene lives by its dynamism.

The *séance à la Chambre* in *A la recherche du temps
perdu* (II, 473-75) is handled to achieve quite a different
effect. This time the center of attention is the prominent

député M. de Guermantes-Bouillon, Prince des Laumes—
the Duc de Guermantes in his youth—and the scene is presented as a commented newspaper transcript of a rather
puerile intervention by the Prince, the subject of which,
significantly, is never mentioned: "The astonishment, I
would not be exaggerating to say the stupor (*strong reaction of approval from the Right*) I felt at hearing the
words of someone who is still, I presume, a member of
the Government . . . (*thunderous applause . . .*)" (Proust's
italics; II, 474). This is only the sham of excitement. It
remains intentionally hollow, for nothing is at stake here.
Meanwhile the narrator's cynical comments ("this 'thunderous applause' breaks down the last shred of hesitation
in the mind of the commonsense reader") dismantle and
devitalize the scene. It belongs to the realm of satire
rather than that of drama. In *A la recherche du temps
perdu* the absence of a connected political plot and the
vagueness of the political elements that remain are mea-
sures of the distance which separates Proust's mature narrative conception from *Jean Santeuil*.[2]

The essence of the Realist paradigm is its portrayal of
the world as a terrain for human action, as a frame for exploits by which men attempt to affirm and transform themselves. The dynamic tone of Realist narration—whose
elemental form is the account of a concrete event—is
precisely what Proust tends to shun in creating the world
of *La Recherche*. Moreover, the *parti pris* against such
narration is quite conscious. As Proust says with regard
to concrete reality: "Tout en haut [de l'échelle intellec-
tuelle], ceux qui se sont fait une vie intérieure ambiante
ont peu égard à l'importance des événements" (III, 728;
"At the summit [of the intellectual scale], those who have
created for themselves an interior life which occupies them
pay little attention to the importance of outside events").

2. Tadié takes a divergent view, seeing the *Jean Santeuil* version as simple
journalism and stressing the richness of the parallel material in *La Recherche:
Proust et le roman*, p. 357.

Of course, it is the shape an event takes in the telling, rather than its bare existence, that determines its influence as an element in the world of a novel. The events in *La Recherche* exhibit a strange diaphaneity. Through the complex of techniques Proust devised to devalue them, they come to lack the solidity that in our ordinary understanding makes an event the fact it is. It is not easy to say when a Proustian event takes place, as Proust suggests in *La Prisonnière*: "Il semble que les événements soient plus vastes que le moment où ils ont lieu et ne peuvent y tenir tout entiers" (III, 401; "Events seem vaster than the moment of their occurrence, and cannot be completely contained within it"). It seems that events in Proust have no fixed location in chronology. Since the narration is retrospective throughout *La Recherche*, the narrator is free at any point to upset time-line telling: "Moreover, let us jump ahead of events to state that . . . " (II, 443). Such interventions are frequent.

Consider this passage from the earliest pages of the novel:

Ou bien en dormant j'avais rejoint sans effort un âge à jamais révolu de ma vie primitive, retrouvé telle de mes terreurs enfantines comme celle que mon grand-oncle me tirât par mes boucles et qu'avait dissipée le jour—*date* pour moi d'*une ère* nouvelle—où on les avait coupées. J'avais oublié cet *événement* pendant mon sommeil, j'en retrouvais le souvenir aussitôt que j'avais réussi à m'éveiller pour échapper aux mains de mon grand-oncle, mais par mesure de précaution j'entourais complètement ma tête de mon oreiller avant de retourner dans le monde des rêves. [I, 4]

(Or perhaps, while asleep, I would have returned effortlessly to an earlier stage of my life, forever gone, and experienced again one of my childhood terrors, such as my great-uncle's pulling my curls, which fear had been effectively dispelled on the day—the first

> *date* of a new *era* for me—when they had been cut off.
> I had forgotten that *event* during my sleep; but the
> memory came back as soon as I had succeeded in wak-
> ing up to get away from my great-uncle; still, as a pre-
> caution, I would bury my head in my pillow before
> returning to the world of dreams.)

Concrete reality has no more prestige for Proust than it did
for Huysmans. This passage makes the point through a
rather tender humor, but its terms reveal how paradoxical
the Proustian event can be. The narrator's thoughts are
voyaging wildly through time as he emerges from sleep. He
conflates several different ages, gently mocking rational
chronology by describing the comic "mesure de précaution" of burying his head under the pillow to protect himself from something which ceased to be a threat many
years before. Though it "took place" (as we naïvely say)
perhaps twenty years previous, the "event"—the cutting of
his hair—even now has not thoroughly happened.

In effect, a Proustian event occurs whenever the teller's
memory falls upon it. The tendency is perceptible in the
nineteenth-century tradition as the logic of the protagonist's mental associations increasingly becomes the logic
of the tale. But by abandoning third-person narration with
its external objective anchor in favor of the multiple "I" of
his first-person, Proust freed the concrete event from rational chronology to a markedly greater degree. Proustian
events diffuse through the texture of his narration. They
hardly ever "occur."

A bit further on is a much more crucial incident, the
"good-night kiss." The narrator uses the same terms we
have already seen to characterize its significance: "Il me
semblait . . . que cette soirée commençait *une ère*, resterait
comme une triste *date*" (I, 38; "It seemed to me . . .
that that evening began an *era*, would remain as a sad
date"). But the subjective effects of such an event are only
understood over the long term, and it is fair to say that for

Marcel this particular event does not "occur" until three thousand pages later, when with infinitely greater lucidity he recalls it in the Prince de Guermantes's library on the afternoon of his revelation (III, 886–87; 1044). Its "occurrence" in the early pages of *Swann* might almost be called fictitious, a pure anticipation by retrospective memory of something not realized until many years later. Yet from our point of view it has already been successfully enacted. The technique is constant. These "prerevelations" are one of the principal means Proust employs to diffuse the facticity of the event over time, space, and the even less measurable dimension of memory.

The most important pattern of prerevelation in *La Recherche* relates to the flight of Albertine. The following passage occurs about three hundred pages before Marcel first learns of her departure: "'Doesn't all that noise from outside bother you?' she asked me. 'I like it myself. But you're such a light sleeper.' On the contrary, I could be a very heavy sleeper at times (as I have already said, but *the event which is to follow* ["l'événement qui va suivre"] obliges me to recall the fact here)" (III, 121). The phrase in italics refers, of course, to Albertine's disappearance, but its chronology ("qui va suivre") is accurate only in the most nominal way. The "événement qui va suivre," through systematic prerevelation, has already occurred a dozen times.

It comes into existence as early as our reading in a table of contents (or in the "Pour Paraître ensuite" of an earlier edition) the title of the volume to follow *La Prisonnière*.[3] Already the shock of the "événement qui va suivre" is being diffused, and the treatment of the story of Albertine depends upon the irony that arises from the experience we are given, long before it "happens," of the shock which

3. The problem of the title of this volume is well known. The early editors chose *Albertine disparue*; the Pléiade edition re-established Proust's choice, *La Fugitive* (he had abandoned it because another novel had appeared with the same title). See Pléiade ed., I, xxiv–xxv, and III, 1094.

Marcel will receive. For us the event does not "take place"; it unfolds with our knowledge of it, and our sense of its authenticity depends hardly at all upon its appearance on the last page of *La Prisonnière*.

Thus in prerevelation, events flow backward to anticipate their accomplishment in the chronology of the story. But in *La Recherche* there is prolongation into the future as well as predisclosure in the past. Proust was conscious of this double projection. Events, he wrote, "débordent sur l'avenir par la mémoire que nous en gardons, mais ils demandent une place aussi dans le temps qui les précède" (III, 401; "events overflow into the future through our memory of them, but they also occupy a place in the time that precedes them"). The latter phenomenon is translated in the technique of prerevelation; the former, which seemed to Proust the key to his narrative originality, becomes the confrontation of ages that occurs in memory, creating a "passé qui ne se réalise pour nous . . . qu'après l'avenir" (III, 87; "a past which we only realize after the future has come and gone"). This radiation of events diffuses even the most crucial of them along the entire time-line of the story. We experience them as increasingly ineluctable atmospheres rather than as moments of decisive occurrence. The prospective or retrospective evocation of an event in *La Recherche* leaves it everything except the clearcut causal precision that, outside the novel, defines events for us.

At the beginning of September 1922, Proust wrote Gaston Gallimard to assure him that "mon prochain volume: *La Prisonnière*, est tout à fait romanesque" (*Lettres à la NRF*, p. 253; "my next volume, *La Prisonnière*, is full of action"). To be sure, the volume contains two portentous reversals in the lives of major characters: Charlus's "exécution" at the hands of Mme Verdurin, and Albertine's escape. But the dramatic energy of these events is systematically drained away by the narrative procedures outlined

above. Proust in his maturity had little use for the "romanesque" in novels. He expresses his disapprobation by
having the Baron de Norpois deliver a sententious en-
comium of the very type of novel Proust wished to dis-
credit—since we understand that whatever Norpois praises,
the narrator condemns. For Norpois, "The novelist's job
is to devise a good story and to edify his readers, not to
fritter away his time etching frontispieces and tailpieces"
(II, 223).[4] The Baron thus criticizes Bergotte: "One never
finds in his enervated works anything you might call a
plot-line. No action—or very little—and, above all, no
range" (I, 473). This de-dramatization is precisely what
drew the young Marcel to Bergotte, and conversely the
"romanesque" elements in Bergotte's novels, the progress
of the intrigue, were what satisfied him the least: "The
passages in which his delight in his own writing was obvious ["les morceaux auxquels il se complaisait"] were the
ones I preferred. . . . *I was disappointed when he resumed
the thread of the story*" (I, 95).[5]

The consequence of these attitudes, the tendency of these
techniques in Proust, is to depreciate the active mode of
narration. The narrative event fades as an element of
construction in *A la Recherche du temps perdu*, and
Proust consciously contrasts his own practice with the
form of the traditional novel—what he calls the "sterile

4. Norpois's preferences also run to authors whose work is "handled with an
agile pen" (I, 453; cf. III, 884, where the expression is used by Brichot). He is
also decidedly hostile to "flute players" (III, 882). Proust's verbal satire can be
very cruel.

5. An even stronger version of the passage appears in one of the notebooks
in the Bibliothèque Nationale: "J'étais presque déçu quand le fil du récit
reprenait et les livres que je préférais de lui quand j'eus [?] connu plusieurs
furent ceux où il y avait le moins de récit" (Cahier XIV, p. 53r; "I was almost
disappointed when the thread of the story began again, and the books of his I
preferred when I had become acquainted with several of them were those in
which there was the least amount of story"). Maurice Bardèche makes some
apposite remarks concerning Proust's willingness to overturn the traditional
forms of the novel; *Marcel Proust romancier*, II, 100–101.

and worthless adventure novel" (II, 68). What results is a comfortable relaxation of the usual linear coherence of plot. Incidents which in natural occurrence form a tension-producing sequence are dissociated so that the element of suspense in them is eliminated. The techniques already outlined, plus several more (suspension, the "feint," the revelation *ex nihilo*) which remain to be discussed have parallel effects. Through their use, Proust sets adrift the temporality of a causal series. What dramatized forms a plot, de-dramatized in Proust's treatment is free to become a collection of expansive, virtually independent scenes.

The unimportance of the novel's frequent internal contradictions shows how relaxed chronology becomes in Proust. Events are misdated or mistakenly occur more than once, but it hardly seems to matter. The stay at Balbec seems to last about six months if we judge by internal indications; Proust tells us it lasted three (I, 952). He twice contradicts the hour at which Swann is refused entry at Odette's although she is at home (see I, 279; 283; 524); and there are numerous other instances. We pass over these confusions because they in no way affect the progress of the intrigue. They have no plot significance. E. M. Forster once observed that in *The Newcomes* Thackeray "by a most monstrous blunder . . . killed Lady Farintosh's mother at one page and brought her to life at another."[6] *La Recherche* reanimates at least fourteen different characters.[7] But the extraordinarily low degree of contingence between events and existences makes it possible for characters in Proust to die a death which does not signify and profit from an absent-minded revitalization without inconveniencing anything or anyone in the world they leave and return to.

Proust dealt himself with his anachronisms, anticipa-

6. Quoted by Edwin Muir, *Structure of the Novel*, p. 51.

7. See Georges Daniel, *Temps et mystification dans "A la recherche du temps perdu,"* p. 96, n. 116. Most of these reanimations of course are attributable to the unfinished state of the novel's later parts.

tions, and other sins against the calendar in a letter (6 August 1922) to Benjamin Crémieux, who had wondered about a possible error of chronology in the novel. The humorous simplicity of Proust's response reemphasizes the fact that, in the absence of a plot which lays crucial importance upon a time scheme precise to the minute, month, or even year, contradictions and confusions make no difference. So he simply dismissed the discrepancy Crémieux had questioned: "Einsteinisons-le si vous voulez pour plus de commodité" ("Let's 'Einsteinize' it to make things easier").[8]

In the active mode of narration, human actions which engage the characters' responsibility direct and pattern the course of the story. Proust's disinclination to exploit active narration makes *A la recherche du temps perdu* an extraordinarily unconstrained structure, and one guided by no coherent plot principle that we can abstract from its texture. A remark by Barbara Hardy concerning Tolstoy applies *a fortiori* to *La Recherche*. Ms. Hardy writes that the looseness of his form "may . . . help to explain why a novel by Tolstoy is for some people difficult to read and for many difficult to remember. There is not the clear diagrammatic pattern of decisive incident and decisive moral crisis to create constant tension, or to act as a useful, if reductive, pattern in memory" (*The Appropriate Form*, p. 190).

A la recherche du temps perdu thus poses a real problem of attention for the reader. Proust recognized the difficulty—and in the main refused to do anything about it. We have seen the pains he took to ridicule attitudes (such as Norpois's) which called upon the writer to make the read-

---

8. Benjamin Crémieux, ed., *Du côté de Marcel Proust*, pp. 167–68. Proust's humorous verb was no doubt suggested by Camille Vettard's article "Proust et Einstein," which appeared in the *Nouvelle Revue Française* on 1 August 1922. Proust immediately telegraphed to thank Vettard for the comparison (*Correspondance générale*, III, 191), and the letter to Crémieux was written four days later.

er's job easier: "They said that the age of speed required
rapidity in art. . . . They warned against fatiguing the
audience's attention" (II, 815). But the complication of
Proust's style of narration works here to his advantage. By
declining the active mode of narration, Proust's manner
obliges us to read with the kind of attention appropriate to
the intricate meaning to be conveyed. In his 1913 interview with Elie-Joseph Bois, Proust was concerned
that understanding of the book he was about to publish
not be distorted by a style of reading appropriate to the
kind of novel M. de Norpois enjoyed:

> *Du côté de chez Swann* n'est pas ce qu'on appelle un
> livre de chemin de fer, qu'on parcourt du coin de
> l'oeil et en sautant des pages, c'est un livre original,
> étrange même, profond, réclamant toute l'attention
> du lecteur, *mais la forçant aussi.* . . . D'action, de cette
> action qu'on est accoutumé de trouver dans la plu-
> part des romans et qui vous emporte, plus ou moins
> ému, à travers une série d'aventures jusqu'à un dénoue-
> ment fatal—*il n'y en a pas.*[9]

> (*Du côté de chez Swann* is not what one might call
> vacation reading, the kind of book you skim through
> with your mind on something else. This novel is or-
> iginal, even strange, profound, requiring all of the
> reader's attention, but *forcing him to give it.* . . . As
> for plot, the kind of plot we are accustomed to finding
> in the majority of novels, the kind that carries you
> emotionally away with it through a series of adventures
> to a tragic conclusion—*there is none.*)

In spite of this effort to prepare the audience, Proust

9. *Marcel Proust: Choix de lettres*, pp. 283–84. The text of the interview
can also be found in *Marcel Proust: Textes retrouvés*, pp. 215–20. Concerning
Proust's part in those sections of the interview in which Bois seems to be
speaking independently, see G. D. Painter, *Marcel Proust: A Biography*, II,
200; and *CSB*, p. 557, n. 2.

suffered because his book was found so difficult to read. He never resigned himself to the fact that other writers gained much wider audiences simply because they had an easier manner, and complained sourly to Gallimard (3 December 1921): "*Nène* [a novel by Pérochon which had already sold 75,000 copies] is the rare case of a Goncourt Prize book which, rightly or wrongly, is thought of as a 'decent novel,' nothing extraordinary. The difference in publication figures between it and *Jeunes Filles* [which had won the previous year's Goncourt] seems astonishing to me. Perhaps it's because *Nène* is *easier reading*" (*Lettres à la NRF*, p. 162).

Though the judgment obviously hurt him, Proust was right. It seems undeniable that the most immediate emotion felt by readers of *La Recherche* is not astonishment, or admiration, but a peculiar tedium. With the suppression of the active mode, no other outcome was possible. To say this is not to depreciate Proust, it is simply to acknowledge one of the conditions of existence of Proustian form. His early admirers confessed the tedium with near unanimity, but pled intense compensating pleasures. As Maugham humorously put it, he "would sooner be bored by Proust than amused by any other writer."[10]

A parallel exists between Maugham's witticism and a judgment of Wagner in *La Recherche*. The Duc de Guermantes has just enunciated one of his characteristic philistinisms: "Wagner puts me right to sleep." The Duchesse reprimands such ignorance: "You're quite wrong. . . . In spite of his intolerable longueurs, Wagner had genius" (II, 491). Her rebuke of Basin must have amused Proust.

10. Quoted by James T. Steen, "Values and Difficulties in the Art of Marcel Proust," p. 81. Other early reactions to Proust's tedium: José Ortega y Gasset, "Le Temps, la distance et la forme chez Proust," pp. 296–97; several of the authors (all admirers) in the English memorial volume, *Marcel Proust: An English Tribute*, ed. C. K. Scott-Moncrieff, particularly E. C. Mayne (p. 91), Violet Hunt (p. 114), and a humorously exasperated Arnold Bennett (p. 145); and Clive Bell, *Proust*, pp. 16–17. Bell's study remains one of the most sensible available on Proust.

Though reduced to lowest critical terms, it represented a justification of his own manner (one imagines with discomfort how cutting Oriane would have been about the longueurs of *La Recherche*). But since we are obliged to admit the existence of Proust's tedium, we ought to consider how tedium functions in his novel.

In January 1921 Proust wrote to Gallimard to reassure him that the utility of his novel's "slow parts [*"lenteurs"*] . . . will become clear later on" (*Lettres à la NRF*, p. 136). Tedium is a favorable condition for the perception of telling in the synthetic mode. In the Realist paradigm, when we are bored, our attention (conditioned to anticipate the next element of the progression) immediately wanders, and the form's solidity collapses. But conditioned to respond to elements of expansion rather than elements of progression, our concentration is heightened as its object dilates, and we penetrate each moment with an ease that grows in proportion to our lack of concern with getting on. Proust's mockery of theories affirming that writers must not "fatigue the audience's attention" was coupled with a defense of his own practice. In the same passage, he continues: "as though we did not have at our disposal different kinds of attention, arousing the finest of which is precisely the artist's task" (II, 815). The "highest attention" for him was clearly the intensive, spreading concentration which obliges us to redefine Proust's tedium as a variety of entrancement.

An image in Walter Benjamin's essay "The Storyteller" (1936) captures the essence of much narration after Flaubert, and evokes the mood of Proust's novel with particular aptness. Benjamin writes: "Tedium is the dreambird that hatches the egg of experience."[11] After belief that the

11. Original text in Benjamin's *Illuminationen*, p. 417. The American translation, *Illuminations*, p. 91, differs slightly. Benjamin (like Spitzer and Curtius) was one of Proust's most brilliant early admirers. As German translator of several volumes of *La Recherche* and author of a fine essay ("The Image of Proust"), he did much to make Proust's work known.

hopes of the individual might be realized in the post-Revolutionary world collapsed, bringing the Realist novel down
with it, the kind of literary entrancement that is described
in Benjamin's image came to take on the role of a thera-
peutic compensation for the failure of real experience.
Mallarmé had already insisted on the way literature had
begun to outshine life. A passage from one of Maurice
Blanchot's essays makes the connection explicit:

> Le monde de l'imaginaire tient entièrement lieu de
> réel, s'y substitue et l'efface: tel est . . . l'idéal de la
> lecture qui veut *prendre* le lecteur, l'envoûter, le
> réduire à sa seule condition de lecteur, qui en somme
> se veut à tel point passionnante qu'elle endorme celui
> qui s'y engage, qu'elle soit comme un sommeil sans
> réveil possible.[12]

> (The imaginary world completely occupies the place
> of the real one, substitutes itself for it and obliterates
> it: this is . . . the quintessence of a kind of reading
> which desires to *take* the reader, cast a spell on him,
> force him to become nothing but a reader; to be so
> completely fascinating that it lulls him to sleep with
> it; desires to become that sleep itself, from which no
> awakening is possible.)

The techniques which organize the narration of *La
Recherche* to this end overturn virtually every aspect of
the Realist paradigm. But for Proust's new fictional system
to operate successfully the expectations of an audience
accustomed to the traditional dramatic novel had to be
forcefully redirected. Tedium is the most unmistakable
sign of this redirection, and in this perspective, Proust's
problem was not how to avoid tedium, but how, fruit-
fully, to create it.

12. "Le Roman, oeuvre de mauvaise foi" [review of J. Pouillon, *Temps et
roman*], *Les Temps Modernes*, p. 1313.

6

The Devaluation of Suspense

Suspense in narrative is the force that throws our expectations ahead, the converse of tedium. For suspense to exist, two conditions are necessary: we must be involved in a situation upon whose resolution some significant interest depends; and the eventual outcome must still be uncertain. We must be made curious, but we can't have been satisfied; we must know something, but we can't yet know everything.

Suppression of either of the two conditions defeats suspense. In Proust, now one, now the other is therefore absent. For suspense is the active mode concretized. It had to be eliminated. Through its deletion Proust created what Gide described as "that extreme leisureliness, that non-desire to go faster, that continual satisfaction" that delighted him in *A la recherche du temps perdu*.[1]

Suspense is the shape taken by the curiosity we feel concerning anything that engages our interest, when this curiosity is experienced within the linear structure of a narrative. Curiosity can take other forms as well, and one of them, infinitely more painful, is Proustian jealousy. From this point of view it is important to note that the compulsion of Proustian jealousy is not toward physical possession but toward *knowledge*: a compulsion which inevitably leads the narrator along "the fatal road, destined to bring pain, of Knowledge" (II, 1115)—"knowledge of whether

1. "Billet à Angèle, à propos de Marcel Proust," reprinted in *Marcel Proust: Lettres à André Gide*, p. 110.

Albertine had lied to me" (III, 514); "knowledge·of which woman she had spent that night with, . . . and what she was experiencing at that moment" (III, 545).

Because it exists in life and not in art, jealousy is a suspense which can have no solution; and Proust's narrator was made aware of how much crueller life became thereby. At grips with the most serious difficulty of his own life, he longs for a relief which he imagines in terms of art: "Novelists often pretend in introductions that, while traveling, they met a person who recounted to them the story of someone's life. . . . How we wish, when we are in love, . . . that we could find such an informant!" (III, 551). Conversely, because Proust sensed a critical irony in the distance which separates what we can know in life and what we can know in books, and installed this irony as an important theme in his own novel, it is a passage involving Marcel's jealousy which explains how the dual conditions for narrative suspense are alternately frustrated in *La Recherche*:

> Je n'aurais pas été jaloux si elle [Albertine] avait eu des plaisirs près de moi, . . . m'épargnant par là la crainte du mensonge; je ne l'aurais peut-être pas été non plus si elle était partie dans un pays assez inconnu de moi et éloigné pour que je ne puisse imaginer . . . son genre de vie. Dans les deux cas, le doute eût été supprimé par une connaissance ou une ignorance également complètes. [III, 30]

> (I would not have been jealous if Albertine had experienced her pleasures in my company, . . . thus sparing me the fear of her lies; I would perhaps not have been jealous either if she had left for a country so unfamiliar and remote that I would have been unable to imagine . . . what her life was like. In both cases, my uncertainty would have been eliminated, by complete knowledge or equally complete ignorance.)

These antithetical means of suppressing Marcel's anguished jealousy precisely parallel the two methods for suppressing literary suspense. The first corresponds to our already knowing the outcome of an otherwise suspenseful situation; the second to our not being aware that a suspenseful situation even exists. The first method is translated technically in the procedure of prerevelation; the second in the Proustian revelation *ex nihilo*, in the digressive suspension, and in a technique which I will call the "feint."

"Suspension" disconnects successive moments. The technique is the same one Auerbach identifies in the recognition scene from Book XIX of the *Odyssey* (*Mimesis*, pp. 3–4). The long description of the origin of Odysseus's scar completely interrupts the account of his old nurse's discovery that he has at last returned. The purpose of such paratactic narration, Auerbach says, is to "relax the tension." When the suspension has sufficient autonomy, as in the example in *Mimesis*, dramatic progression is completely neutralized.

Every reader of Proust has remarked how the account of a conversation or an experience is similarly broken off to permit the narrator to analyze and comment. When events suffer such treatment, they lose their force of presence. In another recognition scene, at the moment when, in Elstir's studio, young Marcel identifies the portrait of Miss Sacripant (I, 860), the narrator begins a passage of reflection on portraits, on Odette's relations with Swann, etc., which lasts for two and a half pages. However interesting we may find the digression, Elstir's studio evaporates. When the narrator's analysis finishes and he wants to retrieve the painter's studio, it seems so distant that he is obliged to inch back obliquely, initially casting Marcel's and Elstir's conversation in indirect discourse, although their words had been directly reported before the suspension: "Was it possible that this man of genius [Elstir] . . . was the foolish, corrupt painter the Verdurins had 'adopted' at one time? I asked him if he had known them, whether by any chance they had nicknamed him Monsieur Biche. He told me that was correct" (I, 863). The revelation is made to seem incidental, and it is another twenty lines before the scene is again sufficiently present for direct dialogue to return.

Suspension is an important characteristic of the narrator's account, in *Le Côté de Guermantes*, of the dinner at Oriane's. The contrivance here is to submerge the description of the meal Marcel is invited to in a flood of material related to the milieu, but having nothing to do with the moment. Finally, dinner is ceremoniously and theatrically announced. "With a vast gyratory, multiple, and simultaneous whir, the double doors of the dining room opened wide" (II, 434). But immediately, the dining room dissolves, and the narrator begins a long description of the mores and foibles of the class to which Oriane and her guests belong. The reality of the evening is diffused by the accompanying analysis, the unconnected anecdotes, the independent subplots which intervene. The suspension allows the descriptive texture to expand extraordinarily. Forty-nine pages after the guests began with such ceremony to enter the dining room, we find (III, 483) that they are just sitting down at table, and the long-awaited dinner finally begins. (It will end as abruptly as it was dilatory in getting started, broken off after yet another sally by the Duchesse, in the middle, no doubt, of the fish course).

The dinner of course is a pretext. Proust's description of Guermantes's society is inconclusive, purposely nondramatic. It is a loose aggregate of moments and portraits; its only plot threads exist more to be dropped than to be followed. Even *L'Education sentimentale* vibrates with excitement compared with Proust's treatment here. The dinner given by Mme Dambreuse in *L'Education* (Part II, ch. 3) is represented as scenic action and has crucial importance in the plot; whatever its lack of dynamism, Flaubert's novel *has* a plot. At his dinner several lines of force converge and, in the persons of three of the women Frédéric Moreau is supposed to be in love with, produce an energetic and economical confrontation. In contrast, the energy of Oriane's dinner is purely local, the product of our curiosity about the tag-line of each successive anecdote. Proust expects no energy from the situation itself. The gathering together of all these people produces no more coherent drama than most such gatherings do outside the novel.[2]

The crudest case of suspension in *La Recherche* occurs toward the end of *Le Côté de Guermantes*:

> Lorsque dans l'après-midi je fus libre de reprendre mon guet, je me mis simplement sur l'escalier. . . . Or cette attente sur l'escalier devait avoir pour moi des conséquences si considérables et me découvrir un paysage . . . moral . . . si important, *qu'il est préférable d'en retarder le récit de quelques instants,* en le faisant précéder d'abord par celui de ma visite aux Guermantes quand je sus qu'ils étaient rentrés. [II, 573]

> (In the afternoon, when I was free to take up my watch again, I simply stood on the staircase [to await the return of the Duc and Duchesse]. . . . This wait on the staircase was to have such considerable consequences for me, and reveal a moral . . . landscape . . . of such importance *that it is preferable to postpone the account of it for a few moments* and precede it by the account of the visit I made to the Guermantes when I knew they had returned.)

These "few minutes" last for over thirty pages; but we forget because the interim is taken up with the brilliant, bitter

2. J.-Y. Tadié discusses the prevalence of such social gatherings in the traditional novel and sees Proust improving on their practice; *Proust et le roman,* p. 344.

account of Swann's visit to the Duc and Duchesse; of
Oriane's high-fantasy response to Mme Molé's calling card;
of the Duc's reaction to his cousin M. d'Osmond's awkward mortal illness; of the Duchesse's red shoes.

Marcel's discovery on the stairway is by now in a different world. When he returns to it, it comes back from
very far away. Yet it is something we have heard of, something we remember waiting for, and that is the effect required. This technique allows Proust to seed the reader's
memory without animating his expectation; it readies us
for the revelation that we know is being prepared, but *without creating suspense.*

In one of the earliest French novels, the *Roman bourgeois*
(1666), Antoine Furetière utilized a rough method for
defeating the delay necessary for suspense, and bantered
with the reader about his procedure:

> Je me doute bien qu'il n'y aura pas un lecteur (tant
> soit-il bénévole) qui ne dise ici en lui-même: "Voici
> un méchant Romaniste! Cette histoire n'est pas fort
> longue ni fort intriguée. Comment! il conclut d'abord
> un mariage, et on n'a coûtume de les faire qu'à la
> fin du dixième tome!"[3]

> (I suspect there's not a reader (however benevolent)
> who won't be saying to himself at this point: "This is
> a very miscreant Novelist! His story is neither long nor
> intricate. What! He starts off by contracting a marriage,
> when by custom that's only done at the end of the
> tenth volume!")

To prevent us from suffering the uncertainty of delay,
Furetière thus contrives to settle his affair almost before it
begins. Unfortunately, this leaves him with one less plot
line and no easy directions for beginning another. Clearly if

3. Antoine Adam, ed., *Romanciers du XVIIᵉ siècle*, pp. 916–17.

he continued to apply the same method, his novel, the victim of its own autosuppression, could only shrivel into silence.

The procedure demonstrates that without delay there is no development, there is in fact nothing at all. What has already been disposed of (like Furetière's love-plot) can no longer serve. The problem is therefore to eliminate suspense and conserve one's material at the same time. This necessity is responsible for the fragmentation of the event in Proust. The event which has been enacted is played out. What Proust required was a way to pre-act events, to pre-reveal denouements, to diffuse occurrences so that their radiation creates in the reader such a familiarity with what is to "happen" that events themselves cease to solicit his concern. Under these conditions our experience of events becomes one of "atmosphere" rather than one of peripety.

The most efficacious of Proust's procedures for creating this atmosphere is prerevelation. It is through prerevelation that events in *La Recherche* live what Spitzer called their "subterranean life,"[4] a life quite as important as the one they lead on the surface. Foreknowledge of events always puts us in ironic relation to the characters who have not yet lived through what we know must happen. We make emotional preparation for the event to come, and its character is irrevocably changed thereby.[5] It gains a kind of mythic inevitability, and gives up the sharp edge of shock its passage would have caused. It becomes *matter of fact*. That is the tone in which prerevelations have always been announced: "They spoke, but none of this would the son of Kronos accomplish"; or "Charlemagne can do nothing to prevent it: they will trick him."[6] But though such prerevelations are uttered neutrally, their rhetorical power

---

4. "Zum Stil Marcel Prousts" (1928), p. 394.

5. See Robert Scholes and Robert Kellogg, *The Nature of Narrative*, p. 241.

6. *Iliad* 3. 302 (trans. Richmond Lattimore); *Chanson de Roland,* 1. 95.

can be immense. They seem to give us an extraordinary hold on the course of events to follow. But in fact, the ultimate effect of prerevelations is to give events an extraordinary hold on us, by transforming them from banal surprises into tragic destinies. In the preface to his translation of *The Bible of Amiens*, Proust spoke of the explanatory notes he had appended throughout the volume suggesting parallels from other of Ruskin's works, as representing an effort to "provide the reader with what might be called an *improvised memory* which I have furnished with recollections of other Ruskin works—a sort of echo chamber" (*CSB*, p. 76, note). The passage describes with great aptness the effect of the prerevelations which were to form an important feature of the novel of ten years later. An improvised memory of what is to follow, giving us the sense of already knowing, deals with suspense decisively.

A passage from *A l'ombre des jeunes filles en fleurs* recalls the one from the Ruskin preface, and suggests that Proust was conscious of the role an improvised memory could play in organizing our perceptions of a work of art (here a piece of music, but the applicability of the observation to the novel is clear):

> Il lui arriva [à Mme Swann] de me jouer la partie de la Sonate de Vinteuil où se trouve la petite phrase que Swann avait tant aimée. Mais souvent on n'entend rien, si c'est une musique un peu compliquée qu'on écoute pour la première fois. Et pourtant quand plus tard on m'eut joué deux ou trois fois cette Sonate, je me trouvai la connaître parfaitement. . . . *Probablement ce qui fait défaut, la première fois, ce n'est pas la compréhension, mais la mémoire.* [I, 529]

> (Mme Swann happened to play for me the part of the Vinteuil Sonata that contained the little phrase that Swann had loved so much. But often one can make no sense of it if one is listening for the first time to a somewhat complicated piece. And yet when later on I had

heard the Sonata two or three times, I found that I knew it perfectly. . . . *Probably what is missing the first time through is not comprehension but memory.*)

Proust's prerevelations of events to come in *La Recherche* function so that our acquaintance with and absorption in the material is "forced" like a hothouse plant, reaching unexpected levels of growth much earlier than would otherwise have happened. Prerevelation dismantles the future; only the present is left operative—precisely the present which enforces itself in the procedure of suspension. We move inside the tale, in the kind of enchantment Blanchot has described. Once inside, the elements of the fiction all become potentially available to us at once, elements of the memory which the telling has improvised within us. Now, any moment in time can be made simultaneous with any other. As chronology is defeated, our responsiveness to thematic patterns multiplies. By making what would otherwise be inaccessible parts of *La Recherche* available, prerevelation allows us a consciousness one step ahead of itself.

The technique deals with every thematic element in *A la recherche du temps perdu,* every incident of importance, every character, even with the structure of the entire novel itself. Proust always made much of the discovery which would close his novel, for him the keynote of a thoroughly meditated architecture. But a sceptical critical current has been very reserved about taking such assurances at face value. Jean-François Revel described his disappointment as follows:

A l'endroit où elle vient, cette révélation si souvent annoncée n'est pas une nouveauté, et *Le Temps retrouvé* n'offre rien que redites sur ce point: Proust a déjà expliqué cent fois ce qu'il considérait comme étant pour lui la source de la "création" littéraire, comme il dit. Pour tant qu'on répète de confiance que

> *Le Temps retrouvé* est la clef de l'oeuvre ... c'est
> là peut-être le passage le moins vivant du *Temps
> retrouvé*, le moins inattendu.[7]

(At the point where it appears, the revelation so often
promised is not new, and *Le Temps retrouvé* only repeats itself on the subject. Proust has already explained a hundred times what he believed to be the
source of literary "creation," as he calls it. People may
bravely claim that *Le Temps retrouvé* is the key to the
whole. . . . But [the revelation] is perhaps the least animated part of the volume, the least unexpected.)

The sense of acquaintance, even overacquaintance, with
the discovery arises from a series of prerevelations which
stretch from one end of *La Recherche* to the other:

> Dès que j'eus reconnu le goût du morceau de made-
> leine ... (quoique je ne susse pas encore et dusse
> remettre à bien plus tard de découvrir pourquoi ce
> souvenir me rendait si heureux). . . . [I, 47]

(As soon as I had recognized the taste of the bite of
madeleine . . . (although I did not understand and had
to wait until much later to discover why this memory
made me so happy) . . . .)

> La meilleure part de notre mémoire est hors de
> nous, dans un souffle pluvieux, dans l'odeur de ren-
> fermé d'une chambre ou dans l'odeur d'une première
> flambée, partout où nous retrouvons de nous-mêmes
> ce que notre intelligence, n'en ayant pas l'emploi,
> avait dédaigné, la dernière réserve du passé, la meilleure,
> celle qui, quand toutes nos larmes semblent taries,
> sait nous faire pleurer encore. . . . C'est grâce à cet
> oubli ... que nous pouvons de temps à autre retrouver
> l'être que nous fûmes. [I, 643]

7. *Sur Proust,* pp. 30-31. Clive Bell said much the same thing in 1929;
Proust, p. 51.

(The best part of our memory is outside of us, in a rainy breeze, in the unaired smell of a bedroom or the odor of the first kindling crackling in a fireplace, wherever we rediscover the part of ourselves which our intellect, having no use for it, had rejected; the final storehouse of the past, and the best, the one which, when all our tears seem to have dried up, can still make us cry. . . . It is thanks to this forgetting . . . that we are able from time to time to recapture the being that we were.)

Dans la suite je retrouvai le genre de plaisir et d'inquiétude que je venais de sentir encore une fois, et . . . un soir—trop tard, mais pour toujours—je m'attachai à lui. [I, 719]

(In the course of time I did recover the kind of pleasure and of anxiety which I had just felt once again, and . . . one evening—too late, but this time forever—I was able to cling to it.)

Les poètes prétendent que nous retrouvons un moment ce que nous avons jadis été en rentrant dans telle maison, dans tel jardin où nous avons vécu jeunes. Ce sont là pèlerinages fort hasardeux et à la suite desquels on compte autant de déceptions que de succès. Les lieux fixes, contemporains d'années différentes, c'est en nous-même qu'il vaut mieux les trouver. . . . On verra combien certaines impressions fugitives et fortuites ramènent bien mieux encore vers le passé, avec une précision plus fine, d'un vol plus léger, plus immatériel, plus vertigineux, plus infaillible, plus immortel, que ces dislocations organiques. [II, 91–92]

(Poets claim that we recapture for a moment the self we had once been when we enter a house or a garden which we had lived in in our youth. These are chancy pilgrimages, which end as often in disappointment as in success. Such fixed locations, contemporaries of different years—we should rather seek them within ourselves . . . . We shall see how certain fugitive and fortuitous impressions carry us back even more effectively toward the past, with a finer precision, with a flight more delicate, more immaterial, more vertiginous, more unerring, more immortal, than these organic dislocations.)

J'éprouvais à les percevoir [les images de lieux passés] un enthousiasme qui aurait pu être fécond si j'étais resté seul, et m'aurait évité ainsi le détour de bien des années inutiles par lesquelles j'allais encore passer avant que se déclarât la vocation invisible dont cet ouvrage est l'histoire. [II, 397]

(I felt in perceiving them [the images of past places] an enthusiasm which might have borne fruit had I been alone, and would thereby have spared me the detour of many useless years which awaited me before the invisible vocation of which this work is the history revealed itself.)

C'était grâce à elle [l'amie de Mlle Vinteuil] . . . qu'a vait pu venir jusqu'à moi l'étrange appel que je ne cesserais plus jamais d'entendre comme la promesse qu'il existait autre chose, réalisable par l'art sans doute, que le néant que j'avais trouvé dans tous les plaisirs et dans l'amour même. [III, 263]

(It was thanks to Mlle Vinteuil's friend . . . that it had reached me, this strange call which I would never cease hearing as the promise that there was something, attainable probably through art, besides the emptiness which I had found in all types of pleasure and even in love.)

La suite le montrera davantage, comme bien des épisodes ont pu déjà l'indiquer—. . . que l'intelligence n'est pas l'instrument le plus subtil, le plus puissant, le plus approprié pour saisir le vrai. [III, 423]

(What follows will demonstrate further, as many episodes have already suggested . . . that the intellect is not our most subtle, nor most powerful, nor most appropriate instrument for seizing the truth.)

Le passé à la recherche duquel j'étais sans le savoir. . . . [III, 555]

(The past which I was searching for without realizing it. . . .)

C'est quelquefois au moment où tout nous semble perdu que l'avertissement arrive qui peut nous sauver. . . . J'étais entré dans la cour de l'hôtel de Guermantes. [III, 866]

(Sometimes it is just when all seems lost that the news arrives which can save us. . . . I had turned into the courtyard of the Hôtel de Guermantes.)

Everything is already present: the problem, the false solutions, the promise of a solution, the nature of the solution, the time of solution, the meaning of the solution. Insofar as it discusses involuntary memory and the revelation of art, *Le Temps retrouvé* is only a gloss on these prerevelations, and it is not surprising that the matter of Marcel's epiphany seems exhausted before it ever "occurs." The desire to create a surprise had to defer to a higher law of structure in *La Recherche*. No event in the novel could be allowed, by creating an impulsion to precipitous reading, to disturb the calm in which, as Benjamin put it, the dreambird's egg must hatch. We need not regret the failure of Proust's climax. Had it succeeded in a final triumph of the active mode, Proust's radically undramatic telling would have been transformed into an ultimately linear plot. But the shape which his conception

of narrative imposed on *A la recherche du temps perdu* is
open, indirect, unmethodical—anything but straight.

In the body of the novel, the prerevelations and the patterns of incident they act upon developed simultaneously
and interdependently. The example of Charlus, aristocrat,
connoisseur, and homosexual, is pertinent. There are two
critical moments in Charlus's development within the
novel: Marcel's discovery of the Baron's inversion, and
Mme Verdurin's brutal severing of his relationship with
Morel—a moment of conjunction, a moment of separation,
which provide two finely-placed articulations of plot. But
both these moments whose potential for drama seems so
great are altered by prerevelation, not to remove their significance, but to permit a significance quite different from
the purely dramatic one we might have supposed.

The Charlus puzzle is set up early in the novel. Just after
Swann has left on the evening of the "good-night kiss,"
while an anguished Marcel at the window waits for his
mother to come up, in the garden the family is talking
about how Swann seems to have aged. "I believe he's
having a lot of difficulty with that awful wife of his, who's
openly been having an affair with a certain M. de Charlus.
Everyone is talking about it" (I, 34). This picture of a
virile Charlus, lover of Mme Swann, is reiterated a number
of times in "Combray." But just before Marcel sees the
Baron near the hawthorn hedge at Tansonville, we are
allowed a vision of him so strange, so oddly emphasized,
that the possibility of a disguise, of a deviation of meaning,
suggests itself: "a little way beyond Mme Swann, a gentleman in a cambric suit, whom I didn't recognize, was
staring at me with eyes which almost seemed to be pop-
ping out of his head" (I, 141).

Charlus does not reappear in "Combray," but at the beginning of "Un Amour de Swann" we are given an image
of him in diametrical contradiction to the one prevalent
so far: here he is one of the most refined of the "high-

society friends" whom Swann enjoyed amusing with zest-
ful accounts of his sexual conquests (I, 193). This almost
parenthetical appearance overturns two of the preconcep-
tions established by our previous exposure to the Baron.
First, it establishes Charlus's lofty social rank. Second, it
situates him not as Mme Swann's lover but on the contrary as one of Swann's most devoted friends. The critical
moment of prerevelation follows immediately when the
hesitant suspicion born in our first view of Charlus at
Tansonville is crystallized by a deliberate comment. Jealous
of Odette and wanting her under surveillance, Swann
calls upon Mémé: "Il était heureux toutes les fois où
M. de Charlus était avec Odette. Entre M. de Charlus et
elle, Swann savait qu'il ne pouvait rien se passer" (I, 315;
"He was happy whenever M. de Charlus was with Odette.
Between M. de Charlus and her, Swann knew nothing
could happen").

The statement thus utilizes a common euphemism to
reveal Charlus's homosexuality. For Swann, whose thoughts
are reported in indirect discourse, this represents no discovery, and there was no reason to give the fact more
relief than it received. From this point on, we become
witnesses to the world's incomprehension of what Charlus
really is. By allowing us the knowledge denied to others,
Proust creates the irony that permits us to analyze, sacri-
fices a potential moment of drama to provide the possibility of more complete comprehension. As the narrator
pointedly puts it at the moment of Marcel's discovery in
Sodome et Gomorrhe, "an error dispelled gives us an
additional sense" (II, 613).

Since we are now in possession of the facts, the actions
of characters who are uninformed become an object of
irony. Saint-Loup is under the same illusion as is everyone
else concerning his uncle Palamède, "very given to physical
exercise, especially long hikes" (I, 749). However, here
Proust intervenes with a minor example of the revelation
ex nihilo. He has set up his scene so that at this point in

A l'ombre des jeunes filles en fleurs we have no way of connecting Robert's uncle with Swann's best friend. In "Un Amour de Swann" Charlus was often called Mémé, but never Palamède. In *Jeunes filles* his surname has not yet been mentioned. His genealogy, like Robert's and Mme de Villeparisis's, is not yet clear enough for us to make the necessary deduction. So there is no reason for any particular interest concerning this personage. Proust makes us wait a few pages more, and even indulges in a final comic deviousness, as Marcel is introduced to the famous uncle:

> —Comment allez-vous? Je vous présente mon neveu, le baron de Guermantes, me dit Mme de Villeparisis, pendant que l'inconnu, sans me regarder, grommelant un vague "Charmé" qu'il fit suivre de: "heue, heue, heue" pour donner à son amabilité quelque chose de forcé. . . .
>
> —Mon Dieu, est-ce que je perds la tête, dit [Mme de Villeparisis] en riant, voilà que je t'appelle le baron de Guermantes. Je vous présente le baron de Charlus. [I, 753]
>
> ("How are you? Let me introduce my nephew, Baron de Guermantes," Mme de Villeparisis said to me, while the stranger, without looking at me, muttered a vague "Charmed!" which he followed by a "hmm, hmm, hmm," to make it clear that his politeness had been forced. . . .
>
> "My heavens, what can I have been thinking of!" Mme de Villeparisis laughed. "Here I am calling you Baron de Guermantes. Let me introduce Baron de Charlus.")

The real object of the irony in this situation is Marcel, who has yet to learn, as he immediately observes himself, that "it is not by asking him to explain them that we learn a person's true intentions" (I, 760). We are given a sense of his naïveté which no direct commentary could have produced. We see him puzzled by Charlus's behavior, sense him looking for the key to its coherence, and failing: "Since Charlus refused to give any explanation, I tried to provide one for myself, and only succeeded in hesitating between several" (I, 760). With every foolish hypothesis, the contrast between our manipulated wisdom and Marcel's naïve groping is emphasized.

The revelation of Charlus's encounter with Jupien, nominally the first critical moment of his existence in *La Recherche*, is thus vitiated more than a thousand pages before it occurs. Moreover, between the discovery we can make through Swann and the discovery we witness in Marcel, a series of clues assure that the reader will realize the truth before Marcel does: Mme de Villeparisis's "pudeur en alarme" ("alarmed sense of modesty") when she hears that Marcel is leaving her matinée with the Baron (II, 283); the strange unfriendliness of M. d'Argencourt who sees the two of them walking together (II, 292); Charlus's refusal to admit to Oriane that he already knows Marcel (II, 379); the revelation of the Baron's attempts to accost Bloch; the assurance that these "curious contradictions" in Charlus's character will be explained "at the end of this volume (*Sodome* I)" (II, 381); and finally the hallucinatory, moonstruck visit to Charlus's hôtel at the end of Oriane's dinner:—the Baron, an aging Apollo in a Chinese dressing gown, screaming wildly at Marcel who, losing his temper, rips a top hat to pieces; then Charlus forgiving as the Pastoral Symphony begins to be heard eerily in the background. But by now we are only forty pages from the Baron's meeting with Jupien, and nothing can surprise us anymore.

Proust wanted much more out of the scene with Jupien than a factual revelation. The revelation therefore had to be situated elsewhere, or he risked having his more subtle effects eclipsed by the blunt specificity of the discovery. His efforts to detach the episode—to the extent of giving it a separate title—from the very "real" scenes surrounding it are obvious. Anyone who reads this idyll of bees and flowers, this fairy ballet, as a scene of straight description will have to find it ridiculous.

Its central effect is created by the coexistence of two languages: on one hand the faint poesy of nature's beauties, of the mysteries of exotic ritual, and on the other the puerile argot of vulgarity which is necessary to Jupien and Charlus to complete their pleasure, much as Mlle Vinteuil spat upon her father's portrait at Montjouvain (II, 608). This conjoining of irreconcilables[8] exists as an image, intentionally somehow askew and awkward, of the homosexual's nature and of the conditions of his "vice" (II, 613). The narrator guides our interpretation of the tone: "The scene was not really comic, however; it was stamped with a strangeness, or if one prefers, with a naturalness, the beauty of which steadily increased" (II, 605). The imagery of the orchid and the bumblebee, for example, would be intolerably precious if its function was simply to serve as a "poetic" replacement for the line of dots that used to intervene in traditional love scenes. But this love scene, if not shown, is at least heard in all its earthy reality (II, 609), while curiously the fertilization of the orchid, the last element of the chapter (II, 632), remains as uncertain for the narrator as the character of the pleasure he has witnessed.

The second critical element of Charlus's existence in *La Recherche*, his liaison with Morel and Mme Verdurin's violent dissolution of it, receives equal prerevelatory treatment. Morel's future existence is hinted at early in *Sodome I*: "M. de Charlus . . . had met the tailor and in him had made the kind of conquest ["bonne fortune"] reserved for

8. For example, "Dans les yeux de l'un et de l'autre, c'était le ciel . . . de quelque cité orientale . . . qui venait de se lever" (II, 605-6) and "Vous en avez un gros pétard!" (II, 610). ("In the eyes of both had risen . . . the sky over some oriental city" and "You certainly have a large behind!")

men of the Baron's type; but, as we shall see, the objects of
such conquests may be infinitely younger and better-look-
ing than Jupien" (II, 607). But the Baron's love affair, carried on under the auspices of La Patronne, is doomed from
the start, for the same reason as Swann's with Odette,
Brichot's with the laundress he wanted to marry and with
Mme de Cambremer, and, in a sense (since the musical
soirée at La Patronne's which she wanted to attend precipitated her flight) even Marcel's with Albertine. The conditions announced at the very beginning of "Un Amour de
Swann" prove fatal for all:

> Si un "fidèle" avait un ami, ou une "habituée" un
> flirt qui serait capable de faire "lâcher," quelquefois,
> les Verdurin, qui ne s'effrayaient pas qu'une femme
> eût un amant pourvu qu'elle l'eût chez eux, l'aimât en
> eux et ne le leur préférât pas, disaient: "Eh bien!
> amenez-le votre ami." Et on l'engageait à l'essai, pour
> voir s'il était capable de ne pas avoir de secrets pour
> Mme Verdurin, s'il était susceptible d'être agrégé au
> "petit clan." S'il ne l'était pas, on prenait à part le
> fidèle qui l'avait présenté et on lui rendait le service de
> le brouiller avec son ami ou avec sa maîtresse. [I, 190]

(If one of the "faithful" had an acquaintance, or one
of the ladies a gentleman friend, who might, now and
then, make them miss an evening, the Verdurins, who
were not afraid of a woman's having a lover so long as
she had him in the group, loved him as part of the
group, and did not prefer him to the group, would say,
"All right, bring your friend along," and they would
take him on approval, to find out if he would be will-
ing to share all his secrets with Mme Verdurin, to see
if he was a candidate for admission to the "little clan."
If he failed, they would take aside the member who
had introduced him and do that person the favor of
breaking up his relationship with the outsider.)

As Swann had another life which Mme Verdurin fiercely envied and which finally turned her against him (see I, 251, 266), Charlus with his princely airs stirs violent jealousy, and the vengeance only requires a little time to organize. The first sign of what will follow is given on the night of Charlus's introduction to La Patronne at La Raspelière. He pointedly fails to notice that she expects him to offer her his seat, and responds to an insolent question of hers with a more brilliantly insolent answer: "'Tell me, Charlus, . . . you don't know of any ruined old nobleman in the *Faubourg* whom I might get as concierge?' 'Why, yes, . . . why, yes, . . . but I wouldn't recommend it.' 'Why not?' 'I'd be afraid for your sake that your society guests might stop in to visit him and you'd never get to see them at all.'" Prerevelation immediately intervenes: "This was the first skirmish between them. . . . Alas, there were to be others in Paris" (II, 967). The coming catastrophe begins to loom larger. A series of warnings follow, pointing out how Charlus fooled himself concerning his standing with the Verdurins (II, 1049), and clarifying the means of their revenge (II, 1062). With the beginning of *La Prisonnière* the warnings become more pressing until, the night in Paris of the Vinteuil septet, it is made clear just after Charlus enters that the moment has come. Then, with a vigor remarkable for its rarity in Proust, Mme Verdurin sets at him: "All right, go fetch Charlus, find some pretext, the time has come" (III, 282). Through the prerevelations, Charlus's decline always precedes him.[9]

For other characters it is their rise which is the object of

9. The final group of warnings of Charlus's disgrace seem much more like portents than prerevelations. Their effect is to increase the sense of foreboding and the suspense, rather than to dissipate it. The reason is simple: until the beginning of the soirée the prerevelations functioned to satisfy our curiosity about the outcome of Charlus's affair so that we might be more sensitive to its subtle evolution; but following p. 229 the announcements are engaged in the creation of a "feint," which will be discussed below.

predisclosure. Rachel's genius is affirmed (II, 168) in spite of her fiasco at Oriane's, and long before public recognition comes to her.[10] The worldly apotheosis of Mme Verdurin is prefigured at a time when her "noyau" still remains as third-rate as in "Un Amour de Swann" (I, 600). Odette's social isolation and her final victory after Swann's death are both foretold (I, 471; cf. 518, n. 4, and 639) long before the evolution of circumstances makes them conceivable. The cosmopolitan ascension of Marcel himself is treated similarly, and we learn long before he penetrates into the *haut monde* that the friendships of the Duchesse and the Princesse de Guermantes are promised him (II, 60, 714).

Prerevelation is the technique used to inform us that Françoise will one day become Marcel's family's own servant (I, 52); that Saint-Loup is a homosexual (II, 405); that Marcel is to meet a great painter, Elstir, at Balbec (I, 489, n. 1; cf. 653, 825); that Morel will abandon Jupien's niece (III, 54); that the scene witnessed at Montjouvain will have vital consequences in Marcel's later life (I, 159); that the musical soirée at Mme Verdurin's will change his ideas concerning art and cause an upheaval in his personal life (III, 198); and even—thereby rendering vain the narrator's fears that he may die before getting his work of art under way—that Marcel had at least three years to live after the Guermantes matinée (III, 951, 952).

Prerevelations thus alter the progression of events by allowing us a vision deep into them before they are even in sight. And while each of the successive subjects of the novel's concern is still present before us, the prerevelations have already evolved to anticipate the next, to prepare a prospective, parallel present toward which the tale must curve. By thus reconceiving the laws of temporal perspective and generating a fourth dimension of narrative, the

10. As usual the prerevelation creates irony. Here, it is a question of discrediting the abusive attacks against Rachel by the "society" at Mme de Villeparisis's matinée.

prerevelations assure that, at any point, whatever is coming has already come.

Marcel's sad love affair with Albertine is the critical experience of his life. Significantly, in the telling it is also the most profoundly fashioned by prerevelation. Nowhere in *A la recherche du temps perdu* are we made to feel greater detachment from an action whose woeful course, for us, is already consummated. Nowhere is our distance from Marcel more accentuated by the techniques of narration.

The coherence of these techniques in the Albertine story demonstrates the control Proust asserted over even his most emotionally-charged material. The portrait of life's possibilities in *La Recherche* is unvarying. The protagonists' experiences run parallel; each is, as the novelist says, a "processus d'angoisses" (I, 858; "a process of anxiety"). Because of this, episodes within the novel echo each other despite the absence of any causal connection. It is not surprising, therefore, that the prerevelations of the Albertine story begin within the story of Swann and Odette, well before Albertine makes her entrance on the beach at Balbec:

> Swann . . . compléta sa pensée en ces mots qui devaient plus tard prendre dans mon souvenir la valeur d'un avertissement prophétique et duquel je ne sus pas tenir compte. "Cependant le danger de ce genre d'amour est que la sujétion de la femme calme un moment la jalousie de l'homme mais la rend aussi plus exigeante. Il arrive à faire vivre sa maîtresse comme ces *prisonniers* qui sont jour et nuit éclairés pour être mieux gardés. Et cela finit généralement par des drames." [I, 563]

> (Swann . . . finished his thought with these words which later in my memory were to take on the character of a prophetic warning, but one which I had not understood well enough to heed it. "However, the danger in this

kind of love affair is that, though the subjection of the woman calms the man's jealousy temporarily, it also makes it more obsessive. He ends up forcing his mistress to live like one of those captives whose cells are kept lighted day and night to make guarding them easier. And generally it ends up very badly.")

It is not long before the whole thematic of *La Prisonnière* and *La Fugitive* is revealed: "describe, at the time of a later love affair, the diverse forms of unhappiness [*chagrin*]" (I, 627).

With Albertine's movement into the foreground of the action, the prerevelatory signals become more frequent and more specific: "even at the time of my deeper—my second—love affair with Albertine" (I, 846; this is well before he has even succeeded in meeting her). Or again: "that evening [with Elstir], the belief, then the fading of the belief, that I was going to be introduced to Albertine, in a few seconds time had made her seem almost insignificant, then infinitely precious to me; some years later, the belief, then the disappearance of the belief, that Albertine was faithful to me brought analogous changes" (I, 857).

Albertine is almost completely absent from *Le Côté de Guermantes*, but in this volume there are three significant prerevelations of what is to follow: concerning the necessity of reading a person's character by actions, not words: "Françoise provided the example (which I was to understand only later on when, as will be seen in the final volumes of this work, it was given to me again, more painfully, by someone much dearer to me) that the truth need not be spoken to be obvious" (II, 66); concerning the disaster that is coming: "Alas, I had not come to the end of my discoveries about Albertine" (II, 361); and concerning the imminence of the painful affair that would change Marcel's life: "I did not see Mme de Stermaria again. It was not she I fell in love with, but it might have been. And perhaps one of the things which made the profound love affair I was soon to be involved in the most agonizing was, recalling that evening, to tell myself that I could easily . . . have fallen in love with someone else" (II, 393).

It is clear from Swann's warning in *A l'ombre des jeunes filles en fleurs* (I, 563, quoted above) that the captive-fugitive motif was deeply ingrained in the novel. It is given further anticipatory force in *Sodome II*: "concerning Albertine, I sensed that I would never learn anything, that I would never be able to sort out the confused profusion of real details and lies. And it would continue like that, *unless I simply imprisoned her (but a prisoner can escape) until the end*" (II, 734). The first announcement of Albertine's death soon appears, combined with the first clear statement of the forgetting that would follow: "Lately I was thinking again about them [the girls who gave him moments of pleasure on the beach], their names came back to me. I counted up twelve who, during that single summer, granted me their adolescent favors. Another name came back later, which made thirteen. . . . Alas, I realized I had *forgotten* the first of them, *Albertine who was no more*, and who made the fourteenth" (II, 789).

As the moment of revelation in the little train approaches, the narrator dwells on the ironic coincidence that would cause his suffering. But this suffering is already real for the reader; the "miseries ["chagrins"] of my life in Paris, the year following" (II, 1006) are already present in tense contrast to the relaxed atmosphere of summer at Balbec. The implications of Albertine's admission coming into the Parville station are immediately explained by the narrator: "At these words . . . an image [Montjouvain] which had been preserved deep within [surged up] . . . like an Avenger, to inaugurate for me a period of torment, . . . a new phase of unsuspected suffering" (II, 1114–15).

With the beginning of *La Prisonnière*, the instability of the relationship tying Marcel and Albertine together provokes a tension as much structural as emotional. The atmosphere of suffering created by the anticipations of *Sodome et Gomorrhe* determines the form of Marcel's experience in *La Prisonnière*: increasing strain and final crisis. But these events continue to be doubled by a superstructure of prerevelation that forestalls the occurrence of drama. What would have been our participation in catastrophe is forced to become a dispassionate appraisal of guilt. We not only experience the disaster, we assign the responsibility.

The means have not changed: we are told things too early. Marcel discovers Albertine's flight on page 414 of the third volume; the reader learns of it on page 24:

> Je ne songeais pas que l'apathie qu'il y avait à se décharger ainsi sur Andrée ou sur le chauffeur du soin de calmer mon agitation, en leur laissant le soin de surveiller Albertine, ankylosait en moi, rendait inertes tous ces mouvements imaginatifs de l'intelligence, toutes ces inspirations de la volonté qui aident à deviner, à empêcher ce que va faire une personne. . . . Or, il peut y avoir dans la vie des hommes . . . (*et il devait y avoir dans la mienne*) un jour où on a besoin d'avoir en soi un préfet de police, . . . un chef de la Sûreté, qui . . . raisonne juste, se dit: ". . . si telle personne s'est enfuie, ce n'est pas vers les buts *a*, *b*, *d*, mais vers le but *c*, et l'endroit où il faut opérer nos recherches est *etc.*" [III, 24]

> (It did not occur to me that the apathy evidenced by my delegating to Andrée or the chauffeur the task of calming my agitation, assigning Albertine's surveillance to them, was paralyzing, rendering inert all those imaginative attempts of the intellect, all those inspirations of the will which help to guess, or prevent, what someone else is going to do. . . . Now it can happen in a person's life . . . (*and it was to happen in mine*) that one day we require within ourselves a chief of detec-

tives, an intelligence analyst who . . . reasons logically, says to himself: ". . . If so-and-so has disappeared, no point in looking in *a*, or *b*, or *d*; but *c* is the place where we ought to search.")

The night of the Vinteuil septet intervenes and Albertine disappears from view for more than a hundred pages. Then follows one of the tensest and saddest of the inquisition scenes, the direct descendents of ones Proust composed as early as *Jean Santeuil*.[11] Marcel, maneuvering, asks Albertine to leave (III, 341), and thereby gets her to agree to stay. But the existence that Marcel has obliged her to accept is too inhuman; her flight is inevitable: "Alors je me disais que cette vie lui était insupportable, . . . et que fatalement elle me quitterait un jour" (III, 392; "Then I said to myself that this kind of life was unbearable for her, that fatally [or "inevitably"] she would leave me one day").

At this point Proust doubles his technique of prerevelation with another procedure, the "feint." The reason is simple: an ordinary prerevelation is pronounced by the omniscient voice of the narrator drawing upon his own lived experience. But as the disaster of the Albertine story approaches, a greater and greater consciousness of it grows in Marcel, and the majority of the prerevelations in *La Prisonnière* come out of his own contemporary—but paralyzed—vision of the situation. Proust gives us the key to an enigma so we can monitor Marcel's reactions as he

11. The section of the Pléiade edition of *Jean Santeuil* that the editors entitled "De l'amour" contains numerous pages which prefigure the anguished tone of Marcel's love affair with Albertine. "L'Aveu," the inquisition scene (pp. 810-13), in which Jean brutally reduces Françoise to tears, could come from *La Recherche*. Proust worked on this material continuously; one of the Bibliothèque Nationale "Cahiers" contains two versions of these episodes, one in the older third-person looking back to *Jean Santeuil*, the other in the first-person of *La Recherche* (Cahier XXV). This material is far from having been invented after the death of Agostinelli. See Painter, *Proust*, II, 208-9 and Bardèche, *Marcel Proust romancier*, II, 230-32.

lives through its solution. The irony concerning Charlus's homosexuality involved the hero's youthful naïveté. In *La Prisonnière* the irony reveals the blindness of Marcel's failure to act in a situation where comprehension was nonetheless increasingly forced upon him. As his consciousness approaches our own complete knowledge, however, we tend to lose the advantage of our omniscience—and Proust, the rhetorical power that the irony gave him over our interpretation of his hero's behavior. Marcel cannot know everything. To reestablish the necessary gap, a feint is employed: "I sensed that she had a secret. *But I was sure that she could not leave me without warning*; moreover, she could hardly desire to (the fitting of her Fortuny gowns was only a week off), nor would it have been seemly, since my mother was returning at the end of the week, as was her aunt" (III, 398-99). The morning of the second day following, she is gone.

No technical procedure can be free of moral meaning, but the prerevelations in *La Prisonnière* support a judgment of the hero grimmer than any other in the novel. The irony which opposes Marcel's ignorance to the narrator's—and thus our—omniscience is here complicated by a graver irony, opposing the narrator's interpretation of his behavior to a truth about it which, even at his most lucid, he does not adequately appreciate. It seems clear that Albertine's death was not an accident (III, 492, 500, 600). She chooses it, and it is on Marcel that the guilt of her suicide must be placed. The thematic of the inquisition has attained its ineluctable end-point, and the prerevelations have freed us to witness every step of the fatality.

Of the two conditions necessary for the existence of suspense outlined at the beginning of this chapter, prerevelation suppresses the second by anticipating the outcome of each uncertain situation. The first condition, concern of the reader over the outcome, can equally be frustrated, by disguising the fact that an uncertain situation exists to begin with. The two techniques which accomplish this, the feint and the revelation *ex nihilo*, have both been touched upon above.

The feint is very simple: it is a false conclusion (one might almost say a false prerevelation) which gives the sense that uncertainty has been resolved—when in fact the real resolution, unsuspected behind this front, conserves its power to overturn the situation without mobilizing suspense because we firmly believe that no surprise awaits. Cases of the feint are numerous in *A la recherche du temps perdu*. For example, with regard to Vinteuil, his music, his daughter and her lesbian friend, Proust sets up a question: "My mother knew that Vinteuil had given up recopying the works of his last years, the insignificant efforts of an old piano teacher. . . . [Only] a few had been noted down illegibly on loose sheets of paper, and would remain unknown. . . . 'Poor M. Vinteuil,' my mother would say, 'he lived and died for his daughter, without any recompense. Will he receive one after his death, and in what form? It could only come from her'" (I, 159-60). To which Marcel gives a definitive response after witnessing the lesbian scene at Montjouvain: "I now knew, for all the suffering M. Vinteuil had endured during his life because of his daughter, what recompense he had received from her after his death" (I, 163). Vinteuil, his music, his daughter and her friend have been classified. When in "Un Amour de Swann" we read this dialogue we have no reason to doubt its accuracy:

> —Je connais bien quelqu'un qui s'appelle Vinteuil, dit Swann, en pensant au professeur de piano des soeurs de ma grand'mère.
> —C'est peut-être lui, s'écria Mme Verdurin.
> —Oh! non, répondit Swann en riant. Si vous l'aviez vu deux minutes, vous ne vous poseriez pas la question. . . . Mais ce pourrait être un parent, reprit Swann, cela serait assez triste, mais enfin un homme de génie peut être le cousin d'une vieille bête. [I, 214]

("I certainly know someone named Vinteuil," said Swann, thinking of my great-aunts' piano teacher.

"Perhaps it's him," cried Mme Verdurin.

"Oh, no," Swann laughed. "If you'd spent two minutes with him you wouldn't even ask. . . . But he might be a relative," Swann continued. "It would be rather sad, but after all, a genius can have a cousin who's some old fool.")

Proust makes us wait eighteen hundred pages for the correction. The first identification of Vinteuil the piano teacher and Vinteuil the genius is given at the moment of Albertine's painful revelation—is in fact the very substance of the revelation—as the little train approaches Parville: "'What musician?' 'My darling girl, if I told you that his name is Vinteuil would you know any more than you already do. . . ?' 'You have no idea how you're amusing me,' Albertine replied as she got up, since the train was coming to a stop. 'Not only does his name mean more to me than you suppose, but . . . I can get you any information you want about him. Remember I told you about my friend who was a little older than me, who has been a mother, a sister to me, . . . well, she . . . is simply Vinteuil's daughter's dearest friend'" (II, 1114).

The trip in the "Transatlantique" is thus doubly deceptive. Two patterns of feint are coupled here and two entirely unexpected revelations (Vinteuil's identity, Albertine's lesbianism) upset the routine jogging of the little train along the coast. Proust situates the peripety at the center of an area of unsuspenseful calm. Its resonances, when they come, are covered by no other sound.[12]

12. There is evidence that virtually all of these procedures for dismantling suspense were quite conscious in Proust. The decline of Realism nurtured a more formalistic paradigm, characterized by more consciously planned, univocal effects, whose growing influence we have seen in Flaubert. The Naturalist period began the great age of theories of fiction, of prefaces which reflect upon the writer's tools and his tasks, of constant, conscious self-examination by novelists of their techniques. Proust emerged from a tradition of extreme

An instance in which the feint produces quite a different effect occurs in *Sodome et Gomorrhe II*, chapter 1, in the section called "Curieuse conversation entre Swann et le prince de Guermantes" (II, 655 ff.; "Strange Conversation between Swann and the Prince de Guermantes"). Having that afternoon told the Duc and Duchesse of his illness, Swann appears at the soirée given by the Prince and Princesse de Guermantes to which Marcel has also gone, though still uncertain whether his invitation is authentic. Preceding and following Swann's entrance, Proust manipulates a feint. He employs traditional suspense to disguise and heighten quite a different revelation whose character required that it remain unsuspected until the final moment.

There are two separate elements in the feint employed. The first, by a great deal the lighter, involves Marcel's fears that his invitation may be a practical joke. Attempting to find out, he visits the Duc and Duchesse that afternoon, and learns of Swann's illness; the Guermantes, however, tell him nothing. *Sodome I* intervenes, but immediately at the beginning of *Sodome II* as he is hesitating to enter the Princesse's mansion, his perplexity returns. The coming moment of resolution is comically postponed by a series of suspense-whetting interruptions. These delays, unlike the sort of suspensions whose effect is to submerge tension, are obviously calculated to heighten it by recalling the awkward situation Marcel is in: the story of the Duc de Châtellerault and the *aboyeur* (II, 634), while Marcel waits nervously on the stairs to be announced; an account of the Princesse's manner of receiving her guests, while Marcel is left wondering if he will ever be admitted among them; the

---

artistic self-consciousness. His essays and letters demonstrate his critical sensitivity and suggest that the details of story-telling in his own novels were rarely the result of chance decisions. The revelation *ex nihilo* in question here, for example, is carefully explained in a letter (end of August 1913) to Lucien Daudet: "I felt it would be more striking to make Vinteuil seem an old fool without suggesting that he is a genius, and in the second chapter ["Un Amour de Swann"] to speak of his sublime Sonata which Swann never thinks of attributing to the 'old fool' " (*Choix de lettres*, p. 192).

description of the footman "dressed in black like an execu-
tioner" (II, 637) and the "bouncers" who may soon be
exercising their office upon Marcel; the crying out of his
name. Finally the comic suspense is dispelled as the Princesse rises to receive Marcel and sends him into the garden
to see the Prince (II, 638).

The second element of the feint, though parallel, is much
more serious. It concerns Swann, whose sad revelation of
the afternoon has gained him our sympathy. The pattern
of the feint is to put Swann in the doubtful position Marcel has occupied. Swann has been a member of the Guermantes milieu for years, but Proust uses the antisemitism
aroused by the Dreyfus affair to create the necessary uncertainty. As the most traditionalist of all the *haute no-
blesse* (II, 570), the Prince de Guermantes's sentiments
concerning the affair have never been in doubt. On the
afternoon of *Sodome I* the Duc asks Marcel not to mention the soirée in front of Swann: "I don't know if he's
invited. Gilbert likes him a great deal, because he believes
Swann is the Duc de Berri's natural grandson, it's quite a
story. (If that weren't the case, can you imagine! My cousin, who has a stroke if he sees a Jew at a hundred yards.)
But it's more complicated now with the Dreyfus affair"
(II, 578).

Swann arrives after Marcel and is immediately led off to
a corner of the garden by the Prince—"some people said
the Prince was asking him to leave" (II, 656). Because we
know of Swann's illness, his fatigue, his demoralization,
the prospect is immensely saddening. At this point Proust
interposes his perversely detailed description of the soirée,
not as suspension but as real suspense, while continued
details emphasize that Swann and the Prince remain in
mysterious conversation in the garden.

Finally Swann returns. Marcel tries to get to him across
the smoking room to find out what has happened, but a
series of obstacles intervene to heighten the tension in the
classic manner of the suspense novel. At the moment that

Marcel observes to his distress how extraordinarily ill Swann appears ("Had he really had an argument with the Prince which had stunned him?" II, 691), Saint-Loup turns up and drags Marcel off in another direction. When finally they drift over toward Swann, Saint-Loup reveals that he has turned anti-Dreyfusard. Finally Swann begins the account of his conversation with the Prince (II, 705). A page later they are interrupted again by Charlus and by the story of Mme Surgis-le-Duc which Proust prolongs for two and a half pages. But when the conversation at last returns, it is for a revelation different from anything we could have supposed: the Prince de Guermantes, contrary to all that we have been told about him, has become convinced of Dreyfus's innocence.[13]

Proust used the feint structurally as well as dramatically as in the example above. Obliged by his publisher to end his first volume a hundred pages earlier than he had planned, he decided to close with the passage on the Bois de Boulogne, giving it a much more prominent position than it was to have had.[14]

Les lieux que nous avons connus n'appartiennent pas qu'au monde de l'espace où nous les situons pour plus de facilité. Ils n'étaient qu'une mince tranche au milieu d'impressions continguës qui formaient

13. A similar example of the feint used to heighten the one dénouement we have been dissuaded from expecting involves Mme Verdurin's "exécution" of Charlus in *La Prisonnière*. The feint here is our knowledge of the Baron's crushing power of invective: "My one consolation was to think that I was about to see Morel and the Verdurins pulverized by M. de Charlus. For a thousand times less [provocation] I had suffered his mad outbursts, . . . a king would not have intimidated him. But an extraordinary thing happened. We saw Charlus mute, stupified, feeling his pain without comprehending its cause, unable to pronounce a single word" (III, 316). The Baron's expected riposte never comes, and the feint enables Proust to concentrate the force of Charlus's emotion in a startling silence.

14. See letters to Lucien Daudet (end of August–September 1913), Daudet, ed., *Autour de soixante lettres de Marcel Proust*, pp. 69, 79-80.

> notre vie d'alors; le souvenir d'une certaine image n'est que le regret d'un certain instant; et les maisons, les routes, les avenues, sont fugitives, hélas! comme les années. [I, 427]

> (The places we have known do not exist only in the geographical world where we map them for our convenience. They were no more than a thin slice amidst the contiguous impressions which composed our life at that time; the memory of a certain image is only nostalgia for a certain moment; and houses, roads, avenues are as fugitive, alas, as the years.)

But this beautiful cadence is false, as Proust observed to Jacques Rivière (7 February 1914): "[The idea] I express at the end of the first volume, in that 'parenthesis' on the Bois de Boulogne which I placed there like a screen [*paravent*] to end up and close off *Swann* . . . is the opposite of my conclusion" (*Marcel Proust: Choix de lettres*, p. 198).

The *paravent* is an apt image for the feint's operation throughout *La Recherche*: it is a false front, a provisional screen which we are made to consider definitive. Proust's design required calm; the structural feint which provides such a serene conclusion to *Du Côté de chez Swann* sets all movement to rest. The closing provides a moment of subtle disenchantment; nothing in the cadence looks forward, all its energy is exhausted. Much later this pessimism will be overturned, but the end of *Swann* contains no hint of it. The walk in the Bois is interesting precisely because it is so completely empty of the future.

The revelation *ex nihilo* is the obverse of the feint. Instead of misleading us to expect a dénouement different from the one that occurs, it misleads by giving no indication of any dénouement at all. Without expectation, there is no suspense, only the Proustian atmosphere of slow, open expansion. In this atmosphere, even crucial discoveries seem damped and are rapidly resorbed by the surrounding

material. The revelations which come out of the void seem
rapidly to return to it. This is true in the case of the reader's discovery that Swann has married Odette. With his
sardonic comment at the conclusion of "Un Amour de
Swann" ("a woman I did not even like"), Odette passes
out of Swann's life and out of the novel. This seems the
final state of the unhappy passion which has occupied
Proust for two hundred pages. But the end of "Un Amour
de Swann" is a feint, and the coming revelation depends
upon it. At the end of "Noms de pays: le nom," Marcel
is walking in the Bois. Through a conversation he over-
hears, and which is no surprise for him, we learn that Swann
in fact married Odette, that Swann's wife is Swann's
cocotte: "'You know who that is? Mme Swann! Can't you
place her? Odette de Crécy?' 'Odette de Crécy? Of course,
those soulful eyes'" (I, 420).

The revelation that Elstir was M. Biche, and of the real
identities of "Miss Sacripant" and the "Dame en rose" are
handled similarly. Only after a hundred pages of the Guermantes reception in *Le Temps retrouvé* does Proust casually mention that the woman whom Marcel has been calling
"Princesse" is not Marie-Gilbert de Guermantes but Mme
Verdurin (III, 955). A world-weary calm always surrounds
these discoveries (for example Elstir's sober show of disabused wisdom in admitting the buffoon's role he played
at Mme Verdurin's, "as if it were a period of his life already rather long ago"; I, 863). The time when they would
have astonished us is made to seem extraordinarily remote.

The announcement of Swann's death is so muffled, so
matter-of-fact, that this most critical of events is made to
seem immensely abstract. Swann alive vividly engaged our
affection; dead, he seems to have no claims on anyone. The
first time he is spoken of dead, it is within the impersonal
atmosphere of administrative detachment: "[Swann]
added a codicil to his will requesting that . . . he be accorded military honors at his funeral as a member of the
Légion d'honneur. Which clause assembled an entire squad

of soldiers around the church at Combray" (II, 713). The second time, he appears so remotely in a context of gossip that his name is not even mentioned: "[The Princesse de Caprarola] had even mentioned her name [Mme Verdurin's] in the course of a condolence call she had made to Mme Swann after the *latter's husband's death*" (II, 870). The great majority of deaths in *La Recherche* are treated with the same abstraction. In spite of the narrator's protest later on ("Swann's death! Swann hardly plays the role of a simple possessive in such a sentence"; III, 199), these oblique death notices epitomize the way the revelation *ex nihilo* can be used to de-energize an event. Albertine is the only character in the novel who "dies at the right time." When the others come to their ends the book closes over their heads and they simply disappear.

The common element in all these techniques—prerevelation, suspension, the feint, the revelation *ex nihilo*—is that whatever they set out to do they accomplish totally. Suspense lives on partiality. What we call a clue works because it gives part of the truth while holding something back. The hint of a coming event acts as an irritant; but a complete announcement—a prerevelation—is rather a calmant. When the feint screens off a future reversal which Proust wants to keep hidden for a time, it does this perfectly, and we see nothing of what it hides. Finally, a suspension entirely supplants the story it interrupts, and absorbs our full attention in its own development.

Seen in active narration, our lives progress from crisis to crisis through objective time. A dialectic between internal and external events, between the subjective and objective frames, is always implied. But the progression of individual moments of which the Realists built portraits of human experience makes no sense to Proust. His techniques for suppressing suspense and the linear motion of narrative fundamentally dislocate this view of experience.

For Proust, more even than for Flaubert, Huysmans or

other post-Naturalists, the logic of our lives resides elsewhere. In his understanding, it is a mistake to try to sort out the relationship between events in the world of concrete social activity and our private triumphs or disasters, since for him our inner existence hardly connects with these anecdotic happenings. At most, our experience is organized in obsessive patterns of response to outward events: psychological themes which we repeat in helpless cycles that betray how unimportant are the specific incidents that trigger them. So at the fundamental level the suppression of active telling denies that experience is progressive. But narrative by its nature is progressive. Reconciling this discord was a serious problem in *A la recherche du temps perdu.*

7

Transitions

Proust's devaluation of the event as building-block for narrative affects every level of his writing. As the ordered dynamism of Realist time gave way to his directionless, atmospheric "Time," the links between the episodes of the tale became exceptionally weak. As a result, transitions between episodes presented a serious problem in *A la recherche du temps perdu*. Proust's difficulty was to make his story go at all, to motivate the scenes no longer linked by the energy of plot.

Proust's transitions need to be analyzed in terms of their function and their form. Traditionally the logic of transitions was based on causal connection. But since Proust's manner of telling makes causality increasingly irrelevant, in *La Recherche* the transition tends to become simply verbal—a conventional narrative punctuation which allows the teller to set aside one subject and take up another. The gracefulness of this movement moreover varies astonishingly.

The transitions in *La Recherche* divide into two dissimilar types, one of which is discursive, abrupt and overtly manipulated, much like the procedures Proust used to devalue the active mode of narration. The other type is unapparent, fluid and elegantly organic, exhibiting significant resemblance to scenic procedures yet to be discussed. While the second type is the product of an impressive artisanship, the first is much more frequent in the novel. Its awkwardness betrays the extent of a problem which the successes of the second type might otherwise have disguised.

The characteristic quality of the first type of transition is how frankly it acknowledges its own artificiality. Its only logic is the subjective logic of the narrator who controls its use. There always seems something improvised in these abrupt deflections of the story, which typically take the form Dickens satirized in *Our Mutual Friend*: "We must now return, as the novelists say, and as we all wish they wouldn't, to the man from Somewhere." The practice which Dickens at once deplores and profits by is constantly present in *La Recherche*. Proust's repeated use of it shows how loosely structured, how almost conversationally free, were the internal details of his own narrative plan.

The narrative simply breaks away from one concern and turns to the next subject in line: "To finish up with this first evening when I met [Albertine] " (I, 876); "I will end this by saying" (II, 381); "Leaving the subject of religion" (II, 1040). These deflections may involve startling chronological jumps. Here is an example from the period of Marcel's grandmother's final illness: "I remember (and here I anticipate) that at the cemetery, . . . my mother . . . could only gently incline her head, showing no tears. Two days before—to anticipate once again before returning immediately to the scene at the bedside where my grandmother lay dying—while they were watching over the body . . . Françoise . . . [etc.] To return now to those final hours . . . " (II, 343). Later the narrator launches a long digression concerning Charlus, tenuously attached to the account of the Princesse de Guermantes's soirée by a memory he had of that soirée while witnessing the scene he is in the middle of describing. He is spying on Charlus: "I emerged from the alley, recalling the evening at the Princesse de Guermantes's (the evening the account of which I have interrupted in this anticipatory parenthesis, but to which I will return)" (II, 716, n. 1). A page later when, as promised, Proust returns to the interrupted soirée, it is only so that the narrator can take his leave of the Prin-

cesse, revealing the factitiousness of the set of links between the two scenes.

There are a whole series of such divagations inserted in
the fabric of the novel's matinées and soirées, which are
made to serve as convenient bases for excursions having
little to do with them. For example (following a long
description of Charlus's relations with Morel after the
separation engineered by Mme Verdurin): "But we have
jumped too far ahead, since all this happened only after
the evening at the Verdurins', which we have interrupted
and which we must take up again where we left off" (III,
312).

"Anticipons" ("let us jump ahead") or its equivalent becomes one of Proust's most frequent narrative punctua-
tions. It permits him to shift to the most distant scenes,
give explanations for the most hidden facts, and thereby
render the laws of objective chronology all the more
irrelevant: "let us jump ahead of our story ["anticipons
sur les événements"] to mention . . ." (II, 443). These
abrupt transitions reveal Proust's haste to get things into
the novel, caring more for the interest of his material than
for the strain put on an already dilated structure. This
tendency became more pronounced toward the end of
Proust's life. But everywhere in the novel, and even in
works antedating La Recherche, we find Proust seizing a
moment, with a discursive announcement that he is doing
so, to include some detail, some anecdote, some explanation which another novelist might have worked less obtru-
sively into the fabric of the telling.

But a certain offhand brusqueness in conducting the narration is of a piece with the fragmentation Proust sought
by a series of procedures that disrupt the fabric of the tale.
Every intervention, however awkward, represents a reasser-
tion of the narrator's controlling voice. Again, there is no
logic natural to events in Proust's view. The logic of his
narrative flows from within the teller, an expression of his
sovereign and irreducible subjectivity. Every time the

skeleton of the work becomes visible, therefore, our impression of its authenticity is reinforced.

This is the sense behind a curious technique appearing at a number of critical moments in the novel, a kind of topic sentence brusquely summarizing or commenting upon material to follow: "Without meaning to, I murmured (though no one else heard): 'I'm done for!' *It did not turn out that way*" (I, 36); "He would have wanted . . . to be able to bid his farewell . . . to Odette . . . whom now he would never see again. *He was wrong.* He was to see her one more time, several weeks later" (I, 378). The same curt reversal in lieu of transition is used at another crisis point much later in the novel: "I abandoned all pride in relation to Albertine, I sent her a desperate telegram entreating her to return on any conditions. . . . *She never returned.* My telegram had just been sent off when I received one . . ." (III, 476).

All of these announcements function to redirect the course of narration toward a new center of interest, to open up a new vein. They do it by proposing an abstract relationship (opposition, reversal, succession) between the passages they link. But they differ from the organic transitions possible in novels whose plots depend upon narrative causality because they never pretext a relationship inherent in the materials joined. The link remains undisguisedly verbal; the development is fortuitous, contrived, even makeshift.

A bizarre example is this transition from *La Prisonnière*: "If a person thought he was not sufficiently popular, I would not tell him to increase his socializing . . . ; I would advise him to refuse all invitations, to remain shut up in his room ["chambre"]. . . . 'Speaking of that, we'll have to begin thinking about your Fortuny dressing gown ["robe de chambre"],' I said to Albertine" (III, 370). What is remarkable is the jump from the use of the word "chambre" in the preceding analytical passage to "robe de chambre" which suddenly Marcel is speaking about with

Albertine. While Marcel speaks of the "robe de chambre," the use of the word "chambre" is the narrator's, and occurs many years after the scene described. The transition is completely factitious. But associations such as this one, because they are always available, never verifiable, and quick, are a favorite means of transition in *La Recherche*.

The disproportion between these summary transitions and the immense scenes they are required to support is immediate evidence of a well-recognized characteristic of Proustian narration: Proust thinks by blocks, by tableaux, not by flow. The rapid movement across scene-boundaries contrasts with the swelling of the scene itself. Not surprisingly, Proust often found it expedient to suppress his transition altogether and pass off this sleight of hand by affecting to notice nothing out of the ordinary. This led to his personal version of the classical *in medias res*.

Typically he turns the illusion by a very simple device, a past or pluperfect tense which assumes action already begun: "M. de Charlus's words about the 'unapproachable Aladdin's palace' his cousin dwelt in did not adequately explain my stupefaction, immediately followed by the fear that I had been taken as the butt of a practical joke, . . . when, perhaps *two months after* my dinner at the Duchesse's, . . . *having opened* an envelope . . . I *read* these words printed on an invitation: 'The Princesse de Guermantes, née Duchesse en Bavière, will be at home on . . . '" (II, 568). In the space of this phrase we pass from the atmosphere of Charlus into the sphere of influence of another Guermantes, whose force (symbolized by her title) is completely formed and has already begun to be felt by Marcel, before the end of the sentence. By the end of this brief account, we have been thoroughly established in a new temporality which will remain the reference point for the crucial events of the next hundred and fifty pages. But characteristically, this reorientation is given no particular relief, is imbedded in a sentence and paragraph whose concerns are apparently elsewhere.

The tendency is particularly noticeable in the *in medias res* launching of new sections of the novel, complete with the pasts or pluperfects which signify already achieved stasis in a set of circumstances unfamiliar to the reader. Proust evokes the new situation with a familiarity that casually omits any account of the interim in which changes took place: "I had arrived at a state of almost complete indifference to Gilberte when, two years later, *I departed* with my grandmother for Balbec" (beginning of "Noms de pays: le pays"); "The early-morning chirping of the birds sounded insipid to Françoise. Every word spoken by the upstairs maids made her jump; disturbed by all their scurrying about, she kept wondering what they could be doing; in other words, *we had moved*" (*Le Côté de Guermantes*); "All day long, in that slightly too countrified house which seemed only a place for a rest between walks or during a storm . . . —*all day long I remained in my room* which looked out on the beautiful greenery of the park and on the lilacs near the entrance, on the green leaves of the tall lake-side trees glistening in the sun, and on the Forest of Méséglise."[1]

The opening of the matinée at Mme de Villeparisis's is the most elaborate example of *in medias res* in *La Recherche*. We never hear of Marcel's arrival, but discover him already there (II, 183–84). The complexity of the eight page transition to this gathering is far from exhausted,

1. In the pre-Pléiade editions, the beginning of *Le Temps retrouvé* was placed here (III, 697; the manuscript does not indicate where the division was to be located). The Pléiade editors chose to begin about seven pages earlier since this avoided dividing the account of the stay at Tansonville (Proust however sometimes cut in the middle of scenes—for example, the beginnings of *Guermantes II* and *La Fugitive*). The original editors' choice had the advantage of giving full weight to the exordium quoted here ("Toute la journée . . ."), which the Pléiade solution tends to bury. Moreover the former beginning is consistent with an important pattern of "distribution" to be discussed below, while the Pléiade's opening is not.

however. Our discovery that Marcel has already been at
Mme de Villeparisis's for "several moments" is surrounded
by an analysis of the social situation of the Marquise and
her salon. The narrator speculates about Mme de Villeparisis's "déclassement" (II, 184; "social decline"), about
the various stages her reputation must have passed through
for her, born a Bouillon, to have reached the point where
only the Duchesse de Guermantes's attendance out of a
sense of family duty lends some elegance to her salon.

Proust then begins (in a Balzacian progression) to compose before us the salon which is the end-point of Mme de
Villeparisis's slow decline: color of the walls, furniture,
portraits of ancestors, the little desk where the hostess has
ceased working on her water colors. Every trace of action
is excluded. The atmosphere consists of acts already accomplished: no movement, only stasis, pure scene: "Mme de
Villeparisis . . . était assise à un petit bureau, où devant
elle, à côté de ces pinceaux, de sa palette et d'une aqua-
relle de fleurs commencée, il y avait dans des verres . . . des
roses, . . . des zinnias, des cheveux de Vénus, qu'à cause
de l'affluence à ce moment-là des visites elle s'était arrêtée
de peindre" (II, 189; "Mme de Villeparisis . . . was seated
at a little desk, on which, in front of her, next to her
brushes, her palette, and a watercolor of flowers which she
had begun, there were some roses in glasses, some zinnias,
a maidenhair fern; which, owing to the number of guests
who had just come in, she had ceased to paint"). Next
comes a summary identification of the people present: an
archivist, a historian, and "my old friend Bloch, now a
rising young playwright" (II, 189).

The sedate analysis moves on, examining the evolutions
of antisemitism and the permanence of races. But in the
midst of this undeviating advance a short parenthesis ruffles
the surface—slightly, but enough to suspend what has
quietly become a spell: for eight dense pages since we
discovered Marcel in the salon, no one has said anything,
no one has thought anything, nothing has moved, there has

been no sound, there has been a complete absence of the kind of social behavior which is normal in such a situation, and which would ordinarily have continued the animated account of Rachel, Saint-Loup, the dancer, and the journalists which directly preceded. The parenthesis in question (with its contrasting context) runs as follows:

> Admirable puissance de la race qui du fond des siècles pousse en avant jusque dans le Paris moderne, dans les couloirs de nos théâtres, derrière les guichets de nos bureaux, à un enterrement, dans la rue, une phalange intacte, stylisant la coiffure moderne, absorbant, faisant oublier, disciplinant la redingote, demeurée, en somme, toute pareille à celle des scribes assyriens peints en costume de cérémonie à la frise d'un monument de Suse devant les portes du palais de Darius. (*Une heure plus tard Bloch allait se figurer* que c'était par malveillance antisémitique que M. de Charlus s'informait s'il portait un prénom juif, alors que c'était simplement par curiosité esthétique et amour de la couleur locale.) Mais, au reste, parler de permanence des races rend inexactement l'impression que nous recevons des Juifs, des Grecs, des Persans. [II, 190–91]

(Admirable power of the race which from the dawn of time has propelled itself to the front, even in modern Paris, on the stages of our theaters, in the offices of our banks, at a funeral, in the street, a solid phalanx, deciding the latest hairstyle, absorbing, putting out of style, disciplining the frock coat, retaining, in fact, much of the appearance of the Assyrian scribes depicted in their ceremonial costumes in the frieze of a monument at Susa before the gates of Darius's palace. (*An hour later Bloch would imagine* that it was out of antisemitic malice that M. de Charlus inquired if he had a Jewish first name, whereas it was simply out of esthetic curiosity and an interest in local color.) But, on the other hand, to speak of the permanence of races

falsifies somewhat the impression we get from the
Jews, the Greeks, the Persians.)

In the midst of such different material, the forecast ex-
change between Bloch and Charlus, appropriately trivial,
prefigures the sort of behavior which has been missing in
these introductory pages. The anticipated presence of
Charlus promises other arrivals; "allait" has something
grammatically prophetic in it that restores energy to the
mummified atmosphere up to this point; "une heure plus
tard" prospectively suggests the center of a new temporality toward which the current one is directed.

In the long silent passage, Proust has been setting up a
forceful re-appearance of movement, while being careful
not to broach the action itself or destroy the contrast before circumstances are ready. The primary characteristic
of the return of movement will be the abrupt sensation of
in medias res which it produces. The pages of dense analysis
represent a subtle sociological preparation of the frame
into which, once it is complete, Proust will audaciously
make the action drop:

> Il me semblait que si j'avais dans la lumière du salon
> de Mme de Villeparisis pris des clichés d'après Bloch,
> ils eussent donné d'Israël cette même image, si trou-
> blante, . . . si décevante, . . . que nous montrent les
> photographies spirites. Il n'est pas, d'une façon plus
> générale, jusqu'à la nullité des propos tenus par les
> personnes au milieu desquelles nous vivons qui ne nous
> donne l'impression du surnaturel, dans notre pauvre
> monde de tous les jours où même un homme de
> génie de qui nous attendons, rassemblés comme autour
> d'une table tournante, le secret de l'infini, prononce
> seulement ces paroles—*les mêmes qui venaient de
> sortir des lèvres de Bloch*—: "*Qu'on fasse attention
> à mon chapeau haute forme.*"
> —Mon Dieu, les ministres, mon cher Monsieur,

était en train de dire Mme de Villeparisis s'adressant
plus particulièrement à mon ancien camarade et re-
nouant le fil d'une conversation que mon entrée avait
interrompue, les ministres. . . . [II, 191–92]

(I felt that if I had taken pictures of Bloch in the
light of Mme de Villeparisis's *salon*, they would have
captured the same . . . disturbing, . . . disappointing
image of Israel which we get in spirit photographs.
More generally speaking, there is nothing, including the
emptiness of the phrases spoken by the people in
whose midst we live, which does not give us the impression of the supernatural, in our poor everyday
world in which even the geniuses, assembled around a
"table tournante," from whom we expect to hear revealed the secrets of the universe, say nothing more
than these words—*the very ones which Bloch had just
spoken*: "*Be careful with my top hat.*"

"My heavens, dear sir, the Cabinet ministers," *Mme
de Villeparisis was saying*, speaking particularly to my
old acquaintance and taking up again the thread of a
conversation that my arrival had interrupted, "the
Cabinet ministers. . . .")

And the matinée, through one of the strangest, most im-
pudently paralogical transitions in *La Recherche*, is
brusquely launched.

The problem of Proust's intentions is an ungrateful one.
Somehow the pattern of coherent practice that in other
works we take as the sign of a formal motive is missing in
La Recherche.[2] The structure of the novel exhibits a peculiar evasiveness, notably in the case of another type of
narrative transition. This second manner of passing between scenes or sections is characterized by a fluidity and
an artisanship which the transitions discussed above seem

2. See on this subject the helpful remarks by Leo Bersani, *Marcel Proust:
The Fictions of Life and of Art*, p. 19.

to refuse. There are two variants of the second type, which can be called "distribution" and "confrontation."

Distribution establishes a program organizing the material to follow. Proust then refers to the program when the appropriate moment of transition arrives. The arrangement gives an authenticity or inevitability to the shift of subject, and tends to unify the structure of the whole through a sense of consistent, natural logic:

> Tout tournait autour de moi dans l'obscurité, les choses, les pays, les années. Mon corps . . . cherchait . . . à repérer la position de ses membres pour en induire la direction du mur, la place des meubles, pour reconstruire et pour nommer la demeure où il se trouvait. Sa mémoire, la mémoire de ses côtes, de ses genoux, de ses épaules, *lui présentait successivement plusieurs des chambres* où il avait dormi. . . . Mon côté ankylosé, cherchant à deviner son orientation, s'imaginait, par exemple, allongé face au mur dans un grand lit à baldaquin, et aussitôt je me disais: "Tiens, j'ai fini par m'endormir quoique maman ne soit pas venue me dire bonsoir," j'étais à la campagne chez mon grand-père, . . . dans *ma chambre de coucher de Combray.* . . .
>
> Puis renaissait le souvenir d'une nouvelle attitude; le mur filait dans une autre direction: j'étais dans *ma chambre chez Mme de Saint-Loup,* à la campagne. . . . Car bien des années ont passé depuis Combray. . . . C'est un autre genre de vie qu'on mène à Tansonville. . . .
>
> Ces évocations tournoyantes et confuses ne duraient jamais que quelques secondes. . . . Mais j'avais revu tantôt l'une, tantôt l'autre des chambres que j'avais habitées dans ma vie, et *je finissais par me les rappeler toutes* dans les longues rêveries qui suivaient mon réveil: . . . parfois *la chambre Louis XVI,* si gaie que même le premier soir je n'y avais pas été trop mal-

heureux ... ;—parfois au contraire *celle, petite et si
élevée de plafond* ... où, dès la première seconde,
j'avais été ... convaincu de l'hostilité des rideaux
violets. ...

Certes, j'étais bien éveillé maintenant. ... Mais
j'avais beau savoir que je n'étais pas dans ces demeures,
... le branle était donné à ma mémoire; générale-
ment je ne cherchais pas à me rendormir tout de suite;
je passais la plus grande partie de la nuit à me rappeler
notre vie d'autrefois *à Combray chez ma grand'tante,
à Balbec, à Paris, à Doncières, à Venise, ailleurs encore*,
à me rappeler les lieux, les personnes que j'y avais
connues, ce que j'avais vu d'elles, ce qu'on m'en avait
raconté. [I, 6–9]

(Everything was circling round me in the darkness,
things, places, years. My body ... sought to determine
the positions of its limbs in order to deduce the location of the wall, of the furniture, to reconstruct and
to give a name to the house where it found itself. Its
memory, the memory of its ribs, its knees, its shoulders, *successively proposed a number of bedrooms*
where it had slept. ... My numbed side, seeking to
guess its position, would imagine itself, for example,
stretched out lying against the wall in a big four-poster
bed, and right away I would say: "Well, I managed to
fall asleep even though Mama never came to say
goodnight": I was in the country at my grandfather's
house, ... *in my bedroom at Combray*. ...

Then the memory of a different position would rise
up; the wall would slide away in another direction: *I
was in my bedroom at Mme de Saint-Loup's house in
the country*. ... Many years have passed since Combray. ... The life at Tansonville is a very different
one. ...

These shifting and confused impressions never
lasted more than a few seconds. ... But I would have
seen again first one, then another of the rooms I had

lived in, and *I would end up recalling all of them* in my long reveries after awakening: . . . *the Louis XVI bedroom*, so pleasant that even the first night I had not been too unhappy in it [at Doncières; see II, 82–83] . . . ; on the other hand, *the small one with the high ceiling* . . . where beginning with the first moment, I had been certain that the violet curtains were hostile to me [at Balbec; see I, 666–67]. . . .

Of course, I was fully awake now. . . . But though I knew I was in none of these houses, . . . my memory was in motion; usually I did not try to fall back asleep right away; I spent the best part of the night recalling our life in the old days *at Combray* with my great-aunt, *at Balbec, at Doncières, at Venice, in still other places,* recalling the places, the people I had known there, what I had actually seen of them, what others had told me.)

This is the "program." Proust utilized it precisely as we would expect, for example in the opening of "Noms de pays: le nom": "Among the bedrooms whose images I called up during my nights of sleeplessness, none was so different from the room at Combray . . . as the one at the Grand-Hôtel de la Plage, at Balbec" (I, 383). The movement has been pre-set by the logic of distribution: this passage which so carefully echoes the novel's opening automatically creates a readiness for the development of a new scene, a new atmosphere, parallel to the scene and atmosphere (Combray) already created. "Chambres" represented a means of ordering each of the novel's successive tableaux, each time referring back to the series sketched in the opening pages of *Du côté de chez Swann*. The transitions motivated in this way have an elegance which grows out of the rationality of the overall plan. The organic coherence of the chain's evolution seems esthetically pleasing.

But the distribution established in the early pages is

worked out so haphazardly that the clarity which made it attractive is lost. Balbec is introduced thanks to this procedure, but on the other hand Doncières, whose "chambre" is evoked exactly parallel with the one at the Grand-Hôtel (I, 8), is arrived at through a transition which has nothing at all to do with the program of "chambres."

There are other beginnings in which the distribution of "chambres" appears. *Le Côté de Guermantes II*, chapter 2, opens with an evocation of the weather, but a page later we read: "It was from my bed that I was today considering these recollections, for I had returned to it to await the moment when, since my parents were away, . . . I was planning to go out this very evening to attend a short play which was being given at Mme de Villeparisis's" (II, 347). However the bedroom setting then quickly evaporates. It is a nice thematic touch, but one with no transitional value. Marcel is in bed again at the opening of both *La Prisonnière* and *La Fugitive*. In the former we read on the first page (echoing *Guermantes II*, chapter 2): "It was moreover principally from my *bedroom* that I perceived life outside during that period" (III, 9). This sentence (specifically reinforcing the distribution established in *Swann*) and the surrounding passage represent a possible use of "chambres" in the later part of the novel. Yet its particular beauty seems the result of its nonconformity to the procedure's logic, which requires that the initial program be specifically referred to as in "Noms de pays: le nom."

The passage chosen by the original editors to open *Le Temps retrouvé* ("Toute la journée . . . je la passais dans ma chambre"; III, 697, quoted above; "All day long . . . I remained in my room") sets out from yet another bedroom and undoubtedly was intended to recall the early anticipation, at that point incomprehensible, of "my room at Mme de Saint-Loup's house" (I, 6; this is the most serious reason why the passage should be reestablished as the opening of the final volume). But the effort of memory required to associate this passage with the original program

would be less had coherent use of the "chambres" distribution through the body of *La Recherche* reinforced
associations structuring each succeeding section. As it is,
these connections seem excessively distant. By the beginning of *Le Temps retrouvé* the largest proportion of the
force of the distribution technique has been lost.

Discussion of "chambres" as a technique of transition
is complicated by the importance of "chambres" as an
atmospheric theme. "Marcel in bed" is one of the con-
stituent images of *La Recherche*, symbolizing at once the
two sides of his nature: the passivity of his relationships
with others, the passion of his curiosity about himself. It
is in this reclining attitude that memory first asserts itself
as his primary faculty for conceiving the world. Nonetheless
the "chambres" distribution at the beginning of the novel
is so fully formed that it seems clear Proust at some point
intended to use it as a continuing means of transition. But
somewhere in the subsequent evolution of the book, the
procedure ceased to be worked out systematically; the list
of bedrooms was modified until it lost its one-to-one connection with the series of tableaux of which the novel
finally came to be composed.[3] We are left with the sense
of a blurred intention. There is too much preparation for
the procedure to have been meant as a purely local effect
in the novel's opening pages; there is too little coherent
development to consider the technique as successfully
constituting, as Proust wrote to René Blum (beginning of

3. Proust long tinkered with the list of bedrooms in the book's early pages.
Although the motif of successive *chambres* dates back to *Jean Santeuil*, in the
earliest sketches for the opening of *La Recherche*, the much less graphic word
"lieux" ("places") appears instead (Cahier IX, pp. 5r-7r, 11r). As for the
contents of the program itself, there are several entries amusingly different
from those in the edition, for example: "je dois être dans un fauteuil, je me
suis endormi au cercle contre la porte, on aura éteint sans me voir. Comment
sortir?" (Cahier IX, p. 9r; "No, I must be sitting in an armchair, I've probably
fallen asleep by the door at the Club, they've closed up without realizing I was
here. How will I be able to get out?") Even in the published versions, Proust
continued to modify the list, since "Doncières" (I, 9) does not appear in the
1913 Grasset edition (p. 10) but was added subsequently.

November 1913), "la tige du livre" ("the backbone of the book").[4]

There are several other systems of distribution in *La Recherche* which divide up the novel's material. Proust early experimented with identifying each individual created atmosphere with one of the novel's women:

> Une femme comme dans un tableau primitif est toujours restée pour moi profilée sur le paysage de nature ou de ville où je l'avais d'abord désirée. . . . Mais surtout par [les femmes], chaque année de ma vie a été placée dans un paysage habituellement inconnu et seulement désiré qui l'accompagne encore plus dans mon souvenir que celui où je l'ai vécue. Dans cette couleur que prend distinctement ainsi dans mon souvenir chaque année de ma vie, je ne saurais démêler si c'était le désir du pays qui me faisait y associer la femme ou si c'était l'amour de la femme qui me faisait désirer le pays. ["Un des premiers états de *Swann*," *Marcel Proust: Textes retrouvés*, p. 175]

> (A woman like the ones in primitive paintings has always remained silhouetted against the land- or cityscape where I had first desired her. . . . But especially because of [women], each year of my life has been placed in a usually unknown landscape, one rather longed for, which accompanies it more completely in my memory than the real one I lived in at that time. In that distinctive shading each year of my life takes in my memory, I would be unable to say if it was desire for the place that made me associate the woman with it, or love for the woman that made me long for the place.)

This initial project appears in the opening pages (in fact it precedes the evocation of the bedrooms): "Sometimes, as Eve was born from Adam's rib, a woman would be born

4. Léon Pierre-Quint, ed., *Comment parut "Du côté de chez Swann,"* p. 62.

from an awkward position of my thigh. . . . If, as sometimes happened, she had the features of a woman I had
known in the past, I would give myself over completely to
the task of recalling her" (I, 4–5). The motif is not developed systematically here, however. It is only near the end
of *Le Temps retrouvé* that the connection made in the
early sketch is consciously expressed; but this time the
periodic quality of the idea is stated with striking lucidity:

> Chacune [des femmes que j'avais connues] s'éle-
> vait, à un point différent de ma vie, dressée comme
> une divinité protectrice et locale, d'abord au milieu
> d'un de ces paysages rêvés dont la juxtaposition qua-
> drillait ma vie . . . ; ensuite vue du côté du souvenir,
> entourée des sites où je l'avais connue et qu'elle me
> rappelait, . . . car si notre vie est vagabonde notre
> mémoire est sédentaire, . . . nos souvenirs, . . . rivés
> aux lieux dont nous nous détachons, continuent à
> y combiner leur vie casanière. [III, 989]

> (Each of the women I had known stood, at a different
> point in my life, like a local tutelary deity, at first in
> the middle of one of those dream-landscapes whose
> juxtapositions marked off the periods of my life,
> . . . later seen from the side of memory, surrounded by
> the places I had known her in, and which she recalled
> to me, . . . for though our life is vagabond, our mem-
> ory is sedentary, . . . our recollections, . . . bound to
> the places which we have left behind, go on there lead-
> ing their everyday lives.)

The "local" influence of the successive women in the novel
at times was used by Proust as a transition technique. The
section of *A l'ombre des jeunes filles en fleurs* titled
"Autour de Mme Swann" opens with the narrator's parents' dinner for M. de Norpois. Mme Swann is nowhere to
be seen. However, Norpois's mentioning her effects the
necessary shift:

—Est-ce que vous étiez hier au banquet des Affaires étrangères?

—Non, répondit M. de Norpois, . . . j'avoue que je l'ai délaissé pour une soirée assez différente. J'ai dîné chez une femme dont vous avez peut-être entendu parler, la belle madame Swann. [I, 465]

("Were you at the Foreign Affairs dinner last night?" "No," M. de Norpois answered, . . . "I must admit I forsook it for a rather different sort of evening. I was invited to dinner by a lady of whom you've perhaps heard, the beautiful Mme Swann.")

The long section "around Mme Swann" then really begins with this remark, and from here on, until the period which closes the section (I, 641), we remain within the sphere of influence of Odette and her projection, Gilberte.

It is Gilberte who serves as the springboard in the next transition, the *in medias res* opening of "Noms de pays: le pays" already quoted ("J'étais arrivé à une presque complète indifférence à l'égard de Gilberte, quand deux ans plus tard je partis avec ma grand'mère pour Balbec"; I, 642; see p. 153). The dominant feminine presence of this part, however, is asserted in another internal shift, marked by the exordium (carefully distinguished from the preceding material by the three asterisks Proust ordered his typist to include at this point)[5] which describes the progress down the beach of the "petite bande" (I, 787–88), the "jeunes filles en fleurs" for whom the volume is named, and in whose shadow its action unfolds.

A number of shifts of atmosphere are accomplished by evoking the women who characterize the section over which they preside. The appearance (II, 11) of a miraculous "fée"—Oriane—defines the particular naïveté of *Le Côté de Guermantes I*. The opening of Guermantes II, as the action passes under the influence of Albertine, recalls the terms

5. See the letter published in André Maurois, *A la recherche de Marcel Proust*, pp. 290–91.

of the exordium (I, 4) in *Swann*: "Le brume, dès le réveil, avait fait de moi, au lieu de l'être centrifuge qu'on est par les beaux jours, un homme replié, désireux du coin du feu et du lit partagé, *Adam* frileux en quête d'une *Eve* sédentaire" (II, 346; "The mist, as soon as I awoke, had made me, not the centrifugal being one becomes in fine weather, but a person withdrawn, longing for hearth and shared bed, a shivering *Adam* searching for a sedentary *Eve*"). And after the long domination of Albertine, present at nearly all the beginnings in the three books devoted to her, the final volume opens at Tansonville under the sign of Gilberte rediscovered after so many years. Yet this is a distribution so imperfectly realized that at times we may be persuaded that we, rather than Proust, imagined it.

There are other distributions which are entirely clear and methodical. The most obvious is the "Stations du 'Transatlantique'" in *Sodome II*. The device is simple, quite successful, and at one point Proust even considerably explains it: "The recollection concerning Morel relates to an incident of a more particular kind. There were others of the same sort, but I am content here, as the little train progresses down the line and the conductor calls out the stops at Doncières, Grattevast, Maineville and so on, to note down what each little resort or garrison town calls up in my memory" (II, 1076). Like "chambres" the device operates by presetting the transitions (here between the successive vignettes) so that the shifts of subject are effected through a simple reference to the next station in the series.[6]

Changing names—of railroad stations or of bedrooms—is a surprisingly widespread motif in *La Recherche*. As in *La Cousine Bette* Balzac systematically marked the stages of

6. Moreover, a marginal note in the manuscript discloses that Proust would willingly have further segmented the anecdotes and emphasized the discreteness of the stations by coordinating them with Brichot's etymologies: "It would be better to have the etymologies given on the trip there; Albertine asks Brichot for them as each station goes by" (II, 1099, n. 2).

his action by giving his protagonist Baron Hulot a new alias each time, Proust arranges for Odette, depending upon the period, to be known variously as La Dame en rose, Miss Sacripant, Mme de Crécy, Mme Swann and Mme de Forcheville. He even provides her with a series of appellations for the English which evolve over time. The detail was conscious (see III, 788). While in *Swann* Odette de Crécy affects a cordial "our neighbors the English" (I, 78), as Mme Swann her affectation is more familiar: "our good neighbors on the Thames" (I, 535); in wartime it is properly militant: "our loyal allies" (III, 788). Such minor details suggest the depth of the distributing tendency in *La Recherche*.

The most coherently worked out distribution in the novel remains to be discussed: the "deux côtés" ("the two 'ways'"). This part of the novel employs distribution with paradigmatic clarity.

Program: "Car il y avait autour de Combray deux 'côtés' pour les promenades, et si opposés qu'on ne sortait pas en effet de chez nous par la même porte, quand on voulait aller d'un côté ou de l'autre: le côté de Méséglise-la-Vineuse, qu'on appelait aussi le côté de chez Swann parce qu'on passait devant la propriété de M. Swann pour aller par là, et le côté de Guermantes" (I, 134).

("For walks, there were two 'ways' in the neighborhood of Combray, in such opposite directions that we left our house by different doors depending on which of the two we had decided to take: one in the direction of Méséglise-la-Vineuse, which we also called Swann's way because we went by Swann's estate on that walk, and the other the Guermantes way.")

First Element: "Quand on voulait aller du côté de Méséglise, on sortait (pas trop tôt, et même si le ciel était couvert, parce que la promenade n'était pas bien longue et n'entraînait pas trop) comme pour aller n'importe où, par la grande porte de la maison de ma tante sur la rue du Saint-Esprit" (I, 135).

("When we had decided to take the Méséglise way, we would leave (not too early, and even if it was cloudy, because the walk wasn't a long one and involved no strain) as we ordinarily did to go anywhere, by the front door of my aunt's house on the Rue du Saint-Esprit.")

Thirty pages of development follow.

Second Element: "S'il était assez simple d'aller du côté de Méséglise, c'était une autre affaire d'aller du côté du Guermantes, car la promenade était longue et l'on voulait être sûr du temps qu'il ferait. . . . On partait tout de suite après déjeuner par la petite porte du jardin et on tournait dans la rue des Perchamps" (I, 165).

("Taking the Méséglise way was relatively easy, but the Guermantes way was another matter, since the walk was long and one wanted to be certain that the weather would hold. . . . We would leave right after lunch by the little garden gate and turn at the Rue des Perchamps.")

Twenty pages of development follow, plus two pages of conclusion, and "Combray" is over.

Before the post-1913 enlargement of the novel upset the pattern, the same configuration was to have served to pre-set the atmosphere of its first two volumes. From the early state of *La Recherche* represented in "Un des premiers états de *Swann*" (1908–1909) to the pages of *La Fugitive* and *Le Temps retrouvé* that no doubt echo the résumé of the thematic in the original third volume, this distribution remains a constant structuring force.[7]

7. The 1908–1909 sketch: "C'est sur le côté de Méséglise que j'ai remarqué les rayons d'or du soleil couchant, . . . c'est du côté de Guermantes que j'ai vu dans les bois où nous nous reposions le soleil tourner lentement autour des arbres" (*Textes retrouvés*, p. 175; "It was on the Méséglise way that I noticed the golden rays of the setting sun, . . . it was on the Guermantes way that I saw the sun circulate slowly around the trees in the woods where we rested").

La Recherche: "Le côté de Méséglise et le côté de Guermantes se touchent" (III, 672; "The Méséglise way and the Guermantes way connect"); "avant tout venaient aboutir à [Mlle de Saint-Loup] les deux grands 'côtés' où j'avais fait tant de promenades et de rêves" (III, 1029; "above all the two main 'ways' where I had so often walked and dreamed both led to Mlle de Saint-Loup").

Yet after "Combray," it too suffers the blurring of contours seen repeatedly above. As in the case of "chambres," the procedure could have spanned the entire novel, and at the moment of conception was probably intended to do so. With the passage of time and the evolution of the book, however, it underwent erosion. There is something constant in the indecisiveness of these executions that fail to sustain the clarity and symmetry of their original patterns.

Confrontation was the procedure Proust hoped might solve the problem of his transitions. Around this use of involuntary memory as a transition technique he built up a metaphysic, claiming that upon it "j'asseois . . . toute ma théorie de l'art" ("I base . . . my whole theory of art").[8] Practically, however, the object of confrontation is simply to make every instant of the narrator's past retrievable at any point in the telling. This requires a sense of intimate relation linking distant elements in Marcel's past, and it is by asserting the existence of such a system of relations that Proust tried to give intellectual substance to the procedure:

> S'il s'agit uniquement de nos coeurs, le poète a eu raison de parler des "fils mystérieux" que la vie brise. Mais il est encore plus vrai qu'elle en tisse sans cesse entre les êtres, entre les événements, qu'elle entrecroise les fils, qu'elle les redouble pour épaissir la trame, *si bien qu'entre le moindre point de notre passé et tous les autres un riche réseau de souvenirs ne laisse que le choix de communications.* [III, 1030]
>
> (If he was thinking only of our hearts, the poet was right to speak of the "mysterious threads" that life snaps. But it is even truer that life weaves others continuously between people, between events, tangling the threads, doubling them up to thicken the weft, *so that*

8. "A propos du 'style' de Flaubert" (1919), *CSB*, p. 599.

between the smallest point of our past and all other
points a dense network of memories only asks us to
choose the connection we wish to follow.)

By evoking the appropriate relation, attention could be
made to pass from virtually any given moment to any
other. Viewed coldly, such subjective motivation of scenes
is just as arbitrary as the manipulated thought associations
examined earlier in this chapter. But the mystique of
involuntary memory adds an element of inscrutability
which resists logical reduction. The semimagical atmosphere surrounding these transitions makes them compelling. If the abrupt "We must now return to the man
from Somewhere" seems to contaminate the fabric of the
narrative, the transition by involuntary memory appears
pure. This is precisely what Proust observed about it in his
most important study of novelistic technique outside *La
Recherche*:

> Sans parler en ce moment de la valeur que je trouve
> à ces ressouvenirs inconscients, . . . et pour m'en
> tenir au point de vue de la composition, j'avais simple-
> ment pour passer d'un plan à un autre plan, *usé non
> d'un fait mais de ce que j'avais trouvé plus pur, plus
> précieux comme jointure*, un phénomène de mémoire.
> Ouvrez les Mémoires d'Outre-Tombe ou les Filles du
> Feu de Gérard de Nerval. Vous verrez que [ces] deux
> grands écrivains . . . connurent parfaitement *ce procédé
> de brusque transition*. Quand Chateaubriand est—si je
> me souviens bien—à Montboissier, il entend tout à
> coup chanter une grive. Et ce chant qu'il écoutait si
> souvent dans sa jeunesse, le fait tout aussitôt revenir
> à Combourg, l'incite à changer, *et à faire changer le
> lecteur avec lui, de temps et de province.*[9]

(Without speaking here of the importance I consider

---

9. *Ibid.*, p. 599. The idea reappears in *Le Temps retrouvé* (III, 728 and 919–
20).

these unconscious recollections to have, . . . and limiting myself to the question of composition, I had simply employed, for moving from one level [or "subject"] to another, *not an event, but something I believe is a purer, more precious transition*, a phenomenon of memory. Open the *Mémoires d'Outre-Tombe* or the *Filles du Feu* of Gérard de Nerval. You will see that these two great writers . . . were perfectly familiar with *this rapid transition technique*. When Chateaubriand is—if memory serves—at Montboissier, suddenly he hears a thrush sing. And this song, which he used to listen to in his youth, immediately brings him back to Combourg, causes him to change, *and to make the reader change with him*, from one time and place to another.)

Maurice Blanchot raised an essential problem concerning this procedure: "Il semble que Proust [in writing *Jean Santeuil*] conçoit alors un art plus pur, concentré sur les seuls instants, sans remplissage, sans appel aux souvenirs volontaires, ni aux vérités d'ordre général formées ou ressaisies par l'intelligence . . . : en somme un récit 'pur' qui serait fait de ces seuls points d'où il prend origine . . . : '. . . Pour n'écrire que quand un passé ressuscitait soudain dans une odeur, dans une vue qu'il faisait éclater et au-dessus duquel palpitait l'imagination et quand cette joie me donnait l'inspiration'" ("It appears that when Proust was writing *Jean Santeuil*, he had a conception of a purer art, concentrating only on moments free of other material, refusing any appeal to voluntary memory or to general truths formed in, or perceived by, the intellect . . . : that is to say, a 'pure' narration made up only of these unique moments in which it arose . . . : ' . . . I would write only when a past came back to life in an odor, a sight, that it expanded, and above which the imagination fluttered; and only when that joy inspired me'").[10] Blanchot (whether or

10. "L'Expérience de Proust" (1954), reprinted in *Le Livre à venir*, pp. 27–28. The passage quoted by Blanchot is from *Jean Santeuil*, p. 401.

not he is right concerning *Jean Santeuil*) poses the question of technical consistency which has come up repeatedly in this chapter, concerning precisely the procedure
that, had it been consistently used, would have assured the
quintessential "récit 'pur.'"

But the reality of the technique in *La Recherche* is
decidedly different. There have been critical disputes concerning exactly how many experiences of involuntary
memory appear in the novel.[11] But in *La Recherche* there
is just one example of confrontation—of involuntary
memory used for transition—and that is the madeleine.
Though it seems extraordinary that Proust should have
failed to re-use such an attractive device, not one of the
other tableaux in the novel is, as he puts it, "[suspendu]
à une sensation du genre de celle de la madeleine" (III,
919; "suspended from a sensation like that of the madeleine").

Only the madeleine episode actually generates within the
novel the exhaustive transcription of the segment of the
past it calls up. The other experiences of involuntary memory tell us in a paragraph or a page how one or another
scene of the past has been resurrected for Marcel, but they
do not signal the beginning of a re-creation in the text
itself. Such is Marcel's discovery of the "intermittences du
coeur" ("the discontinuity of the heart") (II, 755–57), the
emotional revelation of his grandmother's death. The scene
occurs on the first night of the second summer in Balbec,
when Marcel bends down to remove his shoes, something
his grandmother has always done for him. The narrator
begins his account of the moment with a sentence which
from him is astonishing, since it is not a sentence at all:

11. Does one include the steeples of Martinville and the three trees of
Hudimesnil? or the passage in *Jeunes filles* where the hawthorns past their
season re-create the atmosphere of May in Combray (I, 922)? or the one in
La Prisonnière where the smell of kindling recalls autumn in Combray and
Doncières (III, 26)? Roger Shattuck's list is probably the most complete
(*Proust's Binoculars*, pp. 70–74); it contains fifteen examples.

"Bouleversement de toute ma personne." ("Upheaval of my whole being.") Immediately, his grandmother appears before him. What follows, however, is not the evocation of that segment of the past resurrected by involuntary memory (the first summer in Balbec) but instead the continuation of the tale which the sudden discovery had interrupted, the story of the second vacation at the Grand-Hôtel.

The four consecutive experiences of involuntary memory in *Le Temps retrouvé* are no different. It is not possible to support the idea of a cyclical, continuous structure in which these four final incidents would have their transcriptions not following (as the madeleine) but preceding them. The fiction of the novel is reflexive; we pretend that at the end of the narrative Marcel is on the point of setting out to write the novel—the narrative itself. But to give substance to the suggestion that the four incidents of involuntary memory were recapitulated in previous portions of the novel, Proust would have had to provide them with a much more regular content than they have. If for example the resurrections had been of Combray, of Paris, of the first summer in Balbec, and then of the second, we might have seen *La Recherche* as the consecutive unfolding of each of these tableaux—which would have made the series of experiences at the end a reflexive "program" for the entire novel.

But the four incidents have no such regular structure. The first (III, 866) recalls Venice, one of the book's least important episodes. The second (III, 868) recalls only the quiet country scene Marcel had viewed from his train the day before (III, 854-55). The feel of a starched napkin (III, 868-69) recalls the first summer at Balbec; the noise of a water pipe (III, 874) does the same. The only effort at providing a basis for the circularity of the novel is the points of suspension which interrupt Marcel's musing when he sees *François le Champi* in the Prince's library: "C'était de cette soirée, où ma mère avait abdiqué, que datait . . .

le déclin de ma volonté. . . . J'avais pris ma résolution,
j'avais sauté du lit et étais allé . . . m'installer à la fenêtre
. . . jusqu'à ce que j'eusse entendu partir M. Swann. Mes
parents l'avaient accompagné, j'avais entendu la porte du
jardin s'ouvrir, sonner, se refermer..." (III, 1044; these final
points of suspension are in the text); "It was from that
evening [at Combray], when my mother had abdicated,
that the weakness of my will . . . dated. . . . I had made my
decision, had jumped out of bed and gone . . . to the window . . . until I heard Swann depart. My parents had walked
with him, I had heard the garden gate open, heard the little
bell ring, heard the gate shut..."). And one might imagine
that the process of remembering, in the real time of the
novel, began here, with Combray. But if we accept this
idea, the madeleine incident, which equally serves to call
back Combray, loses its logic. The circularity of *La Recherche* does not convert the incidents of involuntary
memory at the end of the novel into transitional elements:
again the systematic working out of the idea is absent.

The transitions of *A la recherche du temps perdu* thus
exhibit a great diversity of forms, among which no ap-
preciable effort is made to exploit the most felicitous. The
patchwork effect makes Proust seem rather gauche, not
much of a technician in this aspect of his craft. Yet the
procedures which might have ensured much-increased
technical refinement were present all the time, were in
fact essential elements in the constitution of the novel. To
wonder why they were not turned to greater account is,
however, to ask another question: whether through
Proust's abstention from refining his transitions, other
aspects of the fabric of the tale are enhanced.

The answer is that when the transition, which is an
element of movement, is ragged, overt, brazenly manipulated, the effect is further to imprison the novel's action in
a static frame, further to suppress the sense of chronological direction which animates the active mode of narra-

tion. Mediating between his tableaux was therefore contrary to Proust's interests, and his experiment with the madeleine stands as proof of this. For although the madeleine rouses a Proustian scene with all the immediacy of its detail, coming in initial position it does not and was not intended to bridge the gap between *two* such scenes. In essence, the madeleine is a creation, not a transition; and there is no *transition* like it in the novel. As for those that do appear, often discordant, always somehow irregular, they exist in spite of themselves, to underline the primacy of tableaux which is the essence of narrative structure in *A la recherche du temps perdu.*

The creation of this scenic structure—by the techniques which function to devalue the active mode of narration, by more positive ones which sustain Proust's new narrative system—carries through the reconception of the Realist paradigm. Since 1830 novelists in France had struggled with the tensions inherent in Realism. But Proust's reformulation of them was the first to produce fiction whose expressive power and moral grasp clearly seem the equal of the Realist masterpieces. Proust's system was to be superseded in its turn by others, but none of these has redirected the tradition as decisively as did his. However much we long for their familiar simplicity, tales in the old style now seem like throwbacks to us. For this, Proust's remaking of the narrative tradition is principally responsible.

8

The Synthetic Mode

The Proustian scene is a closed system. Bounded at its edges by the summary transitions just discussed, its development is internal. Outside the scene, there is nothing; within it, Proust creates a population, an atmosphere, an entire iconography which in their independence refuse conjunction with any others.

One of the few procedures Proust openly admired in another writer is a transition technique in Flaubert: "One of the merits of Flaubert's style which impresses me most, since I find in it the conclusion of my own modest efforts, is that he is able to give a masterly impression of Time. In my opinion, the finest thing in *L'Education sentimentale* is not a sentence, but a blank space." He goes on to quote the famous passage following "Et Frédéric, béant, reconnut Sénécal" ("And Frédéric, open-mouthed, recognized Sénécal").[1] Proust is comparing Flaubert's use of whitespace with his own. But does the "extraordinary change in speed" that he admired in *L'Education* actually exist in *La Recherche*? Proust's movements between scenes made by leaving a blank on the page are usually simple cesuras denoting psychological and temporal discontinuity, separation rather than union:

> Certains jours où je ne l'avais pas vue [Mme Swann] allée des Acacias, il m'arrivait de la rencontrer dans l'allée de la Reine-Marguerite où vont les femmes qui cherchent à être seules, ou à avoir l'air de chercher à l'être; elle ne restait pas longtemps, bientôt rejointe

1. *L'Education*, Part III, ch. 6; "A Propos du 'style' de Flaubert" (1919), *CSB*, p. 595.

par quelque ami, souvent coiffé d'un "tube" gris, que
je ne connaissais pas et qui causait longuement avec
elle, tandis que leurs deux voitures suivaient.

Cette complexité du Bois de Boulogne qui en fait un
lieu factice et, dans le sens zoologique ou mythologique
du mot, un Jardin, je l'ai retrouvée cette année comme
je le traversais pour aller à Trianon, un des premiers
matins de ce mois de novembre. [I, 421-22]

(Certain days when I had not seen Mme Swann in the
Allée des Acacias, I might come upon her in the Allée
de la Reine-Marguerite, where women go to be alone,
or at least to seem to want to be alone; she would not
stay there long, since friends would soon find her, often
gentlemen wearing elegant grey top hats whom I didn't
know and who would speak at length with her while
their carriages followed along.

This complexity of the Bois de Boulogne which
makes it an artificial place and, in the zoological sense
of the word, a Garden, I rediscovered this year as I
passed through on my way to Trianon, one morning
early this November.)

The jump in age and season here, from late Spring to late
Autumn, from youth to full maturity, is too pat, too geo-
metrical, to produce the unexpected effect of temporal
thrust that Proust had admired in Flaubert. In crossing the
white-space in Proust, we are not abruptly precipitated
ahead, we are shepherded carefully over the interim and
find our balance undisturbed on the other side. In *La
Recherche* the blank space hides no drama; it is instead a
version of narrative punctuation—like "disons" or "anticipons," but reduced to a simple visual sign meaning that
one vein has played out, and another is about to be opened.
Like all of Proust's transitions, but more visibly than any
of the others, it stands as a partition between scenes, per-
mitting none of the energy on either side to cross.

A reflection in *Le Côté de Guermantes* reveals how thoroughly this structural discontinuity, so at odds with the practice of novelists before Flaubert, translates a new view of the shape of experience. The terms of the passage show how *inactive* existence has become for Proust, how completely memories have replaced concrete living as the locus for human significance:

> Est-ce parce que nous ne revivons pas nos années dans leur suite continue, jour par jour, mais dans le souvenir figé dans la fraîcheur ou l'insolation d'une matinée ou d'un soir, recevant l'ombre de tel site isolé, enclos, immobile, arrêté et perdu, loin de tout le reste, et qu'ainsi les changements gradués, non seulement au dehors, mais dans nos rêves et notre caractère évoluant, lesquels nous ont insensiblement conduits dans la vie d'un temps à tel autre très différent, se trouvent supprimés? [II, 397]

> (Is it because we live over the years of our past not in their continuous sequence, day by day, but in a memory attached to the coolness or the sunshine of a given morning or evening, or in the shade of some solitary place, a memory enclosed, immobile, fixed and hidden, distant from all others; and that thus the gradual changes not only outside, but within, in our dreams and in our personalities, which have imperceptibly accompanied us from the life of one time to another very different one, are eliminated?)

The number of scenes in *La Recherche* is relatively small. The novel's length is the product of the dilation of each of a few stationary tableaux, rather than of a large number of individual episodes of action. Within the tableaux, the descriptive mood is immensely protracted, perhaps beyond what we find in any other novel. Yet the period of time we are asked to sense passing is surprisingly narrow. Though the novel from Swann's love affair to the Guermantes matinée covers decades, within each scene we have the impression that at most a season elapses. The result of such limited action spread over such an expanse of pages is the snail's pace of *A la recherche du temps perdu*. It is true that in the indeterminate series of days which compose a Proustian scene, from time to time a progressive indication appears ("le lendemain," or "deux jours après"). But these signposts so rarely mark any decisive event that the slowness of the pace becomes, upon occasion, complete immobility. The scenic technique thus tends toward a monumental stasis, far beyond the stasis of plot line in Flaubert.

The discovery of Marcel's vocation seems as if it ought to imply a directed movement toward final insight. But as perceived, the movement within the book rather takes the form of indeterminate immersion in the sea of time. Because the individual tableaux are so thoroughly cut off from their neighbors, passing between them never gives the impression of directional movement. This is why the scenes in *La Recherche* appear not as consecutive but as concurrent; why the experience of reading the novel is one of accumulation, not of progression.

It is the absolute episodicity of the tableaux which allows us to see them as side-by-side rather than as successive.[2] Proust shunned elements within them that might have tended to create links beyond their boundaries. And though the metaphysics developed in *Le Temps retrouvé* preaches a unity of the human personality, in the novel identities are fragmented in such a way that the version each successive scene presents seems thoroughly discontinuous with the others. Because prerevelation immediately resolves concerns which might otherwise have thrown our attention beyond the boundaries of a scene, the sense of forward plot movement is stifled. Since Proust is always free to jump to a point "bien des années plus tard" to draw a conclusion or complete a pattern, the sense of

2. On this subject see the remarks of Georges Poulet, *L'Espace proustien*, p. 133.

measured progression toward this moment which would have developed over the longer term is negated. As Valéry wrote just after Proust died: "On peut ouvrir le livre où l'on veut; sa vitalité ne dépend point de ce qui précède ... ; elle tient à ce qu'on pourrait nommer l'activité propre du tissu même de son texte" ("One can open his book anywhere one likes; its vitality does not depend upon what precedes ... ; it is contained rather in what might be called the immediate life of the very material of which his text is composed").[3]

Because their internal autonomy appears so complete, the scenes, as we read them, do not seem subordinated to any whole. They are free to assimilate a diversity of material which in many other novels would disrupt formal organization. The humor of a remark in *Sodome et Gomorrhe* depends upon this. The narrator has been engaged in a particularly far-fetched divagation on the healthfulness of perspiration. The Marquis de Vaugoubert enters the room, and we read: "The proportions of the present work do not allow me to explain here following upon what youthful occurrences M. de Vaugoubert became one of the only men in society who was, as they say in Sodom, 'in on' M. de Charlus's secrets" (II, 642)—as if this (or any) subject risked disequilibrating the three thousand page bulk of *La Recherche* or appearing too improbable following a digression on sweat.

Proust is satirizing the dimensions of his book. But there is another side to the novel's capaciousness: if nearly anything can find a place nearly anywhere, then the free order of such *matériel de fortune* can produce no more than a minor sense of overall structuring. Once the matter of which a novel is made takes shape in collections rather than successions, the fundamental principles of tight form become irrelevant. From this perspective the sweep of the novel's pattern from beginning to end carries less significance than the impression of fullness created by each of its parts. Whence the primacy of the scene in Proust.

The manner in which the scenes were composed contributed to their independence within the novel's overall plan. Their beginnings and conclusions were generally established well before their substance was completely decided upon. Just as the discovery of Marcel's artistic vocation put a term upon the entire story, the transitions remained as constant end-points during expansions which saw the material within each scene multiply many times. Terminally circumscribed, these structures were internally free. If the saga (as Scholes and Kellogg put it in their discussion of narrative types) is "open-ended,"[4] then Proust's scenes, and the novel which accomodates them, open up from the middle to accomodate Proust's generous expansions.

The continuous increase in the novel's size over the decade and a half of its composition is well known. In letters to friends and publishers, Proust's estimates of its length inexorably inflated.[5] Proust's habit of dilating elements on every level of composition was responsible. His profuse additions to sentences and paragraphs, cramped into the margins of his school notebook pages or his successive sets of galley proofs, are notorious, and the problems they created for his publishers and printers were ex-

4. *The Nature of Narrative*, p. 236.

5. In March 1912 he predicted "800 to 900 pages" to Georges de Lauris (de Lauris, ed., *A un ami*, p. 229); in November of that year he told Gaston Gallimard that his first volume would require 550 pages "if each page has 35 or 36 lines of 45 characters"—"Let's say," as he ingenuously put it, "about the same length as *L'Education sentimentale*"—and that a second volume would be at least as long (*Lettres à la NRF*, pp. 94–95; the holograph of this letter in the Beinecke Library shows that Proust's figure of 550 pages was written over an earlier 600). The post-1913 decision to expand the Albertine story exaggerated this progression. In July of 1918 the book was expected to occupy five volumes, but toward the middle of 1920 it became clear to Gallimard that *Le Côté de Guermantes* would have to be divided in two; and by April 1921, eight volumes were announced. In 1922 this total had risen to ten, and when the editors finished transcribing the posthumous portions the final publication required sixteen.

treme. But it is because of Gallimard's complaints that some elements of Proust's attitude toward his method are available to us. "Cher ami et éditeur" ("Dear friend and publisher"), he wrote Gallimard (May 1919), "You appear to reproach me concerning my system of 'touching up' my manuscript. I admit that it does complicate things. . . . But since you have the kindness to find in my books a slight richness which you enjoy, please understand that this is precisely the result of that overnourishment I infuse into them while I live, which materially speaking is translated into my additions" (*Choix de lettres*, p. 244). The image reappears in *La Recherche*, when Marcel, considering the exigencies of the novel he will write, senses that he must "le suralimenter comme un enfant" (III, 1032; "overnourish it like an infant").

Another letter to Gallimard, written only a month or two before Proust died (end of September or October 1922), spoke more personally about the author's relation to his overflowing material.

> D'autres que moi, et je m'en réjouis, ont la jouissance de l'univers. Je n'ai plus ni le mouvement, ni la parole, ni la pensée, ni le simple bien-être de ne pas souffrir. Ainsi, expulsé pour ainsi dire de moi-même, je me réfugie dans les tomes que je palpe à défaut de les lire, et j'ai, à leur égard, les précautions de la guêpe fouisseuse. . . . Recroquevillé comme elle et privé de tout, je ne m'occupe plus que de leur fournir à travers le monde des esprits l'expansion qui m'est refusé [*Lettres à la NRF*, pp. 269–70]

> (Others, and I am happy for them, can enjoy the world outside. As for me, I can no longer move, nor speak, nor think, nor even experience the pleasure of not having any pain. Since I have been evicted from myself in this way, I have taken refuge in my books which I fondle without being able to read them, and with them I take the precautions of a digger-wasp. . . . Bent over

like the wasp and deprived of everything, I busy myself
only with providing via the world of spirits the growth
of my books that is denied to me.)

Expansion is the key here. The problem for Proust was
to bring out in their full density the forms latent in material already present.

Because the essence of the Proustian scene, abstracted
from the thrust and the drama of the active mode, is
static, the significant pattern to be developed in it took
not the form of movement, but the form of an image. This
is the most constant characteristic of Proust's perception:

> J'ai su pour quelque-unes [des images qui m'avaient
> frappé] découvrir la beauté ou la pensée qu'elles
> contenaient et qui m'avait fait à leur passage dresser
> l'oreille intérieure. Pour d'autres dans ma paresse je
> me disais: il suffit de me rappeler l'image, un jour je
> la prendrai, j'essayerai de l'ouvrir; et c'est ainsi que
> les ateliers de mon passé se sont encombrés de clo-
> chers, de têtes de jeunes filles, de fleurs fanées, de mille
> autres formes. ["Un des premiers états de *Swann*,"
> *Textes retrouvés*, p. 181]

> (For some of the images which had struck me I have
> been able to discover the particular beauty or the idea
> which they held within them and which had made my
> inner ear prick up as they went by. For others, in my
> laziness I said to myself: all I need to do is remember
> the image; some day I will take it, I will try to open it
> up; and thus the ateliers of my past are cluttered with
> steeples, girls' heads, faded flowers, and a thousand
> other forms.)

What is implicit in this fragment is stated clearly in others:
the natural function of memory is to create static images
of the places and people recalled. For example, consider

this passage from one of the early sketches in *Les Plaisirs et les jours*, whose title itself ("Les Regrets; Rêveries couleur du temps XVIII: Tableaux de genre du souvenir" ["Regrets; Reveries in the Color of Time XVIII: Genre Pictures of Memory"]) carries the meaning:

> Tout concourt à faire aujourd'hui de cette époque de ma vie comme une suite, coupée de lacunes, il est vrai, de petits *tableaux* pleins de vérité heureuse et de charme sur lesquels le temps à répandu sa tristesse douce et sa poésie. [*CSB*, p. 131]

> (Everything contributes to making that period of my life seem today a sequence, interrupted by gaps, to be sure, of little *images* full of happy truths and charm over which time has spread its sweet sadness and its poetry.)

This propensity for image-forming becomes the first axiom of Proustian epistemology: what we know of the world outside of us we know because our mind assimilates elements of it in the form of distinct figures:

> Pour entrer en nous, un être a été obligé de prendre la forme, de se plier au cadre du temps; ne nous apparaissant que par minutes successives, il n'a jamais pu nous livrer de lui qu'un seul aspect à la fois, nous débiter de lui qu'une seule *photographie*. [III, 478]

> (To enter into us, a person must have taken on the form, bent to the shape, of time; appearing to us only in successive instants, he can only have given us one aspect of himself at a time, provided us with but a single *photograph*.)

The image of a person or a place at a particular moment dominates the memory that calls it up, and reinforces the discontinuity of the scenes whose identity is the product

of the image-forming process. A number of parallel meta-
phors in the novel describe the phenomenon, the principal
term of comparison being the possibility of concurrent
images in visual art—what Joseph Frank has called "spatial
form." The description in *A l'ombre des jeunes filles en
fleurs* of the different moods of the sky at Balbec employs
several variations of this metaphor: at sunset, reflected in
the panes of Marcel's bookcase, it seemed "like these
different scenes which an old master executed long ago on
a reliquary, and whose separate faces are exhibited side by
side in a museum" (I, 803). At another time the reflections
"appeared to present something like the repetition, characteristic of certain contemporary masters, of one and the
same effect, seized at different times but which now with
the immobility of art can all be seen in the same room"
(I, 805).

But images in *La Recherche* are more complex than simple
snapshots, and Georges Poulet's judgment (*L'Espace proustien*, p. 124) that Proust is principally fascinated by
"l'instantanéité d'une attitude" ("the fleeting quality of an
attitude") is misleading. What is narrated in the novel lies
somewhere between the unique and the habitual, and seeks
to seize not simply an instant, but a whole pattern of
existence. The kind of concentration Proust sought is put
in a letter to Mme Straus, in which he admired a photograph she had given him. It is, he says, "si essentielle, si
contemporaine à vos aspects successifs, en son 'instant
éternel.' C'est l'instantané de ce qui dure dans la personne"
("so essential, so contemporary with your successive
aspects, in its 'eternal instant.' It is the snapshot of what is
constant in you").[6] The play on "instantané" reveals the
complexity of the effect Proust admired in the photograph
and, later, wished to create in his novel. His narration
strives to present the "eternal instant," the essence of characteristic experience—but without blotting out the variety

6. 12 May 1915; *Correspondance générale*, VI, 173. The photograph is re-
produced facing p. 48 of the same volume.

of the original events from which these essential meanings are synthesized. The effort to do this led Proust to the rather audacious solution of disguising habits as incidents, of casting the multiple as if it were individual. Proustian narration thus exists in a paralogical never-never land, neither completely one, nor explicitly many—like Mme Swann's *toilettes* in this curious passage from *A l'ombre des jeunes filles en fleurs*:

> Tout d'un coup, sur le sable de l'allée, tardive, alentie et luxuriante comme la plus belle fleur et qui ne s'ouvrirait qu'à midi, Mme Swann apparaissait, épanouissant autour d'elle une toilette *toujours différente mais que je me rappelle surtout mauve*. [I, 636]

> (All at once, upon the gravelled path, unhurrying, cool, and as luxuriant as the most exquisite flower which would not be fully open before noon, Mme Swann would appear, about her floating a dress which was *never twice the same, but which I remember typically as mauve*.)

The narrator's memory retains both the multiplicity of Odette's numerous costumes and the individuality of one, "surtout mauve." The event which occurred many times, the thing seen repeatedly over a long period, is presented, not explicitly as repetition, but rather with the increased concentration and weight of a single image synthesized in memory.

This is where the Proustian image forms, in creative memory. In an extraordinary expression of his distrust in concrete reality, Proust puts it this way: "*Perhaps because I have lost faith, perhaps because reality forms only in memory*, the flowers I see today for the first time do not seem like real flowers to me" (I, 184). The writer thus "remembers only the essential" (III, 900); the "essence" (III, 718) which characterizes the image is thus built into the structure of retrospective first-person narration, at the

same time as the activity and uncertainty of concrete social
life is increasingly excluded. The synthesizing process has
already taken place.

We rarely perceive this process in operation. At most it
reveals its functioning in phrases like "With diverse variations the following would happen . . . " (II, 799) or "I am
describing one of these dinners, which will give an idea of
what the others were like" (II, 1006). But usually there is
no acknowledgment of the multiplicity of the source
material that the single case narrated will represent: "[En
entrant chez Swann] je ne rencontrais d'abord qu'un valet
de pied" (I, 527; "Entering Swann's house at first I found
[or "would find"] only a footman") or "Voyant que
j'avais à rester longtemps devant les mosaïques qui repré-
sentaient le baptême du Christ, ma mère, sentant la fraîcheur glacée qui tombait dans le baptistère, me jetait un
châle sur les épaules" (III, 646; "Realizing that I would be
spending a long time contemplating the mosaics which
depict Christ's baptism, my mother, feeling the icy cold in
the baptistry, threw [or "would throw"] a shawl over my
shoulders"). These actions seem unique, but in context it
is clear that each epitomizes a fact or gesture repeated
many times, which the narrative has condensed into a
synthetic image. (In the first example the contextual proof
is on the following page: "I would continue waiting, *alone,
or with Swann* and often Gilberte as well"; in the second
example, on the page preceding: "*most frequently* I would
go off to San Marco. . . .") Arriving at Swann's to wait for
Odette, leaving for San Marco to admire the mosaics, were
daily events at a certain period. Memory blurs, and the telling slides lightly over, their day-to-day variations, and the
rich, dense images formed by this distillation of individual
experiences come to represent a higher-order reality.

The poise of Proust's narration between specific events
and generalized abstractions is a delicate equilibrium. The
hardness of unique actions and the progressive thrust of
the active mode had to be deemphasized for this equilib-

rium to exist at all. The image had to remain based on sen-
suous impressions, but not tied to any single instance; and
this delicate balance was achieved in all the finest parts of
A la recherche du temps perdu. Realist structure and
techniques seem very distant from this complex illusion,
which can be called the synthetic mode of narration. Its
full, coherent development shows how far Proust passed
beyond the implications of narrative in Flaubert.

The internal variety of the material telescoped in a synthetic image is still present. In this, the Proustian image is
different from an idealized composite. Proust speaks of
how an artist must have seen many churches to be able to
paint a single one (III, 907). But if the result of these
multiple experiences becomes a Viollet-le-Duc reconstruc-
tion of the "typical" Gothic church, it is not synthetic at
all. What no "typical" composite can show is the irregu-
larity of its sources. It chooses between the quadripartite
vault of Saint-Denis and the sexpartite vault of Notre-
Dame de Paris; between the clarity of Bourges and the
luminosity of Chartres. But the synthetic image is capable
of absorbing such elements of diversity, even of contradiction:

> Dès que j'eus reconnu le goût du morceau de madeleine
> trempé dans le tilleul que me donnait ma tante, . . .
> aussitôt la vieille maison grise sur la rue, où était sa
> chambre, vint . . . s'appliquer au petit pavillon donnant
> sur le jardin, qu'on avait construit pour mes parents
> sur ses derrières (ce pan tronqué que seul j'avais revu
> jusque-là); et avec la maison, la ville, *depuis le matin
> jusqu'au soir et par tous les temps*, la Place où j'allais
> faire des courses, les chemins qu'on prenait si le temps
> était beau. [I, 47]

> (As soon as I had recognized the taste of the bite of
> madeleine dipped in *tilleul* that my aunt used to give
> me, . . . the old house with the grey front where her

room was rose to . . . connect up with the little pa-
vilion on the garden which had been constructed behind the house for my parents (and which was the only
part I had been able to recall until then); and with the
house, the town, *from morning until evening and in
every kind of weather*, the square where I used to go
shopping, the paths where we would go walking if it
was nice outside.)

And the rich image of Combray in the novel contains the
village in all its seasons, all its moods.

The synthesizing function of memory easily subdivides
the image into an array, like the altarpiece the narrator
himself takes as a term of comparison (I, 803), in which
coordinate aspects appear side-by-side to increase the
density and variety of representation. Proust usually establishes his array by a series of adverbial phrases, forming a
miniature "program," as in the transitions discussed above.
For example: "When we wanted to walk along the Méséglise way, we went out" (I, 135); "*Often* the sky clouded
over"; "*But at other times* rain began to fall"; "*Frequently,
too,* we would take shelter" (I, 150); "*Sometimes* the
weather was positively bad" (I, 152); "*If it was already
rainy* in the morning, my parents would give up the
walk" (I, 153), and so on. When the array is simpler and
only one variant of the image requires treatment, a single
adverb suffices: "*often* on the square, as we were returning, my grandmother made me stop " (I, 63); or even "For
a long time, I used to go to bed early. *Sometimes*, with my
candle hardly out, my eyes would close so quickly" (I, 3).

The last example recalls that *A la recherche du temps
perdu* opens squarely in the synthetic mode:

Longtemps, je me suis couché de bonne heure. Parfois,
à peine ma bougie éteinte, mes yeux se fermaient si
vite que je n'avais pas le temps de me dire: "Je m'en-

dors." Et, une demi-heure après, la pensée qu'il était temps de chercher le sommeil m'éveillait; je voulais poser le volume que je croyais avoir encore dans les mains et souffler ma lumière; je n'avais pas cessé en dormant de faire des réflexions sur ce que je venais de lire, mais ces réflexions avaient pris un tour un peu particulier; il me semblait que j'étais moi-même ce dont parlait l'ouvrage: une église, un quatuor, la rivalité de François Ier et de Charles-Quint. Cette croyance survivait pendant quelques secondes à mon réveil; elle ne choquait pas ma raison, mais pesait comme des écailles sur mes yeux et les empêchait de se rendre compte que le bougeoir n'était plus allumé. Puis elle commençait à me devenir inintelligible. [I, 3]

(For a long time I used to go to bed early. Sometimes, with my candle hardly out, my eyes would close so quickly that I would not have the time to tell myself: "I'm falling asleep." And half an hour later, the thought that it was time to try to close my eyes would wake me up; I would try to put aside the book I imagined I was still holding and blow out the light; I had continued while asleep thinking about what I had just been reading, but these reflections had taken a rather odd turn; it seemed to me that I was myself whatever the book was discussing: a church, a quartet, the rivalry between François I and Charles V. That impression would persist for a few seconds after my awakening; it did not shock my sense of logic, but weighed like scales upon my eyes and prevented them from realizing that the candle was no longer lit. Then it would drift into unintelligibility.)

This passage (owing to differences between French and English verbal structures I refer necessarily to the French text) begins by asserting the repetitiveness of the event recounted: *"Longtemps* je me suis couché"; *"Parfois . . .*

mes yeux se fermaient si vite. . . ." But as early as the third sentence of the novel, these adverbial signs disappear, and the series of verbs in the imperfect come to take on the feel of a single progressive narration. By a subtle camouflage, the stages of repeated experience now recalled become stages of an experience that *could be* unique. Delicately but decisively we have been drawn into the unfolding of one quintessential nighttime scene.

Proust thus needed only to allow the drift toward ambiguity to proceed until the original coordinates which situate the scene blurred. Then the synthetic account begins quite automatically. A look at the text of the opening pages will show how freely this kind of narration can move in and out of the synthetic, via the intermediate composite stage governed by adverbs like "parfois," "souvent," "tous les jours."

Navigating within this mode requires a special kind of mental flexibility to pretend there is nothing anomalous in shifting between contradictory versions of the same experience. For example, in the preliminary recollection of Combray (I, 9–10), the narrator tells the story of Golo, among the multiple legends shown on his magic lantern, as if he were seeing it for the first time. He guesses the color of Geneviève de Brabant's castle before it appears—something that could only have happened once. Then, alarmed by the story, he rushes downstairs to the brightly-lit dining room where Françoise serves a "boeuf à la casserole" (I, 10). We cannot assume that the family had this dish every night. Giving the menu, however, increases the impression created by the entire passage: that what is told is a unique occurrence. Yet other details show this is impossible. We cross the blank space (p. 9) and find ourselves in Combray. The characteristic adverbial introduction of a synthetic image follows immediately: "*tous les jours* dès la fin de l'après-midi . . . ." But Proust shades the situation thus established, interposing another adverb, this one ambiguous, which alters the effect of "tous les jours":

A Combray, *tous les jours* dès la fin de l'après-midi,
. . . ma chambre redevenait le point fixe et douloureux
de mes préoccupations. On avait bien inventé, pour me
distraire les soirs où on me trouvait l'air trop mal-
heureux, de me donner une lanterne magique. . . . Mais
ma tristesse n'en était qu'accrue, parce que rien que le
changement d'éclairage détruisait l'habitude que j'avais
de ma chambre et grâce à quoi . . . elle m'était devenue
supportable. *Maintenant* je ne la reconnaissais plus. . . .
Au pas saccadé de son cheval, Golo . . . sortait de la
petite forêt triangulaire. [I, 9]

(At Combray, *every day* at the end of the afternoon,
. . . my bedroom would become the fixed and melancholy focus of my anxieties. To be sure, to distract me
during the evenings when I seemed especially unhappy,
I had been given a magic lantern. . . . But my misery
was only made greater, because even the alteration of
the lighting destroyed the customary familiarity of
my room, thanks to which . . . it had become livable.
Now I no longer recognized it. . . .
Riding at a jerky trot, Golo . . . emerged/would
emerge from the little triangular forest.)

"Maintenant" is indeterminate. Logically, it differentiates
the time preceding the magic lantern's acquisition from the
subsequent period. But its sense vacillates regardless of
logic, and it seems to take on as well the word's more
usual sense, denoting a unique present, an authentic "here
and now"—just the sense it has, for example, on the page
preceding, where Proust, in the temporal ambiguity of
"chambres," writes: "Certes, j'étais bien éveillé *maintenant*" (I, 8; "To be sure, I was fully awake *now*"). The
account of Golo and of Françoise's dinner menu do not
shock us since, through the ambiguity, the mode has passed
from the composite "tous les jours" to the pure synthetic.

The advantage of synthetic over composite telling is

great coherence of representation, a drawing together of
the effect where a cumulative account could not avoid
scattering it. The synthetic is the primary mode of narration in *A la recherche du temps perdu*. Some portions of
the novel are so dominated by it that their entire chronology becomes a projection of the procedure's unifying
tendency. These sections take the form of immense single
images of a "typical" day, and can be called "synthetic
days": Marcel's childhood in Combray; the emotion-filled
autumn of *Le Côté de Guermantes*; the long period of life
in Paris with Albertine as captive; the atmosphere of the
First World War at the beginning of *Le Temps retrouvé*.[7]
Synthetic days are extensions of the pattern observed in
"chambres," where the narration is organized so that the
events recounted seem to have occurred in the course of a
single night of insomnia. But the quantity of material
treated in the synthetic days is enormous.

It seems Proust experimented with the technique in *Jean
Santeuil*, The section the Pléiade editors have entitled "A
Illiers" develops both the daily and seasonal chronologies
that later entered into the conflation of "Combray." The
section opens around Easter (*Jean Santeuil*, p. 277), progresses through May (p. 278), the end of May (p. 313),
summer (p. 327), and finishes very late in the season (p.
352; cf. p. 308). Simultaneously it moves through a daily
cycle beginning at seven o'clock (p. 284), reaching lunch-
time (p. 286) and coffee following (p. 290), the after-
lunch walk (p. 300), just before dinner (p. 316), and the
coming of evening (p. 321).[8] The movement in "Combray"

7. H. R. Jauss was the first critic to describe these important structures in
*La Recherche: Zeit und Erinnerung in Marcel Prousts "A la recherche du temps
perdu"*; the most accessible account of them is probably John P. Houston's
excellent article, "Temporal Patterns in *A la recherche du temps perdu*."

8. As the Pléiade editors note (p. 277, n. 1) it is uncertain that the series of
fragments in this section of *Jean Santeuil* were meant to be read in the order
in which they are printed (which generally follows Fallois's arrangement for
the original edition of the novel). But since the synthetic day technique is
quite clear in "Combray" it does not seem unreasonable to seek its origins
here in this earlier material on the same subjects.

is similar, with the addition of a third evolving scale measured in years, most easily perceptible in the gradual aging and eventual death of Tante Léonie.

The synopsis of the trivial which is so characteristic of "Combray" and the tense, impotent maneuvering condensed into the deception of a winter Sunday (see III, 139, 144, 174) which distinguishes *La Prisonnière* are examples of the way the synthetic day procedure can vividly represent the characteristic tone of a period. Organizing the episodes around the events of one synthetic day captures this tone while reinforcing the novel's pattern of scenic autonomy.

The indispensable element in synthetic narration and in the creation of these synthetic days is the imperfect tense. The imperfect in French expresses a variety of linguistic situations which have no parallel in the English imperfect (this is why imitation of Proust's synthetic mode in English is so unsatisfactory). Particularly, the French imperfect expresses through the same verb form both the durative (or progressive) and the iterative (or habitual) aspects of the verb.[9] The imperfect's ability to carry these two verbal meanings, which are fundamentally unlike, is central to Proust's treatment of past events.[10] The subtle shading

9. "Aspect" describes the manner in which the action expressed by a verb develops, without reference to the action's position in time or the verb's meaning. "I was talking" and "I used to talk" represent in English the durative and iterative aspects in the past tense. French *je parlais* expresses both of these. See Arne Klum, *Verbe et adverbe*, pp. 105ff.; Holger Sten, *Les Temps du verbe fini (indicatif) en français moderne*, pp. 125–83; and Howard Garey, "Verbal Aspect in French."

10. Since synthetic narration depends upon an inherent characteristic of French verbal grammar, it hardly makes sense to say Proust "invented" the technique. He was, however, interested in its history—or more accurately, in the history of evocative uses of the imperfect. His 1919 essay on Flaubert represents the first time critical attention was given to Flaubert's remarkably expressive use of tenses to alter the appearance of narrated material: "That eternal imperfect . . . entirely changes the appearance of things and people" ("A propos du 'style' de Flaubert," *CSB*, p. 590). However, Proust's most

which permits him to move from a composite situation (governed by adverbs like "longtemps" or "tous les jours") to the pure synthetic depends upon his freedom to change the mode without any alteration in the verb form. While the narration goes repeatedly in and out of the pure synthetic, the imperfects simply continue in their indeterminacy.

Moreover, passage from one of the narrative modes to the other is scarcely perceptible as such. The appearance of an adverbial expression like "une fois" permits a specific event to emerge from the flow of remembrance in the synthetic mode. Later, the return of the imperfects quietly effects the resorption of the active. The effect achieved by this easy variation of the modes of narration is an uninterrupted, expansive current of recollection, to which each mode contributes something that the other would have been strained to give.

Some events in the novel, of course, had to be told in the active mode. The first entrance of a character required a shift to capture unique happenings. A large number of the events in the numerous *matinées* and *dîners* (though not as many as one might at first expect) are recounted as individual events, underlined by the specificity of reported dialogue. Most important, the active is the mode of crisis in *La Recherche*.

---

interesting reflections on the use of this tense occur in the essay he wrote to preface his translation of Ruskin's *Sesame and Lilies*: "J'avoue que certain emploi de l'imparfait de l'indicatif—de ce temps cruel qui nous présente la vie comme quelque chose d'éphémère à la fois et de passif, qui, au moment même où il retrace nos actions, les frappe d'illusion, les anéantit dans le passé sans nous laisser comme le parfait, la consolation de l'activité—est resté pour moi une source inépuisable de mystérieuses tristesses" ("Journées de Lecture" [1905], *CSB*, p. 170n.; "I admit that a certain use of the imperfect indicative—this cruel tense that presents life to us as something at once ephemeral and passive, which, at the same time as it retraces our actions, transforms them into illusions, annihilates them in the past without leaving us, as does the preterite, the consolation of activity—has never ceased to be an inexhaustible source of mysterious sadness for me").

But the techniques for devaluating suspense examined above redefine the perspective in which crisis appears. Proust's narration shifts the balance of the dramatic and the scenic, of event and image. We are far from the Realist paradigm: no longer does the novelist struggle to make the events in his plot carry the story's emotional and moral significance.

In terms of the view of human experience expressed in the structure of Proust's narration, it is striking how the synthetic mode leaves behind no feeling of decisive result. The atmosphere which accompanies an action in *La Recherche* is so richly present, the characters are so completely immersed in it, that they seem victims of its timeless evolution. To be indefinitely in the course of becoming is never finally to become. Thus as Proust's duratives expand to embrace every nuance of a tonality from the past, individual actors seem to be struck by a paralysis which prevents them from engaging in their own experience. This is Fabrice's dilemma in *La Chartreuse*, powerfully magnified.

Moreover, this stifling pictorial representation created through the durative imperfects which underlie Proust's synthetic narration gives way, at a very limited number of the novel's critical points, to the present tense—the pictorial tense par excellence. The effect is to create, despite the logic of grammar, an even more immediate illusion. These shifts to the present tense occur in two moments of extreme emotional importance.[11] The best-known is the account of the madeleine:

Accablé par la morne journée, . . . je portai à mes

11. Proust was aware that these shifts to the present seemed facile if overused. He had warned Mme de Noailles (in a letter, 18 June 1905, about her novel *La Domination*) of precisely this danger; *Correspondance générale*, II, 121–22. In addition to the account of the madeleine and the moment in *La Fugitive* to be discussed in the next chapter, Proust also shifted to the present tense to translate Marcel's excitement at discovering his article published in the *Figaro* (III, 568). The technique in this case seems more questionable; indeed, there is some evidence (the variant at the bottom of III, 571) that Proust may have begun to change the tenses here back to the past.

lèvres un cuillerée du thé. . . . Je tressaillis. . . . Un
plaisir délicieux m'avait envahi. . . . D'où avait pu
venir cette puissante joie? Je sentais qu'elle était
liée au goût du thé et du gâteau. . . . Je *bois* une seconde gorgée, . . . une troisième qui m'apporte un peu
moins que la seconde. Il est temps que je m'arrête. . . .
Il est clair que la vérité que je cherche n'est pas en
[le breuvage], mais en moi. . . . Je pose la tasse. . . .
Et je recommence à me demander. . . . [etc.]
    Et tout d'un coup le souvenir m'*est apparu*. Ce
goût, c'était celui . . . [the pasts return]. [I, 45–46]

    (Depressed by the dull day, . . . I raised a spoonful of
the tea to my lips. . . . A trembling went through me.
. . . An exquisite pleasure had entered my body. . . .
Where could such a powerful sense of joy have come
from? I sensed that it was related to the taste of the
tea and the madeleine. . . . I *drink* a second swallow,
. . . a third which brings me a little less than the second. It is time to stop. . . . Obviously the truth I am
looking for is not in the tea, but in myself. . . . I put
the cup down. . . . And I continue to ask myself. . . .
[etc.]
    And suddenly the memory *appeared*. The taste was
. . . [the pasts return].)

The description, governed by "un jour d'hiver" (I, 44)
necessarily begins in the active mode. The effect is careful,
systematic—but remote—recollection. But with the change
of tense (first to the pictorial imperfect, then to the present) the account becomes intimate, actualized. At the
same time, however, Marcel seems momentarily dissolved
in the intense atmosphere, thoroughly confused and unable to make sense of his sudden experience. The qualities
which characterize the synthetic mode operate in these
momentary presents with even greater force.
    A still more impressive instance of the present tense's
abrupt appearance in the texture of an account in the past

occurs in *La Fugitive*. This striking moment is part of the brilliantly orchestrated variation of the modes running through the entire Albertine story. The expressive effects Proust achieved by playing off the modes against each other in this latest part of *La Recherche* show the novel's narrative system at its furthest point of development. The power of the technique is exceptional, and it deserves to be examined in detail.

9

Narration in *La Fugitive*

La Fugitive expresses the pessimism at the heart of post-Flaubertian fiction as clearly as any twentieth-century text. This volume is Proust's brilliant, bitter witness to the catastrophic hostility of the world outside the self, and to the irreducible isolation of the individual. The defensive strategy of withdrawal that has been evident since Stendhal produces in *La Fugitive* Proust's most fully developed conceptualization—and critique—of social experience.

We recall Lucien de Rubempré collapsing by the side of Coralie's grave. Anguish in such situations is elemental; it puts us face to face with one of our most primitive fears. The disappearance of the person who had become his hope for love leaves Lucien momentarily confronting the loneliness and despair which underlie *Illusions perdues* from beginning to end but are nowhere else as naked as here. "Par qui serais-je aimé? se demanda-t-il" (*Illusions perdues*, p. 537; "'Who will love me now?' he asked himself"). The simplicity of the question is eloquent. Along with parallel moments in Stendhal, with the passionate need that drives Emma Bovary, with Frédéric Moreau's somnambulistic perception that something primary is missing in his life, Lucien's question resonates and develops at the center of the novelistic tradition. It is not surprising that the same question defines the gravest crisis in *A la recherche du temps perdu*, in the period after Albertine's death.

But Proust overwhelmingly deepens Balzac's momentary confrontation with emptiness. Increasing pessimism about social relations is basic to the evolution of the novel after the French Revolution. But *La Fugitive* represents an

extraordinary inductive development of the most desolate
implications of earlier fiction. This volume of Proust is the
most fully realized example in the tradition of this constitutive element in novelistic ideology. Lucien's prostration
after Coralie dies, though moving, lasts for less than a page;
the scene in *La Recherche* which corresponds to it is an entire short novel, its anguish so complete that by comparison
earlier novelistic glimpses of unhappiness seem halfhearted.
La Fugitive is a new vision, sustained by new techniques,
of the torment at the focus of social life since the Realists
began exploring it.

The idea of the individual and his chances which Balzac
or Stendhal comes to is not fundamentally less pessimistic
than Proust's; Julien Sorel's suffering when at last he understands he has missed Madame de Rênal is fully as anguished
as Marcel's will be for having lost Albertine. But Stendhal
develops toward his conclusion through a process which, in
essence, dissembles it for the longest portion of the novel.
By contrast, Proust's meaning does not emerge from the
slowly "dawning consciousness" which always announces
psychological revelations in the Realists. The movement in
La Fugitive is violent, primitive. Proust offers no disguise,
prepares everything by prerevelation, lays his meaning immediately bare at the catastrophic opening of *La Fugitive*:
". . . Ces mots: 'Mademoiselle Albertine est partie' venaient
de produire dans mon coeur une souffrance telle que je
sentais que je ne pourrais pas y résister longtemps" (III,
419; ". . . These words: 'Mademoiselle Albertine has left'
had just caused in my heart such suffering that I felt I
would not be able to stand it for long"). The sentence
immediately expresses the involuntary, "totalized" character of experience in this volume. As in Flaubert,
but even more brutally, we are slapped with the novel's
abominable truth, seamless and already fully formed in the
first sentence.

La Fugitive was the last section of *La Recherche* that
Proust reworked virtually as a whole before he died (see

Painter, *Proust*, II, 357). And he had been developing the material for a long time. Its themes are among his earliest and most persistent ("Avant la nuit," *Jean Santeuil*, pp. 167–71, which first states the theme of a lesbian mistress's suicide, dates from 1893). Other versions were sketched in *Jean Santeuil*, in the 1905–1906 proto-*Recherche* which still had Swann as protagonist, and in the 1913–1914 version whose publication was interrupted by the war (see Painter, II, 208-9, 237–39). Swann's affair with Odette, Charlus's with Morel, prefigure Marcel's with Albertine; and there are frequent prerevelatory statements in earlier volumes of the novel (see I, 627 for example) that Proust had reserved his chief treatment of the theme of loss for later on.

The crucial new element in *La Fugitive* is the perfection with which, beyond anything in the novel up to that point, the ideology that underlies *A la recherche du temps perdu* is embedded into the very form of the fiction. In its means of expression *La Fugitive* is the most radically pessimistic book in the entire tradition. With Proust as with the Realists, the evolving dialectical relationship between fictional form and social reality is best traceable in the parallel evolving formal relationship between the hero and the action of the tale. Interpreted in its essentials, *La Fugitive* expresses the modern version of these relationships with paradigmatic clarity. In this volume, Proust has simplified his hero to a recognizably fundamental form: the protagonist as *consciousness of loss*. Coordinately, the action of the volume is precisely the inner experience of isolation suffered by the self. Outward action is already over when *La Fugitive* opens. Albertine has fled, the relationship between the self and the outside world has already reached a new level of unmanageability. And with her death early in the volume, the dialectic between self and other collapses altogether.

When the sense of loss reaches this acute level, existence outside the self is simply abolished in consciousness, the individual's solitude becomes the limit of the world. Reality finally becomes totally mental, as Proust had been insisting all along. In the trance that follows Albertine's death, for the first time Proust thoroughly realizes *in the realm of form* the implications of his own ideology, the meaning of writing "*after* the fall." In *La Fugitive* the "lost paradise" theme fundamental not only to Proust but to the entire tradition functions from within Proust's structure as a total way of experiencing the world—or, what comes to the same thing, of narrating it. It is not just the "subject" of this volume, or a discursive motif. Proust makes it become the form of human experience.

Nearly a century before, Vautrin and Lamiel had been invented to lay bare, in the nakedness of their revolt against the hostile outside, the social crisis that is the ancestor of our own. But the outside won. Marcel in *La Fugitive* expresses a more advanced stage of the crisis through the nakedness of the self which results: so thoroughly isolated in paroxysmic withdrawal from the world of concrete social life that for a time, in a final absurdity, the self pretends what the form suggests, that there is no outside world at all.

La Fugitive emerges from the long "synthetic day" which makes up the body of *La Prisonnière*. This synthetic tableau ends with the event that closes *La Prisonnière* itself, Albertine's flight. Extreme tension has been building beneath the rhythm of Marcel's interrogations and his emotional punishment of Albertine. When she leaves him, time suddenly closes in; the active mode returns and is maintained through Marcel's anxious strategies in the first part of *La Fugitive* to get her to come back to him. But Mme Bontemps's telegram announcing Albertine's death ends these futile maneuvers. At this moment of catastrophe, the active narration reaches its point of highest intensity. Violence, which has always been potential in this mode (as it was in the Realist novel), finally becomes overt. Then the active telling collapses and is replaced by an intense

section in the synthetic mode, describing Marcel's emotional reaction to the disaster. He enters a period of suspended animation—of anesthesia—his mind's defensive
recoil from the disastrous event that has at last occurred:

> Alors ma vie fut entièrement changée. Ce qui en
> avait fait, et non à cause d'Albertine, parallèlement
> à elle, quand j'étais seul, la douceur, c'était justement,
> à l'appel de moments indentiques, la perpétuelle
> renaissance de moments anciens. Par le bruit de la pluie
> m'était rendue l'odeur des lilas de Combray; par la
> mobilité du soleil sur le balcon, les pigeons des Champs-
> Elysées; par l'assourdissement des bruits dans la cha-
> leur de la matinée, la fraîcheur des cerises; le désir de
> la Bretagne ou de Venise par le bruit du vent et le
> retour de Pâques. L'été venait, les jours étaient longs,
> il faisait chaud. . . . Et si Françoise en revenant dé-
> rangeait sans le vouloir les plis du grand rideau, j'é-
> touffais un cri à la déchirure que venait de faire en moi
> ce rayon du soleil ancien qui m'avait fait paraître belle
> la façade neuve de Bricqueville l'Orgueilleuse, quand
> Albertine m'avait dit: "Elle est restaurée." [III,
> 478-79]

(So then my life changed completely. What had made
it—not because of Albertine, but concurrently with
her, when I was alone—pleasant was precisely, at the
call of identical moments, the perpetual resurgence of
moments past. In the sound of the rain, the scent of
the lilacs in Combray came back to me; in the shifting
of the sunlight on the balcony, the pigeons on the
Champs-Elysées; through the noises muffled in the
morning's heat, the cool taste of cherries; the longing
for Brittany or Venice in the sound of the wind and
the return of Easter. The summer was approaching, the
days were long, the weather was warm. . . . And if
Françoise, coming into my room, by accident upset
the folds of the heavy window curtain, I would stifle a

cry of pain at the wound that I had suffered from the
long-ago ray of sun that had made the modern facade
of Bricqueville l'Orgueilleuse seem beautiful to me,
when Albertine had said, "It's restored.")

The eighty-page passage of synthetic narration which begins at this point is the longest and most fully developed
in *A la recherche du temps perdu*. As the pressure of these
painful images grows, synthetic narration permits Proust to
follow Marcel's mental disorientation intimately. His anguish increases until, in another of Proust's sudden presents, this time overtly desperate, we have the most extreme
grammatical dislocation in all of *La Recherche*:

Ne sachant comment expliquer mon soupir à Françoise, je lui disais: "Ah! j'ai soif." Elle sortait, ren-
trait, mais je me détournais violemment, sous la
décharge douloureuse d'un des mille souvenirs invisibles qui à tout moment éclataient autour de moi
dans l'ombre: je venais de voir qu'elle avait apporté
du cidre et des cerises, ce cidre et ces cerises qu'un
garçon de ferme nous avait apportés dans la voiture,
à Balbec. . . . Alors je pensai pour la première fois
à la ferme des Ecorres, et je me dis que, certains
jours où Albertine me disait à Balbec ne pas être
libre, . . . elle était peut-être avec telle de ses amies
dans une ferme où elle savait que je n'avais pas mes
habitudes et où . . . elle usait avec son amie des mêmes
mots qu'avec moi quand nous sortions tous deux:
"Il n'aura pas l'idée de nous chercher ici et comme cela
nous ne serons pas dérangées." Je disais à Françoise
de refermer les rideaux pour ne plus voir ce rayon de
soleil. Mail il continuait à filtrer, aussi corrosif, dans
ma mémoire. "Elle ne me plaît pas, elle est restaurée,
mais nous irons demain à Saint-Martin le Vêtu, après-
demain à . . . " Demain, après-demain, c'était un avenir
de vie commune, peut-être pour toujours, qui *com-*

mence, mon coeur *s'élance* vers lui, mais il n'*est* plus
là, Albertine *est* morte. [III, 479]

(Not knowing how to explain my sigh to Françoise, I
told her, "I'm very thirsty." She went out, came back,
but I turned convulsively away from the painful dis-
charge of one of the thousand invisible memories
which burst constantly around me: I had realized that
she was bringing me cider and cherries, cider and cherries that a farm boy had brought to us in the carriage
at Balbec. . . . Then for the first time I recalled a farm
called Les Ecorres, and I said to myself that, certain
days when Albertine had told me she was not free,
. . . perhaps she had gone with one of her girlfriends to
a farm where she knew I didn't go and where . . . she
told her friend the same things she would tell me when
we went out alone together: "He won't think of looking for us here and so we won't be disturbed." I told
Françoise to close the curtains so I would not see the
ray of sunlight any longer. But it continued to filter
through, just as corrosive, in my memory. "I don't
like it, it's restored, but tomorrow we'll go to Saint-
Martin le Vêtu, the day after tomorrow to . . . "
Tomorrow, the day after, it was a future of shared
life, perhaps for ever, that *begins*, my heart *jumps*
toward it, but it *is* no longer there, Albertine *is* dead.)

The atemporal presents communicate here the vividness of
the pain, the ubiquity of the fact that causes it: everywhere, constantly, with no hope of remission, Albertine is
dead.

This is the purest moment of synthetic narration in the
novel:

Je demandais l'heure à Françoise. Six heures. Enfin,
Dieu merci, allait disparaître cette lourde chaleur
dont autrefois je me plaignais avec Albertine, et que
nous aimions tant. La journée prenait fin. Mais qu'est-

ce que j'y gagnais? La fraîcheur du soir se levait,
c'était le coucher du soleil; dans ma mémoire, au bout
d'une route que nous prenions ensemble pour rentrer,
j'apercevais, plus loin que le dernier village, comme
une station distante, inaccessible pour le soir même
où nous nous arrêterions à Balbec, toujours ensemble.
Ensemble alors, maintenant il fallait s'arrêter court
devant ce même abîme, elle était morte. Ce n'était
plus assez de fermer les rideaux, je tâchais de boucher
les yeux et les oreilles de ma mémoire, pour ne pas
revoir cette bande orangée du couchant, pour ne pas
entendre ces invisibles oiseaux qui se répondirent
d'un arbre à l'autre de chaque côté de moi qu'embras-
sait alors si tendrement celle qui maintenant était
morte. Je tâchais d'éviter ces sensations que donnent
l'humidité des feuilles dans le soir, la montée et la
descente des routes en dos d'âne. Mais déjà ces sensations m'avaient ressaisi, ramené assez loin du moment
actuel, afin qu'eût tout le recul, tout l'élan nécessaire
pour me frapper de nouveau, l'idée qu'Albertine était
morte. . . . Que le jour est lent à mourir par ces soirs
démesurés de l'été. . . . Enfin il faisait nuit. . . .
L'obscurité complète finissait . . . par venir. . . . Ah!
quand la nuit finirait-elle? . . . Bientôt les bruits de la
rue allaient commencer. . . . [III, 480–82]

(I asked Françoise the time. Six o'clock. Finally, thank
God, the oppressive heat which I used to complain
about with Albertine, and which we enjoyed so, would
lift. The day was coming to an end. But what good did
it do me? The coolness of the evening began, the sun
was setting; in my memory, at the end of a road on
which we were returning home together, I made out,
further than the furthest village, what looked like a distant town, too far away to get to that evening, when
we would stop in Balbec, still together. Together then;
now I had to stop short in front of the same abyss, she
was dead. It was no longer enough to close the curtains,

I tried to stop up the eyes and ears of my memory, so
as not to see that band of orange at the setting sun,
so as not to hear those invisible birds which answered
each other from branch to branch on all sides of me
then so tenderly being kissed by her who was now
dead. I tried to avoid the sensations we get from the
wetness of leaves at evening, the up and down of
country roads. But already these sensations had gotten
hold of me again, had brought me far back from the
present, so that it might store up sufficient force to
strike me again: the idea that Albertine was dead. . . .
How slow the day is in dying on these endless summer
evenings. . . . Finally night had fallen. . . . The darkness had come at last. . . . Oh! When would the night
end? . . . Soon the sounds from the streets would start
up again. . . .)

Of course this series of gestures and perceptions—presented
as if they really happened in one extended moment of misery as they are depicted—concentrates the essence of an
indeterminate but prolonged period of emotional desperation. The evening and sleepless night recounted here
(like so many others in the novel) surely are not cast in the
mold of commonsense chronology. But the function of
synthetic narration is to focus the shapelessness of experience into such coherent, heightened patterns. Perhaps
nowhere in *La Recherche* is the power of such a created
narrative image more memorable. Here envelopment within
the moment is so total that the passage succeeds in representing something exceptionally difficult to express
adequately, Marcel's overwhelming disorientation, his loss
of all sense of time.

But the ability to express the mind's slow progression
out of the bewilderment caused by a catastrophe such as Albertine's death is another subtle stylistic resource of the
synthetic mode. Like the loss of equilibrium, its return is
reflected in the essential details of the narrative system. At

the same time another device participates in marking the slow dilution of the synthetic mode over the course of these pages. This is the repetition and progressive modification of the obsessional sentence whose primitive, paradigmatic form we have already seen at the heart of the crisis: "Albertine est morte." In the twenty pages which follow this first appearance, the unmistakable cadence of this phrase re-echoes a dozen times; in the sixty pages of the synthetic passage remaining, it reappears, at the most critical points and with significant changes in form or context, about ten times more.[1] Its diminishing frequency indicates Marcel's gradual emergence from the trance which began with his first comprehension of Mme Bontemps's telegram.

In addition to this insistent refrain, other characteristics sustain the depiction of Marcel's trance-state at this point. As he emerges from it toward stability, the evidence of his recovery will be expressed through changes in precisely these characteristics:

—a sudden absence of specific indications of time, and the substitution of floating suggestions of the type "une de ces fins d'après-midi-là" (III, 480; "one of those late afternoons")

—repeated, cyclical progression through synthetic chronologies of days and seasons, for example, afternoon through morning (III, 479–82 quoted above); summer through winter and the following spring (III, 481–85)[2]

1. These appearances will be found on III, 479, 480 (three times), 488, 489 (three times), 492, 494, 499, 502, 519 (twice), 521, 534, 535, 539 (three times), 557.

2. The *lettre-dédicace* of *Swann* to Madame Scheikévitch (November 1915), in which Proust explained what the volumes not yet published would bring, provides in the résumé of these pages from *La Fugitive* a sense of how consciously meditated was the development of these chronologies. See *Correspondance générale*, V, 239: "... diverses heures, saisons. J'attends que l'été finisse, puis l'automne. Mais les premières gelées me rappellent d'autres souvenirs si cruels ..." ("diverse times of day and seasons. I await the end of summer, then of autumn. But the first frosts call back other memories, so painful ..."). The letter is reprinted (pp. 559–64) in the Pléiade edition of *CSB*.

—immersion in images of the past; for example, the résumé of the synthetic day of *La Prisonnière* (III, 486) or of Marcel's image of Albertine "tour à tour rapide et penchée sur sa bicyclette, . . . ou bien, les soirs où nous avions emporté du champagne dans les bois de Chantepie, la voix provocante . . ." (III, 488 ff.; "now crouched over, coasting on her bicycle, . . . now, on the evenings we had taken some champagne into the Chantepie woods, her voice seductive . . . ")
—absence of physical action
—confinement in a featureless interior, in solitude.
Thus within the circle of the narrator's anguished thoughts, confused mental chronologies coalesce in the pure synthetic mode within the dissolving present.

At this point, however, for the first time since the telegram arrived, an individual memory becomes specific enough to motivate action: Marcel recalls a time when Albertine had blushed at the mention of her "peignoir de douche" and asks Aimé to investigate her conduct at bathing establishments. The decision shows the rigorous logic of detail and the overall irrationality which characterize some types of mental disorganization: Aimé's investigation is of course irrelevant now that Albertine is dead. But Marcel has acted, for the first time since the trance began, and the verbs in the *passé simple* return for a few lines to mark this tentative but important stage in his return to a normal state (III, 492).

Proust's writing problem in this section was to make the movement marked by such stages seem a progressive one. On the level of technique, this meant that the increasing dilution of the synthetic mode had to be as subtle as possible. Since the movement was to be sustained over eighty pages without premature climaxes or grossly schematic manipulation of the elements, the indications of Marcel's return to normality, especially early on as here, had to be implicit and tonal, rather than overtly emphasized. And for a time, each tentative reappearance of the active mode had to be reabsorbed by the still dominant synthetic.

Albertine's death first takes the form of a massive emotional injury to Marcel. In the earliest phases of his trance, the subjectivity of his thoughts is so overwhelming that feeling for Albertine is virtually absent. His returning awareness of others is one of the components of the progression in this long section. It is fifteen dense pages before even a slight sense of another existence becomes visible in his lamentations. Then, finally, he thinks, not of what he has lost in her, but of what she has lost:

> Je venais d'aborder par une nouvelle face cette idée qu'Albertine était morte, Albertine qui m'inspirait cette tendresse qu'on a pour les absentes dont la vue ne vient pas rectifier l'image embellie, inspirant aussi la tristesse que cette absence fût éternelle *et que la pauvre petite fût privée à jamais de la douceur de la vie.* [III, 492–93]

> (I had just come upon from a different direction the idea that Albertine was dead, Albertine who inspired in me the tender feeling which we have for those who are away and whose real appearance does not interfere with our embellished image of them, inspiring also a sadness that she would be away eternally and *that such a dear person should be forever deprived of the pleasure of living.*)

Before long, Marcel has another reaction in specific time:

> Un matin, je crus voir la forme oblongue d'une colline dans le brouillard, . . . pendant que m'étreignait horriblement le coeur ce souvenir de l'après-midi où je l'avais embrassée pour la première fois. . . . Et *je jetai avec colère* une invitation que Françoise m'apporta de Mme Verdurin. [III, 494]

> (One morning, I thought I perceived the oblong shape of a hill through the fog, . . . while my heart was gripped

horribly by the memory of the afternoon I had kissed her for the first time. . . . And *I threw down angrily* an invitation from Mme Verdurin that Françoise had just brought in.)

The outburst of anger represents another type of recognition by Marcel of the world outside. His indignation, that Mme Verdurin and her inconsequential friends should go on living after Albertine has been deprived of life, marks another step in his achievement of perspective. And just four lines below, as if to confirm this new modification of atmosphere, the cadence-phrase reappears with a new tone, seeming for the first time an aching recognition rather than a cruel rediscovery: "*maintenant qu'*Albertine était morte" ("*now that* Albertine was dead").

As Marcel emerges from his trance, not only does his consciousness of the world outside his sorrow increase, but his realization that this is happening gives him evidence of his progress toward recovery. Consciousness of movement thus becomes a fact generating further movement. The distance traveled can be measured in the evolution of emotional tone between two attempts at reassuring himself that he would at last recover. The first of these was the abstract prop his mind had erected in the desperation of the early moments:

Ah! quand la nuit finirait-elle? . . . Je n'avais plus qu'un espoir pour l'avenir—espoir bien plus déchirant qu'une crainte—, c'était d'oublier Albertine. Je savais que je l'oublierais un jour, . . . j'avais bien oublié ma grand'mère. [III, 482]

(Oh! When would the night end? . . . I had only one hope about the future—a hope much more harrowing than any fear could have been—that I might forget Albertine. I knew I would forget her some day, . . . I had surely forgotten my grandmother.)

Twenty pages later, we find instead a disabused, internalized belief whose expression, in another important alteration of the cadence-phrase, only appears to parallel the earlier moment:

> Son corps vivant n'avait point, comme celui de Gilberte, cessé un jour d'être celui où je trouvais ce que je reconnaissais après coup être pour moi . . . les attraits féminins. *Mais elle était morte. Je l'oublierais.* [III, 502]

> (Her living body had not stopped being, as Gilberte's had, the one which possessed what later I realized was my idea of . . . feminine beauty. *But she was dead. I would forget her.*)

The alteration in the rhythm of the cadence, the new matter-of-fact tone, represent the change in meaning of the idea for Marcel.

This change marks a vital intermediate point in the movement of the passage, a kind of tonal boundary between the desperate sorrowing of its initial pages and the resigned sadness of what remains. There is a softening of the early violent tension; the imagery of the continuing synthetic account becomes more peaceful, even conventionally sentimental:

> Mon imagination la cherchait dans le ciel, par les soirs où nous l'avions regardé encore ensemble; au delà de ce clair de lune qu'elle aimait, je tâchais de hausser jusqu'à elle ma tendresse pour qu'elle lui fût une consolation de ne plus vivre, et cet amour pour un être devenu si lointain était comme une religion, mes pensées montaient vers elle comme des prières. [III, 511]

> (My imagination sought her in the sky, on the kind of evenings we had watched it together; beyond the moonlight she loved, I tried to raise my affection up to her,

so that she might have a consolation for no longer being alive; and that love for a being who was so distant was like a religion, my thoughts rose toward her like prayers.)

Even his preoccupation with the secrets of Albertine's behavior is diminished. By now it has taken on the neutral tone of resigned habit, it has lost the urgency which above (III, 492) forced the narration out of the synthetic mode for the first significant time. By now, too, the cadence-phrase has attained forms which, leaving behind the choked parataxis of its early appearances, represent the increasing coherence of Marcel's sense of the world even without Albertine: "*depuis qu*'elle était morte"; "*parce qu*'elle était morte" (III, 519; "*since* she was dead"; "*because* she was dead").

Finally—though in an off-hand parenthesis—an indication of real calendar time returns:

J'essayais de ne penser à rien, de prendre un journal. Mais la lecture m'était insupportable de ces articles écrits par des gens qui n'éprouvaient pas de réelle douleur. . . . Le chroniqueur cynégétique disait (*on était au mois de mai*): "Cette époque est vraiment douloureuse, disons mieux, sinistre, pour le vrai chasseur, car il n'y a rien, absolument rien à tirer." [III, 522]

(I tried not to think about anything, to read the paper. But reading these articles written by people who were experiencing no sorrow was intolerable. . . . The field-and-stream columnist had written (*it was in May*): "This season so far has been deeply depressing, even painful, for the real hunters, for there has been no game, absolutely none.")

In *La Fugitive* the modification of narrative texture precisely parallels the emotional changes in Marcel. The modal variation thus represents mimetically, beyond the power of words and sentences alone, the inward modulations of a profound crisis. Only a narrative texture as unusual as the pure synthetic passage which immediately follows the news of Albertine's death could adequately express the emotional deformation her disappearance causes in Marcel. On the other hand, the emergence of the active mode during the period following her death conveys a return to lucidity and integrated mental behavior, with characteristic one-to-one correspondence to real events. In the pattern of verbal development conveying Marcel's slow reorientation there is a place for the intermediate "composite" mode (in which temporal adverbs like "tous les jours" acknowledge the multiple experiences summed up, whereas the synthetic mode disguises this multiplicity). As the chronologically indeterminate floating of the early phase passes from dominance, a long passage in this composite mode replaces the sense of helpless confusion with a more assured tone conveying the narrator's growing capacity for perspective:

> Les instants que j'avais vécus auprès de cette Albertine-là m'étaient si précieux que j'eusse voulu n'en avoir laissé échapper aucun. Or *parfois*, comme on rattrape les bribes d'une fortune dissipée, j'en retrouvais qui avaient semblé perdus. . . . D'ailleurs mon chagrin prenait tant de formes que *parfois* je ne le reconnaissais plus. . . . Il y avait *des heures* où j'étais décidé à me marier. . . . *Parfois* ma jalousie renaissait dans des moments où je ne me souvenais plus d'Albertine. . . . Mon moi en quelque sorte mi-partie, tandis que son extrémité supérieure était déjà dure et refroidie, brûlait encore à sa base *chaque fois* qu'une étincelle y refaisait passer l'ancien courant. [III, 531-33]

(The moments I had lived with that particular Albertine were so precious that I would have wanted to let none of them go. And *at times*, as one comes across the last remnants of a squandered fortune, I found some which

had seemed lost. . . . My grief assumed so many forms
that *at times* I hardly recognized it. . . . There were
periods when I was ready to marry. . . . *At times* my
jealousy revived in moments when I was no longer remembering Albertine. . . . My divided being, already
hard and cooled at the top, was still burning at its base
each time a spark made the old current pass through it.)

Appropriately, it is at this point that Marcel directly con-
siders his emotional progress. He begins to "reflect on himself" (III, 534). Again, Proust's handling of the material has
avoided anticlimax in the description of the slow progress of
his recovery. Rather than prolong the strange psychological
tone of the trance passage into further and over-subtle gra-
dations, in the new tone of these self-analytical passages he
surprises us by revealing that in fact the cure is further along
than we had any reason to think: "If a physician of the soul
had come to see me, he would have concluded that . . . my
sorrow was recovering" (III, 533). And the crucial change
expressed earlier through tonal means is also made explicit:
"Without my realizing, it was now *the idea of Albertine's
death*—and not the actual memory of her alive—which for
the most part occupied my unconscious musings" (III, 534).
     Marcel has recovered so much mental stability that we
await a decisive move into the active mode. But a surprise
intervenes. At this point in *La Fugitive*, when the dilution
of the synthetic has already progressed quite far and the
composite atmosphere has been clearly established, Proust
reverts to a technique he has used regularly before in structural situations parallel to this (for example, in the "chambres" section at the very beginning of the novel, or at the
most intense moment in the synthetic account of dinner at
Rivebelle [I, 819-20]): narration of a dream. The dream
allows a final reflection of the fantasmagoric bewilderment
of the trance before the movement concludes, and normalcy
—the active mode—returns.:

     Souvent c'était tout simplement pendant mon sommeil

que, par ces "reprises," ces *da capo* du rêve qui tour-
nent d'un seul coup plusieurs pages de la mémoire,
plusieurs feuillets du calendrier me ramenaient, me
faisaient rétrograder à une impression douloureuse
mais ancienne, qui depuis longtemps avait cédé la
place à d'autres et qui redevenait présente. . . . *Parfois*,
par un défaut d'éclairage intérieur . . . mes souvenirs
bien mis en scène me donnant l'illusion de la vie, je
croyais vraiment avoir donné rendez-vous à Albertine. . . . *D'autres fois* Albertine se trouvait dans mon
rêve, et voulait de nouveau me quitter. . . . *D'autres
fois*, sans que j'eusse rêvé, dès mon réveil je sentais que
le vent avait tourné en moi; il soufflait froid et continu
d'une autre direction venue du fond du passé, me
rapportant la sonnerie d'heures lointaines, des siffle-
ments de départ que je n'entendais pas d'habitude. . . .
Je rouvrais un roman de Bergotte. [III, 538–41]

(*Often* it was simply during sleep, in one of those
"repeats," those dream *da capos*, suddenly turning
several pages of memory, several leaves of the calendar,
bringing me back, making me revert to a painful but
past impression, which a long time ago had given way
to others and had now returned into the present. . . .
Sometimes, by a failure of interior lighting, . . . with
some well-staged memories giving me the illusion that
it was true, I distinctly had the impression that I had
made a date with Albertine. . . . *Other times*, Albertine
was in my dream, and threatened to leave me again.
. . . *Other times*, without having dreamed, as soon as I
awoke I felt that the wind had changed inside me; it
blew cold and hard from another direction deep out of
the past, bringing back the chimes of hours now far
away, departure whistles that ordinarily I could not
hear. . . . I reopened a Bergotte novel.)

In the middle of this passage, within what the narrator
appropriately calls one of "these temporary periods of

madness which are our dreams" (III, 540), the pure synthetic mode makes a final appearance. Before the memory
of the trance, once so intensely vivid, but now so atten-
uated, passes away, it echoes one more time, unmistakable
and slightly mad:

Je causais avec [Albertine], pendant que je parlais ma
grand'mère allait et venait dans le fond de la chambre.
Une partie de son menton était tombée en miettes
comme un marbre rongé, mais je ne trouvais à cela rien
d'extraordinaire. Je disais à Albertine que j'aurais des
questions à lui poser relativement à l'établissement de
douches de Balbec et à une certaine blanchisseuse de
Touraine, mais je remettais cela à plus tard puisque
nous avions tout le temps et que rien ne pressait plus.
Elle me promettait qu'elle ne faisait rien de mal et
qu'elle avait seulement la veille embrassé sur les lèvres
Mlle Vinteuil. "Comment? elle est ici? —Oui, il est
même temps que je vous quitte, car je dois aller la voir
tout à l'heure." [III, 539] [3]

(I was conversing with Albertine; while I was talking
my grandmother paced back and forth at the rear of
the room. A part of her chin had crumbled away, as in
a worn marble statue, but that did not seem odd to me.
I told Albertine I had some questions I needed to ask
her concerning the bathing establishment at Balbec and

3. Almost simultaneously, the cadence-phrase recurs three times in fifteen
lines (III, 539), leaving it only one further appearance in the novel.
    The dream passage itself, in the sudden renewal of a nearly exhausted emo-
tion, exactly parallels Swann's final dream of Odette (see I, 378). The two
dreams have a number of elements in common (the facial deformations;
presence of one of the narrator's grandparents). But their functional parallel
is the most important. The dreams allow a final resurgence of the obsession in
all its painful force before it disintegrates and reason returns. "Un Amour de
Swann" ends two pages after the dream about Odette. And while it takes a
bit longer after Marcel's final dream of Albertine for the active mode to
reappear, we clearly feel that the dream represents the final significant moment in this long evolution.

a certain laundress in Touraine, but I would wait until later since we had plenty of time and there was no reason to rush. She swore she had not done anything wrong and that yesterday she had only kissed Mlle Vinteuil on the lips. "What, is she here?" "Yes, and in fact I have to leave now because I'm going to meet her shortly.")

The last stage of this long love story follows, at a disinterested distance from the surreal vividness of the dream. Marcel's thoughts move for the first time beyond Albertine, and his desire finally reorients itself without regard to her at all:

> Me rappelant ainsi soit Albertine elle-même, soit le type pour lequel elle avait sans doute une préférence, ces femmes éveillaient en moi un sentiment cruel, de jalousie ou de regret, qui, plus tard, quand mon chagrin s'apaisa, *se mua en une curiosité non exempte de charme.* [III, 553]

> (As I recalled either Albertine herself, or the type of woman she no doubt preferred, these women called up in me a painful feeling, of jealousy or sorrow, which later, when my grief had calmed, *changed into a curiosity which was not devoid of charm.*)

The end and its coordinate change of atmosphere and mode come quickly now. Four pages following the passage just quoted, the cadence-phrase appears for the last time, in a sentence describing the definitive form of Marcel's memory of Albertine, the form which his reflections would continue to take as he thought of her less and less frequently:

> Elles [the women whom Marcel now brings home with him] ne m'avaient jamais parlé, elles, de la musique de Vinteuil, des Mémoires de Saint-Simon, elles n'avaient pas mis un parfum trop fort pour venir me voir, elles n'avaient pas joué à mêler leurs cils aux

miens, toutes choses importantes parce qu'elles per-
mettent, semble-t-il, de rêver autour de l'acte sexuel
lui-même et de se donner l'illusion de l'amour, mais en
réalité parce qu'elles faisaient partie du souvenir
d'Albertine et que c'était elle que j'aurais voulu trouver.
Ce que ces femmes avaient d'Albertine me faisait
mieux ressentir ce que d'elle il leur manquait, et qui
était tout, et qui ne serait plus jamais, puisque Albertine était morte. . . .

Comme il y a une géométrie dans l'espace, il y a une
psychologie dans le temps, où les calculs d'une psychologie plane ne seraient plus exacts parce qu'on n'y
tiendrait pas compte du Temps et d'une des formes
qu'il revêt, l'oubli; l'oubli dont je commençais à sentir
la force. [III, 556–57]

(The women I would now bring home had never discussed Vinteuil's music or Saint-Simon's Memoirs with
me, they had never put on too much perfume before
coming to see me, they had never played at brushing
eyelashes with me—important things, it would seem,
because they allow us to weave dreams around the
sexual act itself and to give ourselves the illusion of
love, but in reality because they were part of the
memory of Albertine and it was her I would have
wanted to be with. What these women had in common with Albertine made me feel all the more clearly
what of her they lacked, which was everything, and
which would never be again, since Albertine was
dead. . . .

As there is a geometry in space, there is a psychology in time, in which the calculations of plane psychology would no longer be accurate, since they would
fail to take into account Time, and one of the forms it
assumes, forgetting—forgetting, whose power I was beginning to feel.)

The tone of the cadence-phrase by now is one of wistful,
resigned certainty: regret, but no longer revolt. The ab-

stract analytical passage which follows confirms Marcel's
liberation from the confinement, the obsessional solitude
of the period following Albertine's death. This period is
over. All trace now disappears of the mimesis by which the
texture of the narration expressed Marcel's anguish. The
slow erosion of his memories, the slow modulation of his
sorrow, whose very forms became the form of his telling,
now give way to a new discursive, neutral tone:

> Ce n'était pas que je n'aimasse encore Albertine, mais
> déjà pas de la même façon que les derniers temps. . . .
> Et en effet je sentais bien maintenant qu'avant de
> l'oublier tout à fait . . . il me faudrait, avant d'atteindre
> à l'indifférence initiale, traverser en sens inverse tous
> les sentiments par lesquels j'avais passé avant d'arriver à
> mon grand amour. . . . Dans [la voie] que je *suivis* au
> retour, il y *eut*, déjà bien près de l'arrivée, quatre
> étapes que je me rappelle particulièrement, sans doute
> parce que j'y *aperçus* des choses qui ne faisaient pas
> partie de mon amour d'Albertine. . . .
> La première de ces étapes *commença à un début*
> *d'hiver, un beau dimanche de Toussaint où j'étais*
> *sorti.* [III, 558–59]
>
> (It was not that I was not still in love with Alber-
> tine, but already in a different way than I had
> been. . . . And indeed, I was quite conscious that be-
> fore I forgot her completely, . . . before arriving at my
> original indifference, it would be necessary to retrace
> all the feelings I had passed through before I had come
> to profound love. . . . On the route that I *followed*
> back, there *were*, near the end of the journey, four
> landmarks that I particularly recall, no doubt because
> I *perceived* in them things unrelated to my love for
> Albertine. . . .
> The first of these landmarks *came in sight one day at*
> *the beginning of winter, a fine Sunday at the start of*
> *November when I had gone out.*)

All at once, in the space of a few lines, every expressive aspect of the long synthetic trance is overthrown: the verbs in the preterite return; the indications of chronology return; Marcel moves outdoors from the shadowy interior which has confined him since Albertine died; and the formlessness of catalepsy gives way to a geometric plan of the action to follow.

In the desperate moments just after Albertine died, Marcel had tried to reassure himself by rehearsing successive cycles of time, searching for a point by which forgetting might have done its work: "L'hiver finirait par revenir" (III, 483; "Winter would eventually come back"). Now winter has returned and at last suffering has exhausted itself: "Je me disais: 'pauvre petite,' *mais sans tristesse*" (III, 559; "I said to myself, 'Poor Albertine,' *but there was no sadness in it*").

The pages that follow complete the break in action and texture: "Once again, . . . the love of women arose in me, free of exclusive association with any particular woman I had already loved, and floated like those spirits that prior destructions have liberated, . . . asking only to be allowed to inhabit a new body" (III, 561). Suddenly, Marcel is pursuing the mythical, alluring Mlle d'Eporcheville, associated for him in vivid erotic fantasy with a young noblewoman who (according to Saint-Loup) frequents houses of prostitution. The "mad agitation" (III, 565) which characterizes this abortive affair drives the mood of the trance-passage thoroughly out of memory; Saint-Loup's comic telegram which ends the story—"De l'Orgeville, *de* preposition, *orge* the grain, *ville* town, short, dark, plump, is presently in Switzerland" (III, 566)—is thoroughly in the spirit of the new tonality.

About a year following Albertine's death, Marcel has a conversation with Andrée which later seems to him the second of the terminal stages of his forgetting. By this point a patina has so softened memories of Albertine that she has been comfortably reassimilated into his thoughts

about the *petite bande* as if she were only temporarily absent. Andrée's revelations concerning Albertine's lesbianism become, rather than catastrophic shocks, simple
gossip:

> Depuis quelque temps les paroles concernant Alber-
> tine, comme un poison évaporé, n'avaient plus leur
> pouvoir toxique. . . . Je me disais: "Comment! cette
> vérité que j'ai tant cherchée, tant redoutée, c'est
> seulement quelques mots dits dans une conversation!"
> [III, 602]

> (For some time, reminders of Albertine, like a poison
> that has evaporated, no longer had any toxic power.
> . . . I would say to myself: "Really! The facts I tried
> so hard to get at and feared so much amount to
> nothing more than a few words spoken in a conversa-
> tion!")

Meanwhile, an unrelated subplot (the comic story of the
imagined rebuff of Marcel's mother by the Princesse de
Parme, and of her final justification) has been introduced
(III, 612) and mingles on an equal basis with this material which once would have been so dominant.

 In the third, final stage of forgetting, the synthetic mode
typical of the rest of *La Recherche* returns. The two preceding stages employing the active mode for contrast with
the texture of Marcel's trance have isolated the special use
of the synthetic in the section immediately following
Albertine's death from its reappearance here in a much
more familiar form. What returns now resembles the relaxed, intimate, slowly cumulative account of Combray so
well characterized by Tante Léonie as life's "petit train-
train." The analogy between the atmosphere of Combray
and this third stage at Venice, an indeterminate time after
the conversation with Andrée (III, 623), is explicit:

> Ma mère m'y avait emmené passer quelques semaines

et . . . j'y goûtais des impressions analogues à celles
que j'avais si souvent ressenties autrefois à Combray,
mais transposées selon un mode entièrement différent
et plus riche. Quand à dix heures du matin on venait
ouvrir mes volets, je voyais flamboyer, au lieu du
marbre noir que devenait en resplendissant les ardoises
de Saint-Hilaire, l'Ange d'or du campanile de Saint-
Marc. [III, 623]

(My mother had brought me there to spend a few weeks
and . . . I experienced there impressions analogous to
those I had so often enjoyed at Combray, but trans-
posed into an entirely different and far richer key. At
ten o'clock when the servants came in to open my
shutters, I saw glistening, not the black marble that the
slates of Saint-Hilaire used to turn into, but the golden
angel on the Campanile of San Marco.)

And the synthetic portrait of Venice—Venice, about which
Marcel had been dreaming at the moment the catastrophe
of Albertine's departure occurred for him (III, 412-13)—
links up in feeling, beyond the obsessional trance of *La
Fugitive*, with the accounts of Balbec, Doncières, Paris,
which form the principal tableaux of the novel.

The exquisite subtlety of synthetic narration is achieved
at the price of distance from the concrete events of real
life. Maintaining this distance was essential to Proust. Of
course, in the manner of Albertine's death, events do intervene in the novel. But what Proust strove to express in his
telling were the most subtle refractions of events—or
more generally of experiences—as they become images
internalized in feeling. The energy of the narrative is thus
intensive. Technically, Proust's narrative innovations seek
to express the most sensitive definition of a spectrum of
emotional tones whose nuances, through the variation of
the modes, become nuances in the narrative texture itself.

The synthetic account of life's relaxed pace in Combray

parallels the anguished passage describing the narrator's trance following Albertine's death, despite the profound difference in the accompanying emotions. Both of these sections recapture in deeply subjective terms, as emotional contexts in which consciousness is thoroughly immersed, the atmospheres of two crucial periods in the narrator's experience. And it is the same for the other synthetic tableaux in the novel. In "Vacances de Pâques," which appeared just as Proust was preparing *Swann* for publication, he put it this way: "Raconter les événements, c'est faire connaître l'opéra par le livret seulement; mais si j'écrivais un roman, je tâcherais de différencier les musiques successives des jours" (*Chroniques*, p. 107; "Narrating just events is like trying to give the flavor of an opera with just the libretto; but if I were to write a novel, I would try to differentiate the changing melodies of the days").

It is this subjective reflection of outside events that synthetic narration was devised to re-create. But over the whole course of the novelistic tradition, real events in the sphere of concrete social life have determined the development of the very techniques which have tried to write that sphere out of the fabric of fictions. As the evolution of the tradition suggests, as everything up to this point in Proust makes clear, narration focuses on the inside because the evolving world in which the individual is immersed shows itself as increasingly hostile or inaccessible.

To put it another way, the inner world seems to be opened up in proportion to the degree novelists experience it as tragically cut off from the world outside. Every brilliant technical step toward illuminating our "interior monologue" thus reflects a diminishing confidence that authentic dialogue, or dialectical relationship, with the outside is possible. In *La Fugitive* the explicit subject of the long passage of synthetic narration after Marcel learns that Albertine is dead directly parallels the ideological implication of the techniques employed. If this were simply a local effect it would not be decisive. But *all* synthetic narration, no matter what its surface subject or apparent emotional tone, implies a paralysis as total as Marcel's in this volume. Even in "Combray," however benign it appears, synthetic narration re-creates an inert world, brilliantly rich in detail, but from which creative energy is excluded. In synthetic narration the past is not simply located on a time-line continuous with the present, it is transported out of time into a privileged recess of memory, barred by its precious-ness from contact with the world of concrete social ac-tivity. In becoming a rival of the present, it is inaccessible to the present. The past of "Combray" sends us no energy, and has none to send. It puts us to sleep, as Blanchot sug-gests, and our paralysis seems comfortable and reassuring. In this way the subject of a synthetic narration, whether or not he realizes himself captive, is a total prisoner of the past. These pasts may attract him (as the past of "Com-bray" does)—but he immerses himself in them because he flees the present. "Combray" is no less the sign of a crisis in Marcel's life than is the trance after the concrete crisis of Albertine's death in *La Fugitive*.

It is not fiction's task to solve the crises it attempts to portray. It does what it can when it provides (as Proust does through the techniques of synthetic narration) the accurate feeling for reality of which Caudwell speaks. Proust's problem was to express what he saw to be true about the world, to devise the techniques for seizing the disaster which he came to understand was at the center of his view of reality. He develops these techniques furthest in *La Fugitive*, and his appreciation of the volume is uncharacteristically direct: "ce que j'ai écrit de mieux" ("the best thing I've written").[4] He could hardly have judged otherwise his novel's most evocative account of the individual's melancholy isolation.

4. In a letter (probably written in October 1921) to Gaston Gallimard, *Lettres à la NRF*, p. 153.

Conclusion

The meaning of *La Fugitive*—and of synthetic narration there as elsewhere—is that experience outside the self has become completely unmanageable. The temptation to "recuperate" such a dark vision, to find for it the sorts of excuses and explanations that really deny its force, is perhaps inevitable. Appraising coldly, we say that the shock of Albertine's death has driven Marcel temporarily insane, and accounts for his loss of touch with what we insist on calling "reality." And then, we say, Marcel returns to his senses. This soothing view does not deny that crises occur which cut individuals off from the rest of us. But it insists that they represent temporary aberrations. At its most seductive, it maintains that the pessimism expressed in *La Fugitive* about experience outside the self betrays an interesting and prestigious case of neurasthenia.

But the novelists in Proust's tradition seem consistently to disagree. For, in the most significant of their books, has experience ever been less refractory than Proust asserts it to be? Taken as a group, do their protagonists not rather stand with the narrator of *La Recherche* as impressive, persistent examples of the impossibility of self-realization in concrete social activity? The vision of Proust's predecessors confirms his own. *A la recherche du temps perdu* subsumes and powerfully synthesizes a hundred-year developing sense of the isolation of post-Revolutionary man. This is why Proust's protagonist so astonishingly resembles earlier novelistic heroes. The feminized delicacy which charms us in Julien Sorel or Lucien de Rubempré (and denotes their lack of adaptation to the coarse, unmanageable world they move in) is present in Marcel too, but exaggerated into what we call neurasthenia. The Realist hero's isolation becomes in Proust a complete

227

hermit mystique, preaching a retreat more total than Fabrice's to the charterhouse. Balzac's theme of the disappointment that awaits the young bourgeois dazzled by the glamour of high society when he finally penetrates the world of the salons is prolonged in Proust into a radical critique of *all* social life. Similarly, friendship is a grave problem for Frédéric and Deslauriers in *L'Education sentimentale*; Proust simply pronounces friendship impossible (I, 736, 906). Proust's diagnosis identifies the same disease his predecessors had seen, but the malady now seems terminal.

The explicit content of the diagnosis is summed up in one celebrated remark: "Chaque personne est bien seule" (II, 318; "Everyone is completely alone"). This anguished realization is the constant element in Proust's understanding of experience. Much of "Combray" seems sunny, but as the narration there unfolds young Marcel's inner reality, the radical isolation which is its real content is already implied.

Proust's penetration into the narrator's consciousness transcends Realist techniques of psychological analysis on several levels. Not only does Proust draw us deeper "inside," but we are taken further back into childhood in the effort to discover the etiology of Marcel's isolation. The Realists typically began tracing the "formation" of their protagonists in mid or late adolescence because the authenticity and idealism threatened by contemporary existence could still be seized in this period of the hero's life, before the disillusionments of early adult experience which shape the body of these novels. For Flaubert the locus of disenchantment moves back in time: "J'ai eu, *tout jeune*, un pressentiment complet de la vie" (see above, ch. 4, n. 2). Proust again takes the tendency further: after Flaubert, paradise is lost very early on. Proust, Joyce, Freud, all recognize that early childhood holds a secret. One can look only there for the image of hope against which the disappointments of later experience must be measured.

For a time the early portions of *La Recherche* conceal the melancholy reason why the account of Marcel's life needs to be taken up so far back. This is why the valence of "Combray" seems temporarily positive. But concrete experience will negate "Combray" (as, structurally speaking, "Un Amour de Swann" does immediately). No matter how cheerfully they are described, the "two ways" of "Combray" are *both* false paths. What appeared beguiling in the opening section of the novel by its end will thus show itself as terrifying.

As we have seen, synthetic narration, even in sunny "Combray," always portrays a world of latent disaster.[1] As the synthetic mode (at first subtly) underindividualizes concrete events, as we slowly grow accustomed to a certain hollowness and schematism in the contact between subjective consciousness and the outside, the people we could love are progressively disembodied and distanced; the world is quietly going gray. So if we maintain that after the shock of Albertine's death Marcel returned to reality, we have to ask what shape reality took when he came back to it. The answer—the world of the remainder of the novel—is disheartening. Through synthetic narration Proust insists that the locus of human meaning must be elsewhere than in any contact with the hollow world portrayed outside. By the time of *La Fugitive* the crisis of this contact has reached unendurable finality. After this crucial point, there will be something direly spectral in the figures that populate the world outside the self. And, tellingly, there will be no more love affairs for Marcel.

Love relationships are the most intense of all contacts between the self and the outside. From the beginning of the novel, Proust explores the possibilities for human

1. This account of the synthetic mode's underlying pessimism is sustained by Proust's own emotional characterization of the imperfect tense ("ce temps cruel . . . qui au moment même où il retrace nos actions, les frappe d'illusion, les anéantit"), mentioned above. See Ch. 8, n. 10.

realization most centrally in working out his love plots. For him as for his predecessors in the tradition, these are at once the most humanly meaningful and the most technically manageable testing grounds for the novelist's view of concrete social life. The person pursued becomes an immediate symbol of "others" in general; the shape of the pursuit exemplifies the fate of all social relations. The identification is clear from the very earliest novels in the tradition; Balzac concludes *La Peau de chagrin* with a chilling paragraph of disillusionment which makes it obvious:

> —Mais Fœdora?
> —Oh! Fœdora, vous la rencontrerez. . . . Elle était hier aux Bouffons, elle ira ce soir à l'Opéra, elle est partout. *C'est, si vous voulez, la société.* [p. 299]

> ("But what about Fœdora [the woman who inspired Raphaël de Valentin's agonizing and fruitless infatuation]?
> "Oh, Fœdora, you'll see her around town. . . . She was at the theater last night, she'll be at the opera tonight, she's everywhere. *You might call her Society.*")

Love affairs in which the lovers succeed in binding themselves together in opposition to the larger society are exceedingly rare in these fictions. Such couples are throughly outnumbered by those who are internally divided. Love in nineteenth-century novels is portrayed at times as extraordinarily vile (for example, in Pécuchet's low-comic acquisition of venereal disease or, on another scale, in Des Esseintes's depravity). But more than these accounts, the classic Realist portrayals of amorous unhappiness going back to Constant's *Adolphe* are the key precursors of the vein of love in *La Recherche*. Proust begins his image of love where the Realists leave off. From the first moment he defines love as anguish. The "drame du coucher" is the initial example, but it is decisive: "This terrible need for another person, at Combray I came to experience it in the case of my mother, to the point that I would have wanted to die if she had had Françoise tell me she could not come upstairs" (II, 733).

The source of love's impossibility in Proust seems to lie prior to the pattern of imprisonment and flight which is the tragic common experience of all the couples in the novel. This is the mechanism by which affection is destroyed, but the energy for the process seems to rise from deeper in the unhappy lover. Proust constantly defines possession of another person as the figurative (and impossible) fixing of an image: "I knew that I would not possess that young cyclist [Albertine] unless I possessed what was in her eyes as well" (I, 794). But in this passage the narrator's reflections on the "fugacité des êtres" ("the fugacity of others") begin to reveal the impossible situation in which love conceived and experienced as total need has put the Proustian heroes.

"L'amour . . . est *l'exigence d'un tout*. . . . On n'aime que ce qu'on ne possède pas tout entier" (III, 106; "Love . . . is the *need for totality*. . . . One loves only what one does not completely possess"). The whole drama of Proust's search for a totality which would include the self *but not be limited to it* can be felt in this decisive assertion early in *La Prisonnière*. The paroxysmic recoil into total subjectivity which is the most striking aspect of *La Fugitive* is nothing more than the self-defensive obverse of this longing for a wholeness with someone outside the self.

Experience eventually proves that people cannot be fixed like images, but in *La Prisonnière* the drama has not advanced so far. The Proustian lover continues to try for wholeness, and the results continue painful: "Albertine had turned out her light, she was in bed; I remained there motionless, hoping for some lucky chance, but none occurred; and much later, frozen, I went back to get into my own bed, and cried all the rest of the night" (III, 113). Emotionally, of course, this situation with Albertine precisely reproduces the anguish of the childhood "good-night kiss"; but real life refuses to repeat the grace of Combray's miracle. Past childhood, the world outside the self continues unmanageable.

The hostile pressure of the outside always deformed the few moments of real love (Julien in prison, Fabrice in the tower, Lucien by Coralie's deathbed) which earlier novels in the tradition offer. These moments by their nature lead nowhere; they exist only when there is no threat of their continuation, of their becoming free, mature, responsible love. It is a mistake, in romanticizing their magic, to forget that only their impossibility makes them possible. In *La Recherche* Proust finds an equally irremediable structure for the rare moments in the novel when love is not instantly thwarted. Their image is the "sommeil d'Albertine" (III, 69–75), their common characteristic the unconsciousness of one of the partners. There can be no more poignant proof of the solitude of the Proustian lover than this hopeless contemplation of the woman he loves:

> Le pouvoir de rêver que je n'avais qu'en son absence, je le retrouvais à ces instants auprès d'elle, comme si, en dormant, elle était devenue une plante. Par là, son sommeil réalisait, dans une certaine mesure, la possibilité de l'amour. . . . J'avais cette impression de la posséder toute entière que je n'avais pas quand elle était réveillée. [III, 69–70]

> (The capacity to dream which I had only in her absence, I recovered during these moments by her side, as if, in sleeping, she had become a plant. In that way, her sleep created, to some degree, the possibility of love. . . . I had the impression of possessing her completely that I never had when she was awake.)

In Proust the novel still resists total abstraction, total formalization. Proust never wrote a *Bouvard et Pécuchet*. In *La Recherche*, discovering the shape of experience still has to proceed experientially. Despair is progressive in *La Recherche* as in the rest of the tradition. This is what Proust's "lost paradise" means: there have to have been hopes for hope to be annihilated. Whence the pattern, so reminiscent of Flaubert, of the successive love disasters in *La Recherche*: Swann-Odette; Marcel-Gilberte; Marcel-Oriane; Marcel-Albertine; Charlus-Morel; Saint-Loup-Gilberte, and so on. Each catastrophic affair takes us another step toward concluding that we will not require further demonstration of Proust's point in order to believe him.

As with Emma Bovary's suicide, a moment finally comes when there is no material left for any further moments. Except in the surreal atmosphere of *Bouvard*, experience cannot always be drying up without ever exhausting itself. The novel is finite, and inevitably it concludes. On the way, the possibility of satisfying relationships between people has been made to seem increasingly remote.

Proust's brilliant perception of suspicion between man and woman, his extraordinary dissection of the power relationships that poison affection, lead the novel, by the time of *Sodome et Gomorrhe*, almost to declaring the impossibility of heterosexual love. The verse from "La Colère de Samson" which provided the title of Proust's middle volume (see II, 601) evokes its context, Vigny's pessimistic portrait of sexual hostility:

> Bientôt, se retirant dans un hideux royaume,
> La Femme aura Gomorrhe et l'Homme aura Sodome,
> Et, se jetant au loin un regard irrité,
> Les deux sexes mourront chacun de son côté.

> (Retreating into their hideous kingdom,
> Women have Gomorrah; Men have Sodom.
> Exchanging glances hard as stone,
> Two sexes expire, entirely alone.)

Homosexuality emerges at this point as a final fall-back position, while the heterosexual crises of *La Prisonnière*

and *La Fugitive* follow immediately to complete the demonstration in that area. I am persuaded that Proust experienced his homosexuality as a last resort for affection; but
it too proves impossible early in *Le Temps retrouvé*.

The logic of the presentation thus leads, at this final
stage, to a remarkable depopulation of the affective world
outside the self. The characters of central importance
throughout the novel are largely absent from the celebrated
Guermantes matinée. Swann, Albertine—the subjects of
entire sections; Charlus—whose importance is cumulative
but equal to theirs; Bergotte, Vinteuil, Elstir—the models
for the artist in the novel; the narrator's grandmother,
mother and father: all have disappeared by the climactic
scene. The absent characters are, generally, those who
have attempted love; on the other hand, the aged masks
who attend the matinée represent individuals whose social
hollowness has long been known to us. The authentic
presence of "others" in the novel—of people for whom our
affection, like Marcel's, could be more than superficial—is
thus abolished by the final scene. Some are dead, the
remainder (by far the less humanly valuable) are gro-
tesquely caricatured, transformed by the narration into a
gallery of flat, unreal specimens. *A la recherche du temps
perdu* thus seems to move from attempts to describe and
understand human relationships on an affective plane to
the elimination of all "round" characters, of all substantial
relationships, in order to make possible the narrator's experience of absolute selfhood in solitude.

"The individual whose authentic life has been stolen
from him seeks it elsewhere," wrote Barbéris concerning
Balzac's effort to find self-realization in a hostile world.[2]
It is hard to see Proust's revelation of art in any other light.
A la recherche du temps perdu asserts that the only heroic
stance which remains possible is that of the artist-hero who
achieves—or is supposed to achieve—self-realization in

2. "Tout être volé cherche ailleurs la vraie vie"; *Balzac et le mal du siècle*,
I, 351.

imaginative creation, following a disastrous experience of social life. If for Mallarmé and Proust the world exists to end up as a book, it is because, through bitter experience, they failed to discover what else the world might be good for.

But this defensive effort to situate "authentic life" in artistic creation was not totally comfortable for Proust, and did not altogether convince him. He remained too much a part of the long moral tradition of the novel to believe fully that redemption could be found in esthetic joy, in the pure formalism of the imagination's unrestricted play. He is no symbolist, no surrealist, and the magic mental license of Dada is far from his practice.

Consider his frequently quoted plea to readers in *Le Temps retrouvé*: "I would ask them neither to praise me nor to censure me, only to tell me if it seems right to them ["si c'est bien cela"], if the words they read within themselves are truly the ones I've written down" (III, 1033). In inviting us to judge his book by its fidelity to our own experience, the novel begins to uncover its most profound internal contradiction. It asks to be read as a cultural diagnosis, transcending its own unprecedented subjectivity. But its view of reality so completely dissolves the concrete existence of individuals that their very being is called into question.

To whom then is Proust appealing when he asks us to understand his portrait of experience? Where are the people situated to whom the novel is addressed? Proust believes in them—the writing of the novel can only be explained if he believes—*but he cannot write about them*. They exist nowhere *within* the novel; indeed, Proust's techniques function in concert to assure their absence. The world portrayed and the world defined are thus totally discontinuous. The Realist's confidence in the outside has long since disappeared, yet Proust still requires the outside. This is why his so palpable isolation from it, though it is given to us as a triumph, somewhere deep in the texture of the novel is experienced as despair.

Through the domination of the synthetic mode, the concrete world has become almost totally indistinct for Proust. The social gatherings in the novel are increasingly composed of sequences of disembodied voices who come forward to say a few words before receding into grayness. The sense of surrounding reality, which the Realists had striven to create in order to connect the fates of their characters with authentic causation, in Proust fades in increasing vagueness. The social reality of the narrator is uncertain; the sort of hollow assertion we would object to in a second-rate novelist is all the representation we have of him (see for example passages on II, 169 or III, 42). Nor do we know anything about his physical appearance. A search through the novel comes up only with such vague elements as "that odd smile, that uneven moustache" (II, 466). "Marcel," in fact, remains virtually invisible (he was probably not even meant to have a name).

Albertine is invisible too. Her physical portrait omits whole elements of her appearance; her personality, seen through Marcel's obsession, is almost completely diffuse. Her existence becomes more and more tenuous until, as Proust surely planned it, she almost seems an imaginary figure. The presence of *others* in this novel, seemingly so abounding in the life of such a dense population, is thus almost completely problematical well before the Guermantes matinée calls the existence of social relations into final, crucial, question.

"Proustian time" is the shibboleth of Proust criticism. Why is it so distinctive in *La Recherche*, so crucial to our understanding? The new shape taken by time in *A la recherche du temps perdu* is an emanation, a consequence, of the veiling of the subject-object dialectic in the novel after Flaubert. The Realist novel discovers disaster at the end of a long process of experience, and time is consequently the vivifying force in Realist plots. As the century went on, however, the discovery of disaster became internalized, as the dialectical relationship between self

and other became increasingly obscured, increasingly difficult to sense in concrete experience. What had been felt
as a progressive series of determining events began to seem
a pervasive atmosphere of defeat. This is what distinguishes
Julien Sorel's eventual undoing from Frédéric Moreau's
over-determined debacle. In Proust, the consciousness of
disaster as a universal element in experience moves to a
new level of the novelistic texture. There is still ample
experiential material in *La Recherche*. But the image of
this experience is transformed by technical procedures far
more thorough than the "constant obstacle" of *L'Education sentimentale*. Synthetic narration in Proust leaves
experience-to-come none of the freedom it seems to have
had in Stendhal. Time no longer vivifies narrative since at
bottom it is no longer experienced in life.

Despite attempts to assimilate *La Recherche* to existen-
tialist thinking, the ideology of the novel is essentialist.
For Proust, nothing in experience is really contingent, and
Jauss rightly speaks of the novel's systematic "transforma-
tion of events into examples."[3] This is why the moral
lessons of experience in *La Recherche* are always ordered,
on the next level of abstraction, by a series of laws and
maxims which Proust took obvious pride in deriving (see
III, 1041). In the Sartrian sense, *everything* in *La Recherche* is "totalized"; and the entire force of Proust's
view of reality argues that this is necessary.

But maxims live awkwardly within narrative; they are
timeless while narrative requires time to exist. Time in
Proust has always been recognized as achronological. But
being achronological, it is *futureless*. At the deepest level
Proust knows hope is vain, and awaits nothing. *But then
telling a story becomes absurd.* The immense three thousand
page bulk of this gigantic novel is thus at profound odds
with the most crucial metaphysical implication of the view
of experience presented.

This central contradiction in *La Recherche* has remained

3. Quoted by Henri Bonnet, "Une étude allemande sur Proust," p. 313.

central to the novel. Proust, of course, does not stand only as the culmination of the tradition emerging from the Realists. He points forward as well, and the evolution of fiction in the twentieth century proceeds from his work. But the key problem is still seen most clearly in *A la recherche du temps perdu*: Proust's hermit-artist has no friends, needs none, seeks solitude. Yet novels are made up of relationships and love affairs. Similarly, the artist of Proustian Time is beyond *durée*. But beyond *durée* there is no novel. The attempt to join the realm of social action and the realm of personal authenticity, the fundamental tension in the novel since Stendhal, in Proust thus reaches a crucial impasse.

Subsequent fictional systems, whatever our admiration for the courage with which they took on this intractable problem, have not resolved it with any more success than Proust. However heterodox the assertion, novelists since Proust do not strike me as having reconceptualized the relationship between narrative system and objective reality beyond what had been realized during the century of efforts from *Le Rouge et le noir* to *A la recherche du temps perdu*.

Stated schematically, the terms of Proust's impasse defined two possible routes for fiction after *La Recherche*. Writers could attempt to regenerate the narration of meaningful action in the social world; or they could devise systems which dispense even more radically than did Proust with the narrated event in order to immerse themselves in some version of a privileged, static world whose geography might be explored.

Malraux's novels no doubt represent the most prestigious case of the former choice. In their attempt to reunite the realms of inner authenticity and effective action, they reach back precisely to the problem of the early Realist period. In 1830 the frontier of conflict between the individual and the social world was still visibly situated within the borders of Paris (as Balzac clearly asserted in the opening pages of *Le Père Goriot*). But by 1928 or 1933 (dates, respectively, of *Les Conquérants* and *La Condition humaine*), the social dialectic could no longer be experienced directly in France, and logically Malraux found his subject in a region of the world where social development still permitted locating the individual's conflict in a narration of outward action. One need only examine the openings of these books, with their explicit indications of place and date, their tense movement into action so reminiscent of Balzac's setting and then unleashing of his "dramas," to be persuaded that Malraux sought in China or in the Spain of the Civil War places where human significance was no longer private or privileged. His novels struggle to define a world where history might again be felt as the primary force moving reality and creating its meaning for individuals.

But Malraux was a twentieth-century European ("occidental" is his own despairing term), and his effort to regenerate the essential elements of the Realist paradigm was complicated by all that had occurred in Europe since Balzac's time. To recall a term used above in discussing Flaubert, no writer who lived after the fall could naïvely recapture the Realists' openness to experience, their hope—so soon to be abandoned—that the individual might be saved *in the world*. Despite the burning enthusiasm of revolutionary conviction and the optimism of "virile fraternity," Malraux's China and Spain are suffused with the sense that such salvation will not be found. The Chinese in *La Condition humaine* have all been touched in some corrosive way by Europe. This contact, which mediates the coming to consciousness of their individuality, at the same time condemns them to varying forms of alienation from each other and from the society they hope to create. Given to us as proletarian heroes, they fatally resemble Julien Sorel, Stendhal's unlikely peasant: at the deepest level, they, like Julien, are necessarily bourgeois, and their experience lies under the same curse.

Malraux searches through them for access to a humanism

which might abolish the isolation of post-Flaubertian consciousness. The project of his novels seems to be to contradict the grave diagnosis of the individual's possibilities which became explicit in Proust. But no more for Malraux than for the Stendhal of *Lucien Leuwen* is choice of vision free. One cannot create whatever fiction one desires: this is the lesson of novels since the French Revolution. To judge by their plots, there is no escape from history, and the Europe to which Malraux necessarily returns refuses optimistic construction.

The Spanish Civil War had not been lost by the end of *L'Espoir*, but (almost as if Flaubert at his most sardonic had composed it as an epilogue to Malraux's own conclusion) real history was once again to intervene as a constant obstacle to hope. The bitterly ironic light thus cast upon the book's title might stand as an epitaph for Malraux's attempt to avoid Proust's despairing turn toward the past and toward the inside as the only possibility for happiness. (The concept and the title of *Antimémoires* show that Malraux still resists precisely these elements of Proust's solution.)

But how does it work out in the fiction? On the intellectual level Malraux maintains optimism in the last chapter of *L'Espoir*, with its touching invocation of the infinite possibilities of human destiny, of Manuel's discovery of life. But the atmosphere of the narrated action—always a more significant index of the meaning of a fiction than any discursive assertion—is much less certain at the end. It is surely no accident that the music Manuel listens to in this final chapter of *L'Espoir* is Beethoven's *Les Adieux*.[4]

4. Among other novelists who have explored this first route for resolving the contradiction that emerges in Proust, one might name Saint-Exupéry; the Sartre of *Les Chemins de la liberté* (significantly abandoned); the Aragon of the earlier novels, though in *Aurélien* (1945) one senses a very definite infusion of nostalgia, always a significant sign that this vein may be playing out (in *La Semaine sainte* of 1958, Aragon is obliged to return to the period of the Restoration itself in order to recapture some of the historical energy which is essential in these books); the Camus of *La Peste* (another frontier situation); and less important figures, Duhamel, Romains, Martin du Gard. In the United

The mood of this immanent defeat dominatès the other strain in fiction after Proust, defines its atmosphere and its range. In varying ways Sartre's *La Nausée*, the novels of Beckett, the *nouveau roman* all explore it. These worlds work toward total immobility, total abolition of narrative, total ahistorical immersion in the mental images which Proust developed at the center of his system. Beckett's haunting "Where now? Who now? When now?" at the opening of *The Unnamable* asserts through the use of just four words and a brilliantly tensed punctuation mark this fiction's radical denial of the sure grasp of external reality, referable at all times to objective geography, identity, chronology, that characterizes Balzac's worlds. Beckett concentrates in this first line his immersion in the haunted present which was always virtual in Proust, but whose full assertion *La Recherche* had reserved for periods of desperation like the one in *La Fugitive* analyzed above. Beckett lives constantly in the prostration that follows Albertine's death. "Can it be that one day . . . I simply stayed in?" Thus *The Unnamable* continues—but without ever progressing.

It is characteristic of these systems that they are unable to penetrate to the origin of the individual's catastrophe, for if one could get an answer to Beckett's questions— who? what? when?—the curse of total subjectivity would be broken. So writers in this strain "stay in," as Beckett has it: "I am alone here, now, well sheltered" (Robbe-Grillet, opening of *Dans le labyrinthe*.). From this painful "inside," they tell what they are able to see: "yellow and then black for the time of an eye blinking and then yellow again: wings stretched out rapid arbalist form between the sun and the eye" (Claude Simon, opening of *La Bataille de Pharsale*). Simon is brilliantly measuring Lucan's ability to tell a story—the historical Battle of Pharsalus (48 B.C.; 5,000 dead; Pompey dethroned) changed lives

---

States Hemingway stands as perhaps the most significant of any of these figures.

decisively—against his own inability to connect the meaning of a tale with the things that happen to the characters
in it. His sensitivity to the objects of his description is
extraordinary; his descent into the inside, his discovery of
territory still unexplored, are impressive and affecting. But
the direction taken is already evident in Proust, and in no
way—neither in precision nor in desperation—do the novelists in this strain supersede him. They are able only to
follow out his clues with brilliant instinct—for example, in
Simon's extraordinary account in his best novel of the pre-
history of his own isolation, in which he takes Proust's lost
paradise back past the childhood world of "Combray"
and makes it *explicitly* intrauterine:

> . . . la femme penchant son mystérieux buste de
> chair blanche enveloppé de dentelles ce sein qui
> déjà peut-être me portait dans son ténébreux taber-
> nacle sorte de têtard gélatineux lové sur lui-même avec
> ses deux énormes yeux sa tête de ver à soie sa bouche
> sans dents son front cartilagineux d'insecte, moi?
> [End of *Histoire*] [5]

> (. . . the woman leaning her mysterious pale flesh bust
> clothed in lace this breast that perhaps already was
> carrying me in its tenebrous tabernacle a kind of

5. An analysis of the verbal systems in these two strains of post-Proustian
fiction would show that while Malraux strives to recapture the progressive
energy of the active mode of narration (definite chronological specificity,
punctual preterites, vigorous direct dialogue, and so on), accounting for his
misnamed "cinematic" quality, the Beckettian paradigm slips further into the
atmospheric illusion of synthetic telling: the usual texture of floating progressive presents and present participles, already exploited in Flaubert, as Proust
had observed; the frequent omission of the verb altogether, completely opening up the moment of utterance as an all-encompassing temporal void—deepen
the durative feel of the telling, stifle any progressive thrust within it, and
allow the static image of experience an extraordinary power of development.
But all these techniques have their clear precedents; there are virtually no *new*
narrative choices made, or to be made.

gelatinous tadpole coiled upon itself with its two out-
sized eyes its silkworm head its toothless mouth its
cartilaginous insect brow, me?)

If one steps back to examine the course of the tradition
since the Realists, the entropy of fictional worlds after *La
Recherche* seems an emanation from Proust. The difficulty
is thus *not* placing Proust's successors in relation to him.
Impulses in *La Recherche* seem to dominate them despite
their ingeniousness. Writers since Flaubert have *necessarily*
experienced social reality as a negation of their hopes and
a resistance to their dreams of self-realization. What else
could their books communicate? Until outward reality is
altered, until the negation of this negation, in some form
as yet obscure, restores positive energy to the relation between individuals and their world, fictions will continue
trapped in Proust's impasse.

The task is rather to place Proust in the course of the
social dialectic which animates the entire tradition. The
problem is crucial because Proust so firmly resists believing
that any dialectic operates, and denies explicitly that the
situation of the individual depends upon any historical
crisis. But the ideology of a novelistic representation of the
world, its vision of experience, is not identical with its
subject, and still less with its explicit intellectual judgments about the way the world works. Proust's tense and
conflicted relation to history is visible precisely in the
insistence with which he denies it. His novel epitomizes a
system of thinking which arises when the consequences of
exploring the social dialectic have become thoroughly,
painfully apparent. They seem so disastrous that, in its
own defense, creative mind begins to explore situating
the region of human self-realization in imagination, completely independent of outside disasters: "[Les] déceptions de ma vie . . . me faisaient croire que sa réalité devait
résider ailleurs qu'en l'action" (III, 877; "The disappoint-

ments of my life . . . obliged me to conclude that its reality must reside elsewhere than in action").

As the social contradiction attains levels of almost unendurable dissonance in the last part of the nineteenth century, liberty is thus hypostatized as a value to be realized within the soul alone. The external world becomes the domain of blind necessity; the world of the mind the region of unrestricted self-exploration, unprecedented sensitivity, and unrestricted esthetic joy.

This attitude attempts to define history out of the picture. But its crucial contingence *upon the evolution of history* was seen as early as 1802, in Hegel's critique of the process of "internalization" (*Verinnerlichung*) which he foresaw as a consequence of history's movement in the post-Revolutionary period. Hegel clearly felt the temptation to isolate subjective consciousness from the objective world. But at this point in his philosophical evolution, he insisted that the contradiction between personal authenticity and the hostile world could not be abolished by a defensive strategy of introversion. The antagonism between the two realms required resolution in concrete experience. The subject cannot be isolated from the objective world, nor can total immersion in the inner world of the individual lead to his self-realization.[6]

One need not be a Hegelian or a Marxist to sense the sadness that underlies all attempts after Flaubert to discover happiness "inside." No less than the revolutionaries, the writers seem to find internalization disheartening, though their investment in it is immense. So the tradition from Mallarmé to Proust which tries to realize the soul in isolation and to subsume the world in a book requires dialectical interpretation even though its terms strain to deny the dialectic.[7]

6. "Differenz des Fichteschen und Schellingschen Systems," in *Erste Druckschriften*, pp. 18–21; see Herbert Marcuse, *Reason and Revolution: Hegel and the Rise of Social Theory*, p. 47.

7. Those familiar with the Hegel of the *Phenomenology* may find this assertion surprising, since the position that Mallarmé and Proust take is closest to

When one looks in Proust for indices of the dialectic behind the denial, it is easy to see the strategy that disguises it and the terms in which, translated, it nonetheless appears and even dominates. Proust's book for twenty-eight hundred pages is about the past, and this intense effort to trace the shape of the soul's contact with the world that it has passed through is, more than any nineteenth century Realist vision of experience, the most thorough exploration of the individual's relation to the social world that the novel has yet produced. The difficulty is that Proust denied that the shape of this social world outside is in any way contingent upon history. In his view the soul's isolation is ineluctable; the dilemma of the self eternal, universal.

But do we not feel in the passionate concern with which the novelist explores his own past a constant impulse which contradicts this explicit judgment, an attempt to understand the soul's dilemma not as a universal constant but as a product of history? Why else does Proust search for lost time? Discussions of his ideology frequently caricature the novel by forgetting the very Balzacian feel of so much of its texture (particularly the social portraiture), and the Stendhalian character, though hypertrophied, of much of the exploration of love. The Realist's acute attention to the relation between self and other is a preponderant tendency in *La Recherche*, yet in critical discussion of the novel's view of reality, Proust tends to

the philosophical Idealism of Hegel's later works. Hegel's Absolute Knowledge, the triumph of intellectual self-consciousness, is the *Phenomenology*'s solution to the alienation of the individual. But as Jean Hyppolite makes clear, this later position of Hegel's (which is at the origin of Feuerbach's and Marx's criticism of Hegel) seems itself to be the product of Hegel's experience of alienation, rather than the free assertion of Mind as a means for understanding and mastering the world. As Hyppolite puts it: "Pure speculation is unable to resolve a particular historical problem . . ." (*Studies on Marx and Hegel*, p. 85). The loneliness of writers is a powerful demonstration of the point. But perhaps one finds in Hegel himself the most evocative evidence against the position he takes in the *Phenomenology*: the chilling image of Consciousness contemplating itself within a bare skull (*Phenomenology of Mind*, pp. 358 ff.).

become the Proust of *Le Temps retrouvé* exclusively. But there is too much insistence on the world in which the dialectic plays itself out for Proust's meaning to be encompassed in the world where the dialectic has ceased to operate, the realm in which it is irrelevant. There is too much concern in the novel about society and how it fails for the world of art to be the total locus of meaning in *A la recherche du temps perdu*.

In fact, Proust's religion of art is as inadequate to the demands of concrete reality in the twentieth century as was Balzac's reactionary Catholicism to the incoherences of French society during the July Monarchy. Both however are symptomatic of the dilemma of post-Revolutionary man, and neither theology totally duped its theologian. We need to be clear about what art can do. Its task and its skill are not in resolving the contradictions in the world. Art functions more naturally and more powerfully in portraying these crucial dissonances at their source, and with their full problematic quality.

To be sure, Proust's intellectual, idealist solution to the dilemma of experience appears to reduce human alienation. But just as surely, salvation through art is insufficient. No one seriously imagines that all men could live as Proust lived, or attempt to realize themselves in writing personal versions of *A la recherche du temps perdu*.

At the last, Proust's celebration of his "deliverance from time" is unconvincing. If there is joy in his writing, it is the joy of having portrayed outward reality in its most fundamental contradiction, not the joy of having rendered outward reality irrelevant. The real artistic dignity of Proust is to be found here: in the courage with which his depiction of the world confronts the world's resistance. He sees it with exceeding clarity for nearly the whole of *La Recherche*. At the end, his resolution of the tension that he conceptualized more adequately than anyone before him is—necessarily—a false resolution; the self which

Proust defines as highest at the end of the novel is a false self. This incoherence in his system only reflects a level of contradiction in reality which it is not given to the mind alone to abolish.

But to discover how profound is the contradiction that made resolving the dissonance within Proust's esthetic impossible, we rightly examine the fates of people in *A la recherche du temps perdu*. Through Proust's novel, properly interpreted in the light of its tradition, we possess the reality Proust sought to fix, and simultaneously understand why the novel itself could not seize this reality unambiguously.

If *La Recherche* turns upon and contradicts itself in its deepest essence, its most intense assertion, the energy behind this conflict is thus dialectical energy. The novel strives to exclude it, to sustain the synthesis of contraries which emerges precisely where it should most have remained buried, at the conclusion. This dissonance is profoundly revealing about the true configuration of the world the novel portrays. In other words, precisely because it embodies such a powerfully accurate feeling for the reality that generated it, *La Recherche* as a story annihilates itself.

In turn, however, through the paradox of its problematic existence, we are able to comprehend to what extraordinary deformation of the self—which naturally seeks its realization in concrete social activity—Proust was driven when he tried, just short of a century after the Realists began the effort in earnest, to determine, once again, what a person could become in the modern world. The experiences that no one has portrayed better than he—love, loss, loneliness—are experiences of pain. In a brilliant, bitter page of stock-taking near the end of the novel, Proust correctly traced this pain back to "l'impuissance que nous avons à nous réaliser dans la jouissance matérielle, dans l'action" (III, 877; "our inherent powerlessness

to realize ourselves in material enjoyment or in effective
action"). The same pain, for the same reason, has been
at the center of the French novel since the Revolution.
Proust cannot be understood outside this hundred-year
tradition of attempts to understand why living has become
unlivable.

Works Cited

PRIMARY WORKS (with dates of first publication)

Balzac, Honoré. *Eugénie Grandet* (1833). Edited by Pierre-Georges Castex. Paris: Garnier, Classiques Garnier, 1965.
———. *Illusions perdues* (1843). Edited by Antoine Adam. Paris: Garnier, Classiques Garnier, 1965.
———. *La Peau de chagrin* (1831). Edited by Maurice Allem. Paris: Garnier, Classiques Garnier, 1960.
———. *Le Père Goriot* (1835). Edited by Pierre-Georges Castex. Paris: Garnier, Classiques Garnier, 1963.
———. *Splendeurs et misères des courtisanes* (1847). Edited by Antoine Adam. Paris: Garnier, Classiques Garnier, 1964.

Flaubert, Gustave. *Correspondance*. 9 vols. Paris: Conard, 1926–1933. *Supplément*. 4 vols. Paris: Conard, 1954.
———. *Bouvard et Pécuchet* (1881). In *Oeuvres*, edited by Albert Thibaudet and René Dumesnil. 2 vols. Paris: Gallimard, Pléiade, 1952.
———. *L'Education sentimentale* (1869). In *Oeuvres*, edited by Albert Thibaudet and René Dumesnil. 2 vols. Paris: Gallimard, Pléiade, 1952.
———. *Madame Bovary* (1857). Edited by Claudine Gothot-Mersch. Paris: Garnier, Classiques Garnier, 1971.

Huysmans, Joris-Karl. *A rebours* (1884). Paris: Fasquelle, 1965.

Mallarmé, Stéphane. *Oeuvres complètes*. Edited by Henri Mondor and G. Jean-Aubry. Paris: Gallimard, Pléiade, 1945.

Musset, Alfred de. *La Confession d'un enfant du siècle* (1836). Edited by Claude Duchet and Maurice Allem. Paris: Garnier, Classiques Garnier, 1968.

Proust, Marcel. *A la recherche du temps perdu* (1913–

1927). 3 vols. Edited by Pierre Clarac and André Ferré. Paris: Gallimard, Pléiade, 1954.

——. Cahiers. Sixty-two school notebooks, containing sketches and reworkings of passages from all sections of *A la recherche du temps perdu* and from other works of Proust. Bibliothèque Nationale, Département des Manuscrits.

——. *Chroniques* (1927). Paris: Gallimard, 1949.

——. *Contre Sainte-Beuve* (contains *Pastiches et mélanges* and "Essais et articles"). Edited by Pierre Clarac and Yves Sandre. Paris: Gallimard, Pléiade, 1971. Cited as *CSB*.

——. *Correspondance générale*. 6 vols. Edited by Robert Proust, Paul Brach, Suzy Mante-Proust and Philip Kolb. Paris: Plon, 1930–1936.

——. *Jean Santeuil* (contains *Les Plaisirs et les jours*). Edited by Pierre Clarac and Yves Sandre. Paris: Gallimard, Pléiade, 1971.

——. *Lettres à la NRF*. In Les Cahiers Marcel Proust, No. 6, pp. 89–273. Paris: Gallimard, 1932.

——. *Marcel Proust: Choix de lettres*. Edited by Philip Kolb. Paris: Plon, 1965.

——. *Marcel Proust: Textes retrouvés*. Edited by Philip Kolb and Larkin B. Price. Urbana: University of Illinois Press, 1968.

Stendhal [Marie Henri Beyle]. *La Chartreuse de Parme* (1839). Edited by Antoine Adam. Paris: Garnier, Classiques Garnier, 1973.

——. *Journal.* In *Oeuvres intimes*. Edited by Henri Martineau. Paris: Gallimard, Pléiade, 1955.

——. *Lamiel* (1842). In *Romans et nouvelles*. Edited by Henri Martineau. 2 vols. Paris: Gallimard, Pléiade, 1952.

——. *Lucien Leuwen* (1834–1835). In *Romans et nouvelles*. Edited by Henri Martineau. 2 vols. Paris: Gallimard, Pléiade, 1952.

——. *Mélanges intimes et marginalia*. Edited by Henri Martineau. 2 vols. Paris: Divan, 1936.

——. *Le Rouge et le noir* (1830). Edited by Pierre-Georges Castex. Paris: Garnier, Classiques Garnier, 1973.

CRITICAL WORKS

Adam, Antoine, ed. *Romanciers du XVIIe siècle*. Paris: Gallimard, Pléiade, 1958.

Adams, Robert M. *Stendhal: Notes on a Novelist*. Paperbound edition. New York: Noonday Press, 1959.

Albaret, Céleste. *Monsieur Proust*. Paris: R. Laffont, 1973.

Auerbach, Erich. *Mimesis: The Representation of Reality in Western Literature*. Translated by Willard Trask. Princeton: Princeton University Press, 1953.

Barbéris, Pierre. *Balzac et le mal du siècle: Contribution à une physiologie du monde moderne*. 2 vols. Paris: Gallimard, Bibliothèque des idées, 1970.

——. *Balzac: Une Mythologie réaliste*. Paris: Larousse, Thèmes et Textes, 1971.

——. *Le Père Goriot de Balzac: Ecriture, structures, significations*. Paris: Larousse, Thèmes et Textes, 1972.

——. "Mal du siècle ou d'un romantisme de droite à un romantisme de gauche." In *Romantisme et politique 1815-1851*. Colloque de l'Ecole Normale Supérieure de Saint-Cloud, pp. 164–82. Paris: A. Colin, 1969.

——. *Le Monde de Balzac*. Paris: Arthaud, 1973.

——. *Mythes balzaciens*. Paris: A. Colin, 1972.

Bardèche, Maurice. *Marcel Proust romancier*. 2 vols. Paris: Les Sept couleurs, 1971.

Béguin, Albert. *Balzac lu et relu*. Paris: Seuil, 1965.

Bell, Clive. *Proust*. New York: Harcourt, Brace, 1929.

Benjamin, Walter. *Illuminationen: Ausgewählte Schriften*. Edited by Siegfried Unseld. Frankfurt a. M.: Suhrkamp, 1961.

——. *Illuminations*. Translated by Harry Zohn. Paperbound edition. New York: Schocken, 1969.

Bersani, Leo. *Marcel Proust: The Fictions of Life and of Art*. New York: Oxford University Press, 1965.

Blanchot, Maurice. "Le Roman, oeuvre de mauvaise foi."

Les Temps Modernes, no. 19 (April 1947), pp. 1304–17.
——. "L'Expérience de Proust" (1954). In *Le Livre à venir*, pp. 18–34. Paris: Gallimard, 1959.

Bois, Elie-Joseph. Interview with Marcel Proust. *Le Temps*, 13 November 1913, p. 4. Quoted according to *Marcel Proust: Choix de lettres*, pp. 283–89. Also reprinted in *Marcel Proust: Textes Retrouvés*, pp. 215–19.

Bollème, Geneviève. *Le second volume de "Bouvard et Pécuchet."* Paris: Denoël, 1966.

Bonnet, Henri. "Une étude allemande sur Proust." Review of H. R. Jauss, "Proust auf der Suche nach seiner Konzeption des Romans." *Revue d'Esthétique* 9 (1956): 312–21.

Brombert, Victor, "Stendhal, Analyst or Amorist?" *Yale French Studies*, no. 11 (1953), pp. 39–48. Reprinted in *Stendhal: A Collection of Critical Essays*, edited by Victor Brombert, pp. 157–66. Englewood Cliffs, N.J.: Prentice-Hall, 1962.

——. *Stendhal: La Voie oblique*. Paris: Presses Universitaires de France, 1954.

Caillois, Roger. Preface to Montesquieu, *Oeuvres complètes*. Paris: Gallimard, Pléiade, 1949–1958.

Caudwell, Christopher. *Illusion and Reality: A Study of the Sources of Poetry*. New York: International Publishers, 1963.

Crémieux, Benjamin, ed. *Du côté de Marcel Proust, suivi de lettres inédites de Marcel Proust à Benjamin Crémieux*. Paris: Lemarget, 1929.

Curtius, Ernst-Robert. "Les Bases sociales de l'oeuvre de Proust." *Le Rouge et le Noir*, April 1928, pp. 31–36.

——. *Marcel Proust*. Translated by A. Pierhal. Paris: Editions de la Revue Nouvelle, 1928.

Daniel, Georges. *Temps et mystification dans "A la recherche du temps perdu."* Paris: Nizet, 1963.

Daudet, Lucien, ed. *Autour de soixante lettres de Marcel Proust*. Les Cahiers Marcel Proust, No. 6. Paris: Gallimard, 1929.

Durry, Marie-Jeanne. *Flaubert et ses projets inédits*. Paris: Nizet, 1950.

Feuillerat, Albert. *Comment Marcel Proust a composé son roman*. New Haven: Yale University Press, 1934.

Forster, E. M. *Aspects of the Novel*. Paperbound edition. New York: Harcourt, Brace & World, Harvest, 1954.

Frank, Joseph. "Spatial Form in Modern Literature" (1945). In his *The Widening Gyre*, pp. 3–62. New Brunswick, N.J.: Rutgers University Press, 1963.

Garey, Howard B. "Verbal Aspect in French." *Language* 33 (1957): 91–110.

Gide, André. "Billet à Angèle, à propos de Marcel Proust." *Nouvelle Revue Française* 16 (1921): 586–91. Reprinted in *Marcel Proust: Lettres à André Gide*, edited by André Gide. Neuchâtel and Paris: Ides et Calendes, 1949.

Guizot, François. *Mémoires pour servir à l'histoire de mon temps*. 8 vols. Paris: Michel Lévy, 1872.

Hardy, Barbara. *The Appropriate Form*. London: Athlone Press, 1964.

Hegel, G. W. F. *Erste Druckschriften*. Edited by G. Lasson. Leipzig: Felix von Meiner, 1928.

——. *Phenomenology of Mind*. Translated by J. B. Baillie. 2nd revised edition. London: George Allen and Unwin, 1949.

Hobsbawm, E. J. *The Age of Revolution, 1789–1848*. Paperbound edition. New York: New American Library, Mentor, 1962.

Hommage à Marcel Proust. Les Cahiers Marcel Proust, No. 1 (republication of special number of *Nouvelle Revue Française* of 1 January 1923). Paris: Gallimard, 1927.

Houston, John P. "Temporal Patterns in *A la recherche du temps perdu*." *French Studies* 16 (1962): 33–44.

Hyppolite, Jean. *Studies on Marx and Hegel*. Translated by John O'Neill. Paperbound edition. New York: Harper & Row, Torchbook, 1969.

Jauss, Hans Robert. *Zeit und Erinnerung in Marcel Prousts*

"A la recherche du temps perdu." Heidelberg: Winter, 1955.

Kahler, Erich. *The Inward Turn of Narrative.* Translated by Richard and Clara Winston. Princeton: Princeton University Press, 1973.

Kermode, Frank. *The Sense of an Ending.* New York: Oxford University Press, 1967.

Klum, Arne. *Verbe et adverbe.* Stockholm: Almqvist and Wiksell, 1961.

Kolb, Philip. *La Correspondance de Marcel Proust: Chronologie et commentaire critique.* Illinois Studies in Language and Literature, vol. 33, nos. 1–2. Urbana: University of Illinois Press, 1949.

de Lauris, Georges, ed. *A un ami*: *Correspondance inédite, 1903–1922.* Paris: Amiot-Dumont, 1948.

Levin, Harry. *The Gates of Horn.* New York: Oxford University Press, 1963.

Lukács, Georg. *Studies in European Realism.* Paperbound edition. New York: Grosset & Dunlap, Universal, 1970.

Malraux, André. "Laclos." In *Tableau de la littérature française XVIIe–XVIIIe siècles,* preface by André Gide. Paris: Gallimard, 1939.

Marcuse, Herbert. *Reason and Revolution: Hegel and the Rise of Social Theory.* Boston: Beacon Press, 1960.

Maurois, André. *A la recherche de Marcel Proust.* Paris: Hachette, 1949.

Muir, Edwin. *The Structure of the Novel.* London: Hogarth Press, 1963.

Muller, Marcel. *Les Voix narratives dans la "Recherche du temps perdu."* Geneva: Droz, 1965.

Ortega y Gasset, José. "Le Temps, la distance et la forme chez Proust." In *Hommage à Marcel Proust,* q.v., pp. 287–99.

Painter, George D. *Marcel Proust: A Biography.* 2 vols. London: Chatto and Windus, 1959–1965.

Pierre-Quint, Léon, ed. *Comment parut "Du côté de chez Swann": Lettres de Marcel Proust à Renè Blum, Bernard Grasset, et Louis Brun.* Paris: Kra, 1930.

Poulet, Georges, *L'Espace proustien*. Paris: Gallimard, 1963.

——. *Etudes sur le temps humain*. Paris: Plon, 1950.

Revel, Jean-François. *Sur Proust*. Paris: Julliard, 1960.

Richard, Jean-Pierre. "Connaissance et tendresse chez Stendhal." In his *Littérature et sensation,* pp. 15–116. Paris: Seuil, 1954.

Rogers, B. G. *Proust's Narrative Techniques*. Geneva: Droz, 1965.

Rousset, Jean. *Forme et signification*. Paris: Corti, 1964.

Sartre, Jean-Paul. "A propos de *Le Bruit et la fureur*: la temporalité chez Faulkner." In his *Situations I*, pp. 70–81. Paris: Gallimard, 1947.

——. *L'Idiot de la famille: Gustave Flaubert de 1821 à 1857*. 3 vols. Paris: Gallimard, Bibliothèque de philosophie, 1971–1972.

Scholes, Robert, and Kellogg, Robert. *The Nature of Narrative*. New York: Oxford University Press, 1966.

Scott-Moncrieff, C. K., ed. *Marcel Proust: An English Tribute*. London: Chatto and Windus, 1923.

Shattuck, Roger. *Proust's Binoculars*. New York: Random House, 1963.

Spitzer, Leo. "Zum Stil Marcel Prousts" (1928). In his *Stilstudien II*, pp. 365–497. Munich: Max Hübner, 1961.

Starobinski, Jean. "Stendhal pseudonyme." In his *L'Oeil vivant*, pp. 193–244. Paris: Gallimard, 1961.

Steen, James T. "Values and Difficulties in the Art of Marcel Proust." In *Six Novelists*, foreword by Austin Wright, pp. 67–81. Carnegie Series in English, no. 5. Pittsburgh: Carnegie Institute of Technology Press, 1959.

Sten, Holger. *Les Temps du verbe fini (indicatif) en français moderne*. Danske Videnskabernes Selskab, Historisk-Filologiske Meddelelser, no. 33. Copenhagen: Munksgaard, 1952.

Suzuki, Michihiko. "Le 'Je' proustien," *Bulletin de la Société des Amis de Marcel Proust et de Combray*, no. 9 (1955), pp. 69–82.

Tadié, Jean-Yves. *Proust et le roman*. Paris: Gallimard, Bibliothèque des idées, 1971.

Valéry, Paul. "Hommage." In *Hommage à Marcel Proust*, q.v., pp. 105–10.

Waters, Harold A. "The Narrator, not Marcel." *French Review* 33 (1959–1960): 389–92.

Wolitz, Seth. *The Proustian Community*. New York: New York University Press, 1971.

Woolf, Virginia. *A Writer's Diary*. Edited by Leonard Woolf. Paperbound edition. New York: Harcourt, Brace, Jovanovich, Harvest, 1973.

——. "How It Strikes a Contemporary." In her *The Common Reader, First Series*. New York: Harcourt, Brace, 1953.

Zima, P. -V. *Le Désir du mythe: Une Lecture sociologique de Marcel Proust*. Paris: Nizet, 1973.

Index

Action: in Balzac and Tolstoy, 47;
  motivation of, 54; Balzac's belief
  in, 57; Proust's attitude toward,
  57–58; in Malraux, 238–40
Active narration. *See* Narrative types
  and techniques
Adams, Robert M., 16
Adventure novel, 98; in Stendhal, 31;
  in Proust, 58; Proust criticizes,
  105–06
Albaret, Céleste: quoted, 89
Albertine, character in *A la recherche
  du temps perdu. See* Simonet,
  Albertine
Alienation: characteristic of post-
  Revolutionary period, 15; in
  Stendhal, 24; of Stendhal's heroes,
  30; and self-alienation in Stendhal,
  34; in Malraux, 239
Aragon, Louis, 240*n*
Aspect, verbal, 194

Balzac, Honoré de, 83, 85, 87, 166,
  234; place in novel tradition, 9;
  dialectic of experience in, 20; and
  Vidocq, Vautrin, 35; resisted
  fragmentation of narrative energy,
  39; and Stendhal, 39; traced narrative connections, 41; prisons in,
  41; protected enclaves in, 41;
  psychology, 46–47; and Tolstoy,
  46–47; materialist causation in, 48;
  pessimism in, 51; fates of heroes
  in, 52; judged by Proust, 55–57;
  belief in history, 57; and Flaubert,
  58–59; referents in concrete social
  world, 62; conception of experience, 63; values in, 69; insistence

on social dialectic, 92; Proust
  echoes, 154; and Proust, portrayal
  of unhappiness in, 200; Proust
  continues theme of disillusionment, 228; love in, 230; religious
  views, 246
—*La Cousine Bette,* 166
—*Eugénie Grandet:* materialist
  causation, 42; immaturity of
  structure, 42–43; love *vs.* money
  in, 43; love inadequate in, 43;
  corrosion of Eugénie, 43–44;
  purity and defeat in, 44–45; end
  ambiguous, 45
—*Illusions perdues,* 46, 199;
  classicism and romanticism discussed, 11; form of novel in, 11;
  more pessimistic than *Eugénie
  Grandet,* 45; at heart of novel
  tradition, 48; central to post-
  Restoration fiction, 48–49. *See
  also* Rubempré, Lucien Chardon de
—*La Peau de chagrin,* 44; place
  in Balzac's evolution, 49; causation in, 49–50; love in, 230. *See also*
  Valentin, Raphaël de
—*Le Père Goriot,* 50, 51, 77
  238–39. *See also* Rastignac, Eugène
  de
—*Splendeurs et misères des
  courtisanes:* quoted, 53–54. *See
  also* Rubempré, Lucien Chardon de;
  Vautrin
Barbéris, Pierre, 4, 65, 92, 234; on
  literary evolution after Restoration, 10–11; on *La Peau de chagrin,*
  49; on Rubempré and Rastignac,
  50, 52–53

257